Corporate Finance

Practical Applications

Second Edition

Steven M. Bragg

Published by AccountingTools, Inc., Centennial, Colorado.

For more information about AccountingTools® products, visit our Web site at www.accountingtools.com.

ISBN-13: 978-1-938910-98-2

Table of Contents

Chapter 1 - Overview of Corporate Finance...1

The Nature of Finance 1

Corporate Finance Topics 2

Financial Management 4

External Players...7

The Balancing Act of Corporate Finance 8

Chapter 2 - Capital Structure..11

Optimal Capital Structure..11

Capital Structure Analysis 12

The Financial Leverage Concept 13

    Leverage Risk 16

    Impact of Compensation on Leverage 18

Line of Credit Issues 18

Tax Shield Effects...18

Future Financing Flexibility 19

Market Timing..19

Loan Covenant Issues 20

Maturity Structure of Debt...20

Creditor Position Considerations 21

Debt Paydown...22

Cost of Capital Reduction 22

Market Signals 22

Planning for a Bond Rating 23

Timing of Changes to the Capital Structure...............................25

Chapter 3 - Financial Planning 26

The Cash Forecast 26

    The Short-Term Cash Forecast 27

    The Medium-Term Cash Forecast 30

    The Use of Averages 31

The Reliability of Cash Flow Information...................................32

    The Impact of Special Events 34

The Master Budget..35

The Budgeted Income Statement 35
Components of the Budgeted Balance Sheet 36
Additional Estimation Elements 43
The Cash Line Item 44
The Budgeted Balance Sheet 45
The Financing Budget 47

Chapter 4 - Early-Stage Financing **50**

Angel Investors *50*

Venture Capital *50*

Dangers of Venture Capital *52*

Chapter 5 - The Initial Public Offering **54**

Reasons for and Against an IPO *54*

Preparation for the IPO *56*

The Initial Public Offering *58*

Share Lockup Period *64*

Blue Sky Laws *64*

Chapter 6 - Other Capital Raising Alternatives **67**

Regulation D Stock Sales *67*
Regulation D Rules 67
Regulation D Process Flow 68
The Form D Filing 70

Rule 506(c) *71*

The Accredited Investor *72*

Regulation A+ Overview *73*

Private Investments in Public Equity *74*

Crowdfunding *75*
Requirements 75
Disclosures 76
Limits on Advertising and Promoters 78
Restrictions on Resale 79
Exemption from Section 12(g) 79
Bad Actor Disqualification 79

Seasoned Equity Offerings *80*

The Rights Offering *81*

Dilution *82*

Chapter 7 - Debt Financing **84**

Overview of Debt Financing *84*

The Line of Credit *85*

The Borrowing Base *86*

Invoice Discounting *87*

Factoring *88*

Receivables Securitization *89*

Inventory Financing *90*

Loan Stock *91*

Purchase Order Financing *91*

Hard Money Loans *91*

Mezzanine Financing *92*

The Long-Term Loan *93*

Bonds *94*

Agency Financing *95*

Debt for Equity Swaps *96*

Chapter 8 - Leasing **98**

The Lease Arrangement *98*

The Lease or Buy Decision *99*

Leasing Concerns *100*

Leasing Advantages *101*

Chapter 9 - The Cost of Capital **103**

Cost of Capital Derivation *103*

    Cost of Debt 103

    Cost of Preferred Stock 104

    Cost of Common Stock 104

    Weighted Average Cost of Capital 105

Variations in the Cost of Capital *105*

Adjustments to the Cost of Capital *108*

Cost of Capital as a Threshold Value *109*

Chapter 10 - Discounted Cash Flows **111**

Time Value of Money *111*

Present and Future Value Tables *113*

Net Present Value *115*

Internal Rate of Return...116

Incremental Internal Rate of Return 117

Terminal Value..118

Inclusions in Cash Flow Analysis 119

Chapter 11 - Working Capital Management **121**

The Impact of Working Capital on Corporate Finance 121

Accounts Receivable Enhancements 121
    Credit Enhancements 122
    Billing Enhancements 123
    Collection Enhancements 124
    Accounts Receivable Policies 125

Inventory Enhancements 126
    Product Design..127
    Product Record Keeping...128
    Inventory Acquisition 128
    Inventory Ownership 129
    Manufacturing Process Flow 129
    Fulfillment 130
    Inventory Disposition 130
    Inventory Policies 131
    Departmental Cooperation...131

Accounts Payable Enhancements..132
    Terms Renegotiation..132
    Early Payment Discounts...132
    Payment Processing Frequency 134
    Accounts Payable Policies 134

Researching Working Capital Enhancements..134

Working Capital Forecasting..135

Working Capital Strategy..135

Chapter 12 - Capital Expenditures **137**

Overview of Capital Expenditures 137

Net Present Value Analysis 138

Breakeven Analysis 141

The Profitability Index 142

The Payback Method..143

Real Options..145

Constraint Analysis 147

Capital Expenditure Proposal Analysis 148

The Outsourcing Decision..*150*

Complex Systems Analysis *151*

Chapter 13 - Investment Alternatives..**153**

Investment Guidelines...*153*

Cash Availability Scenarios..*156*

Investment Strategy..*157*

Types of Investments *160*
    Repurchase Agreements 160
    Time Deposits..161
    Certificates of Deposit 161
    Bankers' Acceptances...161
    Commercial Paper 162
    Money Market Funds..162
    U.S. Government Debt Instruments...162
    State and Local Government Debt..163
    Bonds...163

The Primary and Secondary Markets...*164*

The Effective Interest Rate *165*

The Discounted Investment Formula *165*

Chapter 14 - Dividends and Other Payouts **167**

Dividend Mechanics..*167*

Types of Dividends..*168*

The Investor Viewpoint *169*

The Company Viewpoint *170*

The Stock Buyback Option *171*

Deciding Between a Dividend and a Buyback *173*

The Stock Dividend *174*

Chapter 15 - Mergers and Acquisitions....................................**176**

Acquisition Strategy..*176*
    The Sales Growth Strategy 176
    The Geographic Growth Strategy 177
    The Product Supplementation Strategy 177
    The Full Service Strategy 178
    The Vertical Integration Strategy..178
    The Adjacent Industry Strategy 179
    The Diversification Strategy 179
    The Market Window Strategy...180
    The Bolt-on Strategy...181

The Low-Cost Strategy 181
The Industry Roll-up Strategy 182

Valuation of a Target Company 182
Liquidation Value 183
Real Estate Value 183
Relief-from-Royalty Method 184
Enterprise Value 184
Multiples Analysis 185
Discounted Cash Flows 188
Replication Value 190
Comparison Analysis 192
The Strategic Purchase 193
The Control Premium 193
The Valuation Floor and Ceiling 193

Payment Structures 195
The Stock-for-Stock Exchange 195
The Exchange Ratio 196
Issues Impacting the Stock Payment Decision 197
Stock Payment Based on Fixed Share Count or Fixed Price 198
The Debt Payment 200
The Cash Payment 200
Practical Considerations 201

Chapter 16 - Foreign Exchange Risk Management **204**

Foreign Exchange Risk Overview 204

Foreign Exchange Risk Management 206
Take No Action 206
Avoid Risk 207
Shift Risk 207
Time Compression 208
Payment Leading and Lagging 209
Build Reserves 209
Maintain Local Reserves 209
Hedging 209

Types of Foreign Exchange Hedges 211
Loan Denominated in a Foreign Currency 211
The Forward Contract 211
The Futures Contract 213
The Currency Option 213
The Cylinder Option 215
Swaps 216

Netting 216

Chapter 17 - Interest Rate Risk Management **218**

Interest Risk Overview 218

Interest Rate Risk Management *218*
 Take No Action..219
 Avoid Risk 219
 Asset and Liability Matching..219
 Hedging 219

Types of Interest Rate Hedges..*220*
 The Forward Rate Agreement...220
 The Futures Contract 222
 The Interest Rate Swap 224
 Interest Rate Options 226
 Interest Rate Swaptions 229

Chapter 18 - Supply Chain Financing **231**

Supply Chain Financing...*231*

Chapter 19 - Corporate Finance Measurements **234**

Corporate Finance Metrics...*234*

Cash Conversion Cycle...*235*
 Days Sales in Accounts Receivable..236
 Days Sales in Inventory 236
 Days Payables Outstanding 237

Actual Cash Position versus Forecast *238*

Earnings on Invested Funds..*239*

Ability to Pay Measurements *240*
 Interest Coverage Ratio 240
 Debt Service Coverage Ratio..241
 Fixed Charge Coverage Ratio...241
 Cash Coverage Ratio 242

Debt to Equity Ratio...*243*

Average Cost of Debt..*244*

Borrowing Base Usage *246*

Glossary..**248**

Index **253**

Preface

Even the best organization, with excellent products and processes, cannot survive without proper attention to its finances. This is because finance represents the flow of money through an organization – without money, no activities can last for long, and the business will die. *Corporate Finance* addresses the practical aspects of fund raising and the deployment of cash. If the concepts addressed in this book are followed, an organization can improve its ability to raise funds at a reasonable price, while driving down the amount of its working capital requirements and directing funds into those activities that will be best able to generate cash.

Corporate Finance covers the financial planning process in Chapters 2 and 3, addressing the factors that can alter an organization's capital structure as well as the construction of cash forecasts and finance budgets. The book then turns to the sources of equity and debt funding in Chapters 4 through 8, covering early-stage financing, the initial public offering, debt financing, and several related topics. The discussion then shifts to financial evaluation tools in Chapters 9 and 10, where the cost of capital and the formulation of discounted cash flows are covered. The best possible deployment of funds is discussed in Chapters 11 through 15, which delve into the management of working capital, the analysis of proposed capital expenditures, the implications of dividend payments, the valuation of acquisition targets, and investment vehicles. Other topics include risk management, supply chain management, and the use of measurements most applicable to corporate finance.

You can find the answers to many questions in *Corporate Finance* that can be of immediate practical use, such as:

- Which factors could change my company's capital structure?
- How do I develop a short-term cash forecast?
- What are the steps involved in an initial public offering?
- Which types of debt funding do not require collateral?
- Which analysis tools are available for the examination of capital expenditures, and what are their weaknesses?
- Which mix of methods should I use to derive a valuation for an acquisition target?
- How do I mitigate the risk of losses from payments in a foreign currency?
- How can I lock in a specific interest rate, despite having a variable rate loan?

Corporate Finance is designed for both professionals and students. Professionals can use it as a handy reference tool for dealing with practical day-to-day issues, while students will find that it clarifies a number of the more arcane finance topics. The book also provides references to the author's popular Accounting Best Practices podcast, which provides additional coverage of many finance topics. As such, it may earn a place on your book shelf as a reference tool for years to come.

Centennial, Colorado
November 2017

About the Author

Steven Bragg, CPA, has been the chief financial officer or controller of four companies, as well as a consulting manager at Ernst & Young. He received a master's degree in finance from Bentley College, an MBA from Babson College, and a Bachelor's degree in Economics from the University of Maine. He has been a two-time president of the Colorado Mountain Club, and is an avid alpine skier, mountain biker, and certified master diver. Mr. Bragg resides in Centennial, Colorado. He has written the following books and courses:

7 Habits of Effective CEOs
7 Habits of Effective CFOs
7 Habits of Effective Controllers
Accountant Ethics [for multiple states]
Accountants' Guidebook
Accounting Changes and Error Corrections
Accounting Controls Guidebook
Accounting for Casinos and Gaming
Accounting for Derivatives and Hedges
Accounting for Earnings per Share
Accounting for Inventory
Accounting for Investments
Accounting for Intangible Assets
Accounting for Leases
Accounting for Managers
Accounting for Stock-Based Compensation
Accounting Procedures Guidebook
Agricultural Accounting
Behavioral Ethics
Bookkeeping Guidebook
Budgeting
Business Combinations and Consolidations
Business Insurance Fundamentals
Business Ratios
Business Valuation
Capital Budgeting
CFO Guidebook
Change Management
Closing the Books
Coaching and Mentoring
Conflict Management
Constraint Management
Construction Accounting
Corporate Cash Management
Corporate Finance

Cost Accounting (college textbook)
Cost Accounting Fundamentals
Cost Management Guidebook
Credit & Collection Guidebook
Crowdfunding
Developing and Managing Teams
Effective Collections
Employee Onboarding
Enterprise Risk Management
Fair Value Accounting
Financial Analysis
Financial Forecasting and Modeling
Fixed Asset Accounting
Foreign Currency Accounting
Fraud Examination
Fraud Schemes
GAAP Guidebook
Governmental Accounting
Health Care Accounting
Hospitality Accounting
How to Audit Cash
How to Audit Fixed Assets
How to Audit for Fraud
How to Audit Inventory
How to Audit Receivables
How to Run a Meeting
Human Resources Guidebook
IFRS Guidebook
Interpretation of Financial Statements
Inventory Management
Investor Relations Guidebook
Lean Accounting Guidebook
Mergers & Acquisitions
Negotiation
New Controller Guidebook

(continued)

Nonprofit Accounting | Records Management
Partnership Accounting | Recruiting and Hiring
Payables Management | Revenue Recognition
Payroll Management | Sales and Use Tax Accounting
Performance Appraisals | The MBA Guidebook
Project Accounting | The Soft Close
Project Management | The Statement of Cash Flows
Public Company Accounting | The Year-End Close
Purchasing Guidebook | Treasurer's Guidebook
Real Estate Accounting | Working Capital Management

On-Line Resources by Steven Bragg

Steven maintains the accountingtools.com web site, which contains continuing professional education courses, the Accounting Best Practices podcast, and thousands of articles on accounting subjects.

Corporate Finance is also available as a continuing professional education (CPE) course. You can purchase the course (and many other courses) and take an on-line exam at:

www.accountingtools.com/cpe

Chapter 1
Overview of Corporate Finance

Introduction

The intent of this book is to give the reader an understanding of all aspects of corporate finance, and the practical methods used to ensure that funds are cost-effectively raised and deployed. To do that, we must first address the nature of finance, so that one can understand the prevalence of finance in the modern corporation. In this chapter, we cover the full scope of the finance topic: the nature of corporate finance, the topics comprising it, who is responsible for it, and the outside parties who must be dealt with.

The Nature of Finance

The founders of a company are interested in creating a product or service. However, upon starting operations, they find that a key impediment is a lack of funds to pay for employees, facilities, inventory, receivables, and more. As the business increases in size, they will once again find that a lack of funds is constraining them from entering into new activities. For example, they land a large new customer account, but the customer demands lengthy credit terms. There is a good chance that the fledgling business cannot support sales to this customer, since it cannot afford to pay for the goods and services being provided. Or, the owners may be offered a chance to buy a competitor at an excellent price – but cannot do so, because there is not enough cash to pay the stockholders of the competitor. The common theme in these situations is that starting a business and expanding it requires funds that may not be available.

Besides the startup and expansion issues just noted, the founders will find that they must maintain tight control over operations, or else the company will bleed so much cash that it will be necessary to continually add funding infusions to the business. Proper management of the business calls for an awareness of how much inventory is being kept on hand, the payment terms being offered by suppliers, and the amount of credit being granted to customers. These areas, known as working capital, tend to not be monitored closely, and so can result in a gradual loss of ready cash from a business.

And what if a business proves to be successful, and begins to spin off excess cash that is not needed to maintain operations? Once again, the founders must make decisions about finance – should they pay out dividends, reinvest the funds in fixed assets, engage in acquisitions, or simply invest the funds in order to build a cash reserve for the organization?

Yet another aspect of finance that tends to intrude on a business is the risk of losses from financial activities. If the company is being financed with debt, there is a risk that the interest rates being paid will increase over time. Or, if the company is obligated to make payments in a different currency, there is a risk that the exchange rate will change in an unfavorable direction before the payment is due, so that the entity is obligated to pay more than was originally intended.

All of these issues fall into the corporate finance category. The founders of a business may have had no knowledge of or interest in this topic when they decided to start the company, but will inevitably find that they must build up a notable level of expertise in this area – or risk seeing their organization fail.

Corporate Finance Topics

There are a multitude of topics that comprise corporate finance. In this section, we give a brief overview of each topic, for which much more complete discussions are available in the following chapters. The topics are:

- *Capital structure*. An issue of immediate concern to any startup company is the structure of its funding, which is called its capital structure. This structure describes the mix of funding sources, which may include shares sold to investors, debt obtained from lenders, and/or some mix of the two, such as debt that is convertible into shares. A startup business will find that its access to debt will be severely limited, unless the founders want to personally guarantee repayment of the debt. As the business expands and builds up its asset base while also creating a history of profitability, lenders will be more amenable to granting loans. An additional consideration is the ability of a business to pay off loans. Some entities have such wildly variable cash flows that it is far too risky to commit to a long series of loan payments, in which case debt financing is not a realistic option. Other organizations have such steady and reliable cash flows that they can easily pay off loans. See Chapter 2, Capital Structure, for more information.
- *Financial planning*. In order to determine when to take on more financing and in what amount, it is first necessary to create at least a cash forecast, if not an entire annual budget. The cash forecast is needed for short-term planning, and the budget for a view of the long-range outlook. Both types of planning systems must be crafted with care and monitored closely. Otherwise, company managers may be surprised by a sudden funding shortfall that requires a scramble to find cash, or which may even send the business into bankruptcy. See Chapter 3, Financial Planning, for more information.
- *Equity funding*. Equity is the funding of a business through the sale of shares to investors. There are many ways in which to obtain equity funding. It may be possible to sell shares to an angel investor, who usually invests only at the earliest "proof of concept" stages of a business. Or, if it appears that the company may be headed toward a robust growth path, perhaps a venture capital firm would be willing to invest a larger amount. As the organization increases in size, it may be able to sell shares through a number of other alternatives, possibly culminating in an initial public offering. These con-

cepts are discussed in Chapters 4 through 6, Early-Stage Financing, The Initial Public Offering, and Other Capital Raising Alternatives.

- *Debt funding.* Debt is the funding of a business by lenders. There are a large number of possible variations on the debt concept, including invoice discounting, a line of credit, leasing, inventory financing, bonds, and long-term loans. Each one is designed for a different situation, and has differing lender requirements and costs. The full range of debt alternatives are covered in Chapters 7 and 8, Debt Financing and Leasing.

- *Evaluation tools.* There is a cost associated with funds, which is referred to as the cost of capital. This is comprised of the weighted average costs of debt and equity. A business should always engage in activities that generate a return at least as high as the cost of capital, or else the organization is generating a negative return for its shareholders. In addition, managers should be aware of the concept of discounted cash flows, where decisions are made based on the present value of the expected cash flows arising from various decisions. These evaluation tools are needed to make many decisions involving corporate finance. The concepts are covered in Chapters 9 and 10, The Cost of Capital and Discounted Cash Flows.

- *Uses of funds.* Managers must be exceedingly deliberate in how they allocate available funds, since there is a limited supply of cash, and it must be carefully apportioned to generate the maximum possible return. This can be done by being mindful of the level of working capital, and by using a rigid analysis system for buying fixed assets. Also, the board of directors should understand the implications of initiating dividend payments, as well as the size and frequency of those dividends. Further, there should be a logical strategy behind the selection of acquisition targets, as well as a standard methodology for pricing these targets. In all of the preceding cases, a certain amount of regimented analysis is needed in order to reduce the risk that funds will be mis-spent. If there are no further investments to be made in company operations or acquisitions, then there are a number of investment vehicles available in which funds can be parked, depending on the liquidity, risk, and return objectives of the company. These topics are addressed in Chapters 11 through 15, covering working capital management, capital expenditures, investment alternatives, dividends and other payouts, and mergers and acquisitions.

- *Risk management.* A business can incur significant losses if it engages in foreign currency transactions and is caught in an adverse currency exchange rate position. Similarly, a sudden climb in interest rates can trigger a sharp increase in interest expense, especially if a company has taken on a large amount of debt. In these situations, it is possible to manage the amount of risk by using different payment methods, forward contracts, futures contracts, currency options, swaps, swaptions, and netting arrangements. While some of these alternatives are complex, they can mitigate the risk of several types of losses. These techniques are discussed in Chapters 16 and 17, Foreign Exchange Risk Management and Interest Rate Risk Management.

- *Supply chain financing.* The financial health of a company depends, to some extent, on the financial health of its suppliers. If they are short on funds, they will have a more difficult time making deliveries, and will not be able to invest in their own infrastructure. A business can assist its suppliers by setting up a supply chain financing arrangement, where a bank agrees to pay the company's payables to its suppliers at an accelerated rate in exchange for a discount on the payments. This financing alternative is covered in Chapter 18, Supply Chain Financing.
- *Metrics.* A well-designed system that supports corporate finance requires a feedback loop, in order to determine how well it is functioning. This calls for measurements that monitor cash usage, cash forecasting, cash at work, and solvency. Key among these measurements is the cash conversion cycle, which tracks the amount of time that it takes to pay cash for inventory, convert the inventory to finished goods, sell them, and receive cash back from customers. Other measurements are noted in Chapter 19, Corporate Finance Measurements.

The preceding points should make it clear that elements of corporate finance can be found throughout an organization. Thus, one must be mindful of the sources and uses of funds in all functional areas.

Financial Management

Given the pervasive nature of corporate finance, it makes sense to create a management structure that assigns specific responsibility for financial issues to a high-ranking member of management. This person is the chief financial officer (CFO). The CFO's responsibilities cover the following five general areas:

- *Planning.* The formulation of the strategic direction of the business and the tactical plans, budgeting systems, and performance metrics required to achieve that direction.
- *Operations.* The direct oversight of a number of departments, as well as coordinating the operations of those departments with other areas of the business. It can also include the selection, purchase, and subsequent integration of acquired businesses.
- *Financial information.* The compilation of financial information into financial statements, and the presentation of this information to various internal and external recipients.
- *Risk management.* Understanding the current and potential risks to which the business is subjected and taking steps to mitigate those risks.
- *Financing.* Monitoring projected cash balances and arranging for either additional financing or investment options, depending on the amount of expected cash balances.

More specifically, the CFO's job includes the following tasks:

Planning

- Develop a strategic direction for the business, along with supporting tactics
- Monitor the progress of the company in meeting its strategic goals
- Oversee the formulation of the annual budget
- Develop a system of performance metrics that support the company's strategic direction

Operations

- Manage the accounting, treasury, tax, human resources, and investor relations departments
- Oversee the activities of any supplier to which functions have been out-sourced
- Participate in the functions and decisions of the executive management team
- Implement operational best practices throughout his or her areas of responsibility
- Engage in acquisition selection, purchase negotiations, and acquiree integration into the business

Financial Information

- Oversee the compilation of financial information into financial statements, with accompanying disclosures
- If the company is publicly held, certify the financial statements filed with the Securities and Exchange Commission
- Report financial results to management, the board of directors, and the investment community

Risk Management

- Understand the current and potential risks to which the business is subjected
- Take steps to mitigate risks, including the use of control systems, shifting risk to other parties, and insurance coverage
- Report on risk issues to the board of directors
- Ensure that the business complies with all regulatory and other legal requirements
- Monitor known legal issues involving the company, as well as legal issues impacting the entire industry
- Review and act upon the findings and recommendations of internal and external auditors

Financing

- Monitor projected cash balances
- Arrange for financing to meet future cash requirements
- Invest excess funds based on projected cash balances
- Invest funds on behalf of the company pension plan
- Maintain relationships with banks, lenders, investors, investment bankers, and outside analysts

Some of the activities in the preceding job description do not address the corporate finance topic, such as outsourcing oversight, best practices implementations, and financial reporting. Nonetheless, the majority of tasks are directly related to corporate finance.

The CFO is by no means the only person in an organization who is tasked with finance responsibilities. The following organizational chart of positions reporting to the CFO clarifies the extent to which finance issues pervade the CFO's area of responsibility.

Finance Organizational Structure

Note how virtually all of the activities of the treasurer relate to corporate finance. In addition, the controller is responsible for multiple finance-related areas: billings, budgeting, cash receipts, collections, and payables. Though less obvious, the investor relations officer can assist with the sale of shares to investors. Also, the tax manager can oversee tax strategies that reduce the effective tax rate of the business, thereby increasing the amount of available cash flow.

External Players

The group of people within a company who are charged with managing corporate finance must also deal with a number of external players, some of which can have a profound impact on the firm's ability to raise and invest funds. These external players include the following:

- *Banks*. A bank is a financial institution that is licensed to receive deposits. These heavily-regulated entities also issue loans to individuals and businesses. The typical organization will offload a large amount of its financial transactions to a bank, including the processing of checks and electronic payments, as well as short-term investment activities. There is likely to be a line of credit with a bank for dealing with short-term cash shortfalls. Banks may also offer additional products, such as lock boxes, payables management, and a number of risk management services.
- *Non-bank lenders*. There are several types of entities that lend money, but which do not receive deposits. Instead, they borrow money and then loan it out, making money by lending at a higher rate than they borrow funds. These lenders can engage in a variety of non-traditional lending arrangements, such as hard money loans, factoring, and inventory financing.
- *Investors*. If a company wants to sell shares, it must maintain relations with the investment community. For a private company, this may mean fund raising through a small core group of investors. For larger equity sales, this can involve using an investment banker's network to reach out to a larger group of investors. If a company goes public and sells shares to a large number of investors, then it is useful to maintain an in-house investor relations function, which manages earnings conference calls to discuss the latest results of the business, issues press releases, maintains the investor relations section of the company website, and conducts road shows to meet with individual investors.
- *Capital markets*. A capital market is an organized market in which both individuals and business entities (such as pension funds and corporations) sell and exchange debt and equity securities. This is a key source of funds for an entity whose securities are permitted by a regulatory authority to be traded, since it can readily sell its debt obligations and equity to investors. When a publicly-held company sells its securities in the capital markets, this is referred to as primary market activity. The subsequent trading of company securities between investors is known as secondary market activity. Examples of highly organized capital markets are the New York Stock Exchange, American Stock Exchange, London Stock Exchange, and NASDAQ. Securities can also be traded "over the counter," rather than on an organized exchange. These securities are usually issued by entities whose business fundamentals (such as revenue, capitalization, and profitability) do not meet the minimum standards of a formal exchange, which forces investors to use other avenues to trade the securities.

- *Stock transfer agents.* When a company is publicly-held, it hires an outside agency to manage its shareholder records. This stock transfer agent is responsible for maintaining a list of investors, issuing share certificates, cancelling certificates, and counting ballots for shareholder meetings.
- *Rating agencies.* If a company wants to issue bonds to the investment community, it will soon find that no one will purchase the bonds unless a rating has first been issued by a rating agency. To obtain such a rating, the company must pay a rating agency to conduct a detailed review of its finances. It may be necessary to adopt a more conservative financial structure in order to obtain a higher credit rating. The higher the rating, the lower the interest rate that investors will accept, since the perceived risk of the issuance is reduced.
- *Regulatory agencies.* If a company plans to sell its securities to the public, it must first comply with the detailed reporting requirements of a regulatory agency. In the United States, this is the Securities and Exchange Commission (SEC). The SEC has very specific requirements for the frequency and types of information reporting for publicly-held companies, as well as a detailed review process for certain types of reports filed with it. The SEC is particularly careful about examining the initial information filings of companies offering securities for sale to the public for the first time.
- *Auditors.* Many investors and lenders will refuse to buy shares in or lend funds to a company unless its financial statements have been examined and certified by an outside auditor. To obtain such a certification, a business must use the accrual basis of accounting (where revenue is recognized when earned and expenses when incurred) and produce consistently accurate financial statements. A business should expect to undergo an audit following the completion of its year-end financial statements.
- *Investment bankers.* Investment banking is an industry that provides several types of services, which can be generally clustered under the heading of being an intermediary between companies and investors. They can assist a CFO in the pursuit of funding. This means creating a presentation of the business and its cash needs, establishing interest among the bankers' contacts, and organizing a series of presentation meetings. The banker then assists in hammering out the final terms of a deal package. Investment bankers also assist in locating possible target companies to purchase, valuing the targets, and assisting with acquisition negotiations. Other services include underwriting the sale of shares, assistance with corporate reorganizations, and consulting services.

The Balancing Act of Corporate Finance

What is the goal of corporate finance? One possibility is to increase the overall return for shareholders. This could mean funding the business primarily with debt, in order to minimize the amount of shareholder investment and thereby enhance the return on investment percentage. It could also involve funding a rapid expansion of the business, which requires a large investment in working capital and fixed assets. Another variation that leads to an increased return is cutting back on certain discretionary expenses that are not absolutely critical in the short-term, such as maintenance, advertising, and research.

There are several problems with these activities. An organization might incur so much debt that even a modest downturn in its cash flows could trigger a debt default, and perhaps even bankruptcy. Also, rapid expansion tends to result in a loosening of cost controls, as well as expansion into less-profitable product lines. Further, the reduction of discretionary expenses is harmful over the long-term, when the effects of reduced maintenance, advertising, and research will result in a decline in profits. Consequently, an excessive focus on the return on equity could be harmful.

We might take an alternative path and instead emphasize a stable, highly liquid entity that has a low risk of bankruptcy. Under this approach, growth is sharply curtailed, with an emphasis only on the highest-profit niches that spin off large amounts of cash, and which do not require inordinate fixed asset or working capital investments. However, the growth rate of the business under this approach may be so slow that its market share dwindles as more aggressive competitors snap up customers and issue new products into more markets at an increasing rate.

These two alternatives represent the extreme ends of a continuum, somewhere along which a company places itself. There is typically a significant amount of pressure from investors to increase their returns, so most organizations tend to place themselves further along the continuum in the direction of shareholder returns. However, this must be tempered by the risk of financial failure. Consequently, the CFO must continually examine the ability of the organization to raise funds, the cost of those funds, the ability to pay back debt, and the projected returns on the uses to which funds can be put. Out of this analysis comes a balancing act, where a reasonable level of shareholder return is targeted, as is a low risk of financial failure.

Summary

The chapter has provided an overview of the general nature of corporate finance, the areas commonly considered part of corporate finance, and how it is managed. We have also noted the outside parties that a business must deal with when engaged in finance activities, as well as the types of corporate finance goals. In the succeeding chapters, we explore each of the areas of corporate finance in more detail.

When perusing the information in the following chapters, keep in mind that certain activities will only be necessary at different stages of the life of an organization. For example, angel investing is only an option during the early stages of a new business, while foreign exchange risk management is unlikely to be an issue until management decides to expand into overseas markets. The following table notes the topics most applicable to startup companies, mature organizations, and large entities; the topics listed roughly correspond to the titles of the following chapters.

Applicable Finance Topics

Startup Companies	Mature Organizations	Large Entities
Early-stage financing	Capital structure analysis	Capital structure analysis
Other capital-raising alternatives	Financial planning	Financial planning
Debt financing	The initial public offering	Debt financing
Leasing	Other capital-raising alternatives	Leasing
Working capital management	Debt financing	The cost of capital
Capital expenditures	Leasing	Discounted cash flows
	The cost of capital	Working capital management
	Discounted cash flows	Capital expenditures
	Working capital management	Investments
	Capital expenditures	Dividend analysis
	Investments	Mergers and acquisitions
	Dividend analysis	Foreign exchange risk management
	Mergers and acquisitions	Interest rate risk management
		Supply chain financing

Chapter 2
Capital Structure

Introduction

The capital structure of a business is the mix of long-term funds that it employs, which involves both equity and debt. In all likelihood, the average business has a capital structure that was not planned. Instead, the company has taken whatever types of funding were available. The resulting capital structure may not be one that best meets the needs of the company or its shareholders. In this chapter, we address a number of issues that should be considered in regard to capital structure, and which may lead to a different mix of funding sources.

Optimal Capital Structure

The optimal capital structure can be defined as the point where the cost of any additional incremental funds will be too high to generate a positive net present value on any additional projects that require the expenditure of capital. The concept is best viewed through an example.

EXAMPLE

The management of Grissom Granaries believes that there is a large market for its grain storage facilities throughout the Midwest region of the United States. Each of these facilities costs $20,000,000, and Grissom can potentially construct over a hundred of the facilities. The net present value of these facilities is greater than zero, as long as the discount rate used does not exceed 14%. The company is closely held, and the shareholders have not expressed any willingness for the company to raise funds through the sale of additional equity.

Grissom's CFO meets with lenders to see how much additional debt the company can obtain, and summarizes her findings as follows:

Funding Tranches	Cost of Funds
1st $100,000,000	10.0%
2nd $100,000,000	13.5%
Additional funding	18.0%

Based on this information, the company can elect to acquire an additional $200,000,000 of debt, which will allow it to generate a positive return on ten more grain storage facilities. If the company wants additional funding beyond the initial $200,000,000, lenders will assign a much higher risk premium to the associated debt, which will render all additional projects unprofitable on a net present value basis.

It may initially appear that the derivation of the optimal capital structure is a simple quantitative calculation. This is not the case. There are a number of additional issues to be considered, none of which involve a formula. Instead, company management must integrate into its capital structure the points raised in the next section.

Capital Structure Analysis

Capital structure analysis is a periodic evaluation of all components of the debt and equity financing used by a business. The intent of the analysis is to evaluate what combination of debt and equity a business should have, which varies over time based on the costs of debt and equity and the risks to which the business is subjected. The analysis may be on a regularly scheduled basis, or it could be triggered by one of the following events:

- The upcoming maturity of a debt instrument
- The need to find funding for the acquisition of a fixed asset
- The need to fund an acquisition
- A demand by a key investor to have the business buy back shares
- A demand by investors for a larger dividend
- An expected change in the market interest rate

When engaging in a capital structure analysis, it may be worth considering the following questions, and how they impact the mix of debt and equity that a company has obtained:

- How much financial leverage is the company currently employing, and is it safe to increase the level of debt to further extend the amount of leverage? See the Financial Leverage and Line of Credit sections in this chapter.
- Does the business generate a sufficient amount of income to offset the tax deductions generated by interest expense? If the organization is not able to do so, then the cost of its debt will increase. See the Tax Shield Effects section.
- Does management want to maintain additional flexibility in its ability to obtain additional debt financing in the future? See the Future Financing Flexibility section.
- Is the price of the company's stock unusually high or low at the moment? This can impact the willingness of managers to sell equity. See the Market Timing section.
- Does the company have trouble paying off its line of credit each year? See the Line of Credit Issues section.
- How does the current or projected capital structure impact any loan covenants, such as the debt to equity ratio? If the effect is negative, it may not be possible to acquire any additional debt, or existing debt may need to be paid down. See the Loan Covenant Issues section.

12

- What is the maturity structure of the company's debt? Ideally, company operations should always have sufficient cash flow to pay off debt as it comes due for payment. See the Maturity Structure of Debt section.
- Are shareholders sensitive about allowing creditors a claim on company assets in the event of a corporate liquidation? If so, the amount of debt that can be obtained may be severely limited. See the Creditor Position Considerations section.
- Are there any expensive tranches of debt that can be paid down? This involves a discussion of alternative uses for any available cash, which could be more profitably employed elsewhere. See the Debt Paydown section.
- Can the company's cost of capital be reduced by altering the capital structure? This can be of some importance when a large investment is needed in the business. See the Cost of Capital Reduction section.
- Are the uses for cash within the company's business beginning to decline? If so, does it make more sense to return cash to investors by buying back shares or issuing more dividends? See the Dividends and Other Payouts chapter.
- Does the investor relations officer want to establish a floor for the company's stock price? This can be achieved by engaging in an ongoing stock repurchase program that is triggered whenever the stock price falls below a certain amount. See the Stock Buyback Option section in the Dividends and Other Payouts chapter.
- Does the company want to send a signal to the investment community regarding its confidence regarding the level of future earnings? A higher level of confidence in earnings means that a higher level of debt burden can be sustained. See the Market Signals section for more information.
- Does the company want to achieve a certain rating for its bonds? If so, it may need to restructure its financing mix to be more conservative, thereby improving the odds of investors being repaid by the company for their purchases of the company's bonds. See the Planning for a Bond Rating section.

The following sections expand upon these questions.

The Financial Leverage Concept

The essential concept behind financial leverage is that the return on equity of a business can be increased by funding new projects with debt, rather than equity. Doing so freezes the equity portion of the return on equity calculation, so that any incremental profits generated by the debt-funded activities will automatically increase the return to shareholders. This is called *positive leverage*. If profits decline as a result of debt financing, it is known as *negative leverage*.

In short, when used properly, debt financing allows you to increase the numerator in the following return on equity measurement, while freezing the denominator:

Capital Structure

	Return on Equity Formula		Effect of Funding with Debt
Net income		=	Increases when leverage is positive
Equity		=	No impact on equity

The concept is best illustrated with an example, as follows.

EXAMPLE

The management team of Grissom Granaries wants to invest in five barges and a tugboat, which it will use to transport grain down the Mississippi River. The cost of these assets is $10,000,000. The company expects to generate an annual $2,000,000 profit by operating the barges and tugboat. The company can elect to fund the purchases either by selling shares or issuing bonds at an interest rate of 8%. The current amount of equity held by the company is $50,000,000, and it typically earns $5,000,000 per year for an average return on equity of 10%. The results of the alternative forms of financing appear in the following table:

	Equity Funding	Debt Funding
Current equity	$50,000,000	$50,000,000
Additional equity	10,000,000	
Total equity	$60,000,000	$50,000,000
Existing profit	$5,000,000	$5,000,000
Profit from invested funds	2,000,000	2,000,000
Less: debt cost		-800,000
Total profit	$7,000,000	$6,200,000
Return on equity	11.7%	12.4%

Based on the information in the table, Grissom's shareholders can earn a greater return on equity by directing the company to fund the fixed asset purchase with debt. By doing so, the denominator in the return on equity calculation (i.e., equity) is held constant, thereby boosting the return on equity with profits from the new venture.

The preceding example illustrates the benefits of financial leverage at the simplest possible level, without also factoring in the beneficial effects of income taxes on debt funding. When a company borrows money, the related interest expense is tax deductible in most taxing jurisdictions, so the net amount of profit generated is actually higher than was indicated in the example. In the following example, we adjust the calculation to reveal the effects of taxation.

EXAMPLE

Grissom Granaries is subject to a 35% incremental income tax rate. The return on equity table from the preceding example is adjusted below for the beneficial effects of this tax rate:

	Equity Funding	Debt Funding
Current equity	$50,000,000	$50,000,000
Additional equity	10,000,000	
Total equity	$60,000,000	$50,000,000
Existing profit	$5,000,000	$5,000,000
Profit from invested funds	2,000,000	2,000,000
Less: debt cost		**-520,000**
Total profit	$7,000,000	$6,480,000
Return on equity	11.7%	13.0%

Once the effects of taxes are included in the return on equity calculation, Grissom's management sees that the return on equity has now increased from 12.4% to 13.0%, which makes the use of debt an even more attractive option.

If a company is not currently earning a profit, then the tax-deductible status of interest expense is a moot point, and should not be included in the calculation of earnings to be achieved through the use of leverage. However, it may be possible to include the tax effect if the current lack of income is expected to be of short duration, since tax losses can be rolled forward and applied as net operating loss carryforwards against future earnings. The impact of taxation is discussed further in the Tax Shield Effects section.

In short, we have established that financial leverage can be a substantially beneficial alternative. However, there is also a downside to the use of debt. If the borrower cannot generate a net positive return on the borrowed funds, then the result can be a major decline in overall profitability, as well as some risk that the company cannot pay back the borrowed funds. The issue is illustrated in the following example.

EXAMPLE

The financial analyst of Grissom Granaries hears about the prospective sale of $10,000,000 in bonds (from the earlier examples) to pay for barges and a tugboat, and is concerned that the profits from this operation will be too variable to support payment of the related interest expense. As proof, she notes a recent study that the depth of the Mississippi River has been too low in four of the past 10 years in the area where Grissom intends to use the barges to support the draft of the barges. This results in a binary situation – either the company can

15

operate the barges fully or it cannot operate them at all. In the latter case, there will be no income from the invested funds, while the company must still pay the $520,000 after-tax cost of the debt. If this situation were to arise, the result would be as noted in the following table:

	Debt Funding
Total equity	$50,000,000
Existing profit	$5,000,000
Less: debt cost	**-520,000**
Total profit	$4,480,000
Return on equity	9.0%

The table indicates that a combination of debt financing and a low-water season on the Mississippi will result in a net decline in Grissom's net income, to a point below the 10% that the company was earning prior to its contemplated investment in the barges and tugboat.

The result of this preliminary analysis should be a detailed review of the odds of low-water conditions on the Mississippi during the period when the related debt is outstanding, whether management wants to sustain reduced earnings during these periods, and also whether lower-draft barges can be obtained that would make the fleet usable even in low-water seasons. If management is risk averse, it may choose to avoid these problems by either using additional equity to fund the asset purchases, or by not investing in the assets at all.

Stated another way, financial leverage increases the fixed cost base of a business by adding interest expense. This means that the breakeven point of a business rises, so that additional sales must be generated in order to provide sufficient additional contribution margin to pay for the added interest expense.

In short, financial leverage can provide a boost to the return on equity by providing funding for the generation of additional earnings, but at the risk of incurring a debt load that may prove to be unmanageable if incremental earnings cannot be created.

Leverage Risk

The downside of funding a business with a large amount of debt is that positive leverage can turn negative under the following circumstances:

- Lenders will only issue funds at a variable rate of interest, and the short-term after-tax interest rate increases to the point where it exceeds the incremental profitability of the business; or
- Lenders reduce the amount of debt they are willing to extend, requiring a business to replace the funds with more expensive financing; or

- The company's incremental earnings rate drops below the after-tax tax rate charged by lenders.

Some of these circumstances may be combined during an economic contraction, where banks routinely cut back on the amount of funds they are willing to loan, while company profits plunge. These combined effects routinely lead to the bankruptcy of those firms that employed leverage too much during the good times, without regard to what would happen under more adverse circumstances.

Examples of situations under which financial leverage can be best employed or where it should be avoided are noted in the following table.

Condition	Favorable for Leverage	Unfavorable for Leverage
Barriers to entry	When it is difficult for new competitors to enter a market, there is less downward pressure on prices, so it is easier to earn a profit on additional funds invested	When there are low barriers to entry in a market, there is a risk that a new competitor will enter at a low price point, driving down profits for all existing companies in that market, and turning their positive leverage into negative leverage
Competition	A near-monopoly situation is favorable for leverage, since a business can more easily maintain prices	It is unwise to maintain much leverage when there is a large amount of competition, since it is more likely that profits will be driven down over time, impacting the ability to pay back debt
Interest rates	If money can be borrowed at a fixed interest rate, the company has no risk of a rate increase over the term of the loan, and so can borrow more funds as long as the invested cash can yield a return greater than the fixed interest rate	If money can only be borrowed at a variable interest rate, then there is a risk of a rate increase eliminating all positive leverage
Lending environment	If there is a credit crunch where bankers are retracting credit, it may not be possible to obtain funds at any reasonable interest rate	When the lending environment allows for easy credit terms and low interest rates, this is an ideal time to engage in leverage, especially if the funds can be obtained at a fixed interest rate
Product life cycles	When product life cycles are long, it is easier to reliably forecast profits into the future, so there is a low risk of an unanticipated profit decline	When there are short product life cycles, a company may find that its newest products are not catching on in the market, so it can no longer support the debt payments associated with its financial leverage

The senior managers of a company may elect to engage in a large amount of financial leverage, even knowing that the preceding factors will put their companies at risk of negative leverage. The reason may be an excessive degree of optimism, where they assign a lower probability of occurrence to the preceding factors. In such cases, it is useful to keep management informed of changes in the various factors that can contribute to negative leverage. By doing so, it may be possible to take early action to reduce debt levels enough to mitigate the effects of negative leverage before the business is imperiled.

Impact of Compensation on Leverage

The management team of a business is typically given a compensation package that issues bonuses if the company can achieve a higher level of profitability. This can yield an unfortunate side effect, which is that managers can increase their bonuses by expanding the financial leverage of the firm. This is most likely to occur when bonus plans cover short periods of time, and do not address the financial *position* of a business. In this case, a manager is not penalized for loading large amounts of debt onto the company's balance sheet, and so has no incentive *not* to employ leverage.

This unfortunate situation can be mitigated by altering the type of bonus compensation paid, so that rewards are based on the long-term market value of a business. For example, consider offering stock options or stock grants that vest over a number of years. By doing so, managers are less likely to place the company at risk during the period when they expect to have an equity stake in the business.

Line of Credit Issues

A line of credit is a commitment from a lender to lend funds to a company as needed, up to a predetermined maximum amount. The intent of a line of credit is to fund the short-term cash shortfalls of a business, not its long-term funding requirements. To reinforce this point, lenders generally require that a line of credit balance be dropped to zero at least once a year. If the business is unable to pay off the line of credit, it is likely that long-term funding needs are being mixed with the short-term cash requirements of the business. If so, arrange for a longer-term loan that offloads some of the cash requirements currently being fulfilled by the line of credit. If the lender providing the line of credit has senior rights to the company's assets, then the provider of the longer-term loan may require a higher interest rate in exchange for accepting a junior rights position.

Tax Shield Effects

When a company takes on debt, the related interest expense will be tax deductible in most government jurisdictions, thereby reducing the after-tax cost of the debt. This reduction in taxable income is referred to as a tax shield. However, the tax shield only operates if a business has taxable earnings from which interest expense can be deducted.

A common scenario for a growing business is that it needs to incur debt in order to build operations that will eventually generate taxable income – but there may be little or no taxable income during this growth stage. If so, the net cost of debt will be the full amount of the debt, with no tax shield effect, until such time as enough taxable income is being generated to offset the interest expense.

One could make the case that any tax losses in the current period can be rolled forward and applied against future taxable income as a tax loss carryforward. However, if a company is expanding into new lines of business, there is no certainty that this taxable income will ever appear. If so, it makes sense to assume that the capital structure will result in interest expense that has not been reduced by the effect of the tax shield. A possible outcome of this situation is that management elects not to take on any additional debt.

Future Financing Flexibility

If a business acquires a large amount of debt, this may close off debt financing in the future, because lenders may then feel that the company is too highly leveraged to take on additional debt. This is particularly likely to be the case if the current lender has encumbered the bulk of the company's assets, leaving few assets available as collateral for additional rounds of financing.

To maintain flexibility in the capital structure, management might want to emphasize equity financing, or only entering into debt agreements that do not require collateral or overly restrictive covenants. This is an especially common issue in tight credit markets where debt can only be acquired at a high cost, and with tight restrictions.

Market Timing

The managers of a publicly-held company likely have a keen awareness of the current market price of their company's stock. They also know how this number compares to historical price points. Further, they should have an expectation for the future performance of the firm. The result of these inputs is a strong opinion regarding whether investors are currently placing a fair price on the company's shares in comparison to management's expectations. If there is a current need to sell more equity, managers will be more willing to do so if the current market price is high in relation to their expectations. Conversely, if the market price is low, they will be more likely to either use debt financing or internally generated funds, or simply hold off on capital projects until the price of the stock eventually increases. This behavior is quite rational, since managers will believe they are selling shares too cheaply at a low price, and would rather wait. Conversely, if the share price is perceived to be inordinately high, management may sell more shares than it was planning to, just to take advantage of the situation.

Loan Covenant Issues

When a company takes on new debt, the associated debt agreement may contain any number of loan covenants that the company must meet over the period of the loan. If the company cannot do so, then the lender can force the immediate repayment of the loan. Typical covenants include:

- Maintaining a certain minimum profit amount or profit percentage
- Keeping the current ratio higher than a certain percentage
- Keeping the interest coverage ratio higher than a certain percentage
- Not issuing dividends to investors
- Freezing or limiting compensation levels for senior managers

Covenants are designed to protect the assets of the lender. For example, limiting dividends and compensation keep the borrower from shifting borrowed funds outside of the company, where the lender cannot recover the funds. Similarly, if certain performance or financial position ratios decline, the lender is in a better position to reclaim loaned funds at once, before the company's finances decline further.

In situations where restrictive loan covenants are in place or will be imposed, a company may conclude that the negative effects of the covenants supersede the benefits of having additional debt. If so, management may conclude that no additional debt should be obtained, or that existing debt should be paid off – thereby freeing the company from loan covenants. Doing so means that the optimal capital structure of a business may involve no debt at all.

Maturity Structure of Debt

A key element of the capital structure is the mix of maturity dates linked to corporate debt. Ideally, debt should mature shortly after the company is scheduled to liquidate a sufficient amount of assets to pay off the debt. This means that the company has the capability to liquidate debts through internal cash flows, rather than having to rely upon third parties to roll over the debt to a later period. Here are several examples of maturity structure issues:

- A company borrows $20,000,000 in order to purchase an office building. The payoff structure of the loan should approximately match the cash flows that the company earns from the building's tenant rental payments.
- A company borrows $500,000 to buy a machine that should produce goods for the next five years at an even rate. The payoff structure of the loan should be matched to the cash flows generated by the machine.
- A company borrows $50,000,000 to acquire a competitor, using a bond issuance. If it is not possible to estimate the timing and amounts of cash flows resulting from the acquisition, it may be best to design an attractive conversion feature into the bond, thereby encouraging bond holders to convert their bonds into the company's common stock.

- A company engages in separate borrowing transactions to fund several different projects. The analyst recommends adjusting the terms of these debt instruments so that their maturity dates are staggered. Doing so keeps the company from being dependent on lenders for a large amount of debt repayment within a short period of time.

The maturity structure of debt may be of less concern to a large, well-capitalized and publicly-held business that routinely raises funds in the capital markets. However, even in these cases, economic downturns can increase the cost of funds dramatically from time to time. To avoid these situations, it may sometimes make sense to take advantage of times when credit is cheap, and the business can refinance existing debt at these lower rates.

When designing an appropriate maturity structure for corporate debt, plan for a gradual build-up of cash prior to debt repayment dates, so that the company is not suddenly faced with a large cash shortfall that is difficult to roll over.

A major trap that many CFOs fall into is the belief that interest rates will decline in the future. This belief leads them to continually finance company operations with short term debt, since they are always waiting for a decline in interest rates. A common result is that interest rates do *not* decline; instead, the company is subjected to short-term swings in interest rates, as well as the availability of short-term debt, which can lead to significant funding problems. Consequently, a prudent person should arrange for a large portion of company debt to have a longer maturity. If interest rates eventually decline, then this longer-term debt can be refinanced at the new, lower rate.

Creditor Position Considerations

If a company is liquidated, the proceeds from sale of its remaining assets are paid to those creditors having the most senior claim on those assets. These creditors usually include lenders who have required that collateral be included in their debt agreements. If the claims of these senior creditors are fully paid off, then the claims of junior creditors are paid. Only after all of these claims have been settled can any residual funds be distributed to shareholders. Because of this positioning at the bottom of the creditor pecking order, shareholders may not be interested in the acquisition of debt, and may instead opt for growth that is only fueled by internally-generated cash flows.

Concern about the rights of creditors is of more importance to shareholders in organizations that have such shaky financial structures and earnings that the right to residual funds is a real concern. It may also be an issue in a family-controlled business where the assets of the organization represent the primary source of wealth of the family.

Debt Paydown

A business could have locked itself into an expensive cost of debt when it acquired debt at some earlier point in time. Management may have an interest in paying off this higher-cost debt under a variety of circumstances. Doing so will alter the capital structure of the business, as well as its weighted-average cost of capital. Here are several issues to consider when engaging in a debt paydown:

- *Bank relationship.* The bank issuing debt to the company may require unusually oppressive loan covenants, as well as require that all of the company's bank accounts be shifted to it. If so, the benefit of paying down high-cost debt may be enhanced by management's need to sever the banking relationship. If so, the nature of the lending relationship may drive the decision to accelerate the pay down of debt.
- *Alternative uses.* The company may not have adequate internal uses for its excess funds, so the pay down of expensive debt becomes the most economical use of the funds.
- *Balance sheet clean up.* The company may be preparing its financial statements for viewing by outside parties, and wants to reduce the amount of expensive debt listed on its balance sheet. This situation may arise when a company is applying for credit with a key supplier, going public, or is considering being acquired.

Cost of Capital Reduction

As noted in the Cost of Capital chapter, the cost of the funds employed by a business is derived from the weighted average cost of equity and debt. The cost of equity is much more expensive than debt in most cases, so a business wanting to reduce the weighted average cost of its capital would logically want to use as much debt as possible. With a lower cost of funds, it is then possible to invest in projects that have lower returns on investment.

As an example of this concept, a company that leases copier machines can offer its customers lease rates at lower prices than a competitor, if the company's cost of capital is lower than the competitor's cost of capital. As long as the company can continue to obtain debt funding at a lower cost than the competitor, it will have a definitive pricing advantage that may translate into additional sales.

A reduction in the cost of capital is of much less concern in a business that requires little capital investment. In this situation, there are few projects requiring capital investment, so the cost of funds is irrelevant.

Market Signals

When management foresees a low level of earnings in the immediate future, there will be little point in obtaining additional debt, since the added interest expense cannot be used to shield any income. Instead, there will be a tendency to maintain or reduce debt levels. Conversely, if there is a strong sense that the corporate level of income will soon increase, management will be more likely to take on additional debt in order to fund operations. The interest expense associated with the extra debt can be used to offset taxable income. In addition, taking on extra debt sends a signal to the investment community that management is so confident about the company's future that the risk associated with paying back the added debt is not considered to be an issue. If investors are watching closely, they will interpret this altered debt load as a market signal, and may react by bidding up the price of the company's stock.

The market signaling concept is only applicable when a company is publicly-held and its shares are trading on a stock exchange. A private company with a small number of shareholders will have no interest in the market signaling aspects of its capital structure.

Planning for a Bond Rating

A credit rating agency is an entity that assigns credit ratings to either the issuers of certain kinds of debt, or directly to their debt instruments. There are three major credit rating agencies that provide ratings for the bulk of all debt issuances. They are authorized for ratings work as Nationally Recognized Statistical Rating Organizations (NRSROs) by the SEC. The three agencies that collectively control most of the market are:

- Moody's Investor Service
- Standard & Poor's
- Fitch Ratings

The ratings issued by these agencies are used by investors to determine the price at which to buy debt (usually bonds). In addition, the investment policies of many entities require them to limit their investments to debt issuances having certain minimum credit ratings. It is difficult to issue debt without a credit rating, since the issuance may be undersubscribed or can only be sold at a high effective interest rate.

The rating classifications used by the agencies vary from each other to some extent. The following table presents a comparison of the credit rating classifications of the three largest agencies. Debt issuances rated as investment grade in the table are considered suitable for investment purposes. The ratings classified as speculative are generally avoided by those entities looking for safe investments.

Credit Rating Comparison

Risk Level	Moody's	Standard & Poor's	Fitch
Investment grade:			
(highest investment grade)	Aaa	AAA	AAA
	Aa1	AA+	AA+
	Aa2	AA	AA
	Aa3	AA-	AA-
	A1	A+	A+
	A2	A	A
	A3	A-	A-
	Baa1	BBB+	BBB+
	Baa2	BBB	BBB
(lowest investment grade)	Baa3	BBB-	BBB-
Speculative grade:			
(highest speculative grade)	Ba1	BB+	BB+
	Ba2	BB	BB
	Ba3	BB-	BB-
	B1	B+	B+
	B2	B	B
	B3	B-	B-
	Caa1	CCC+	CCC+

Note: There are additional lower speculative grades than those listed in this table.

Only a large company with a stable business model and conservative financial practices can hope to qualify for one of the top-tier investment grades. Indeed, so few AAA ratings are issued that the recipients tend to use them as marketing tools to impress customers, suppliers, and employees. Since the AAA rating is well out of reach for most companies, the primary goal is simply to obtain a mid-level investment grade rating. By doing so, investors will not demand an excessively high interest rate on bond issuances. Companies certainly do not want their debt instruments to be classified as speculative, since investors will not buy them unless the company is willing to pay a very high interest rate.

A debt issuer may find that the credit rating agencies assign different credit ratings to different bond issuances, even though the bonds are all being issued by the same entity. This variation is caused by differences in the amount of collateral (if any) assigned to the debt, the level of subordination to other debt instruments of the issuer, and other debt terms.

Credit ratings and the objectives of a business are intertwined. If senior management wants to achieve rapid growth, it may need to issue more debt than a rating agency might consider prudent, resulting in a lower credit rating. Conversely, if it is considered more important to maintain a high credit rating, doing so will mandate a level of fiscal prudence that cannot support a rapid rate of growth. In short, it is difficult to obtain both a high growth rate and a stratospheric credit rating – management has to choose which objective is more important.

If the management team is interested in altering the capital structure of the business by adding debt, it may make sense to pay a consulting firm or one of the credit rating agencies to advise the company on the amount of additional debt that can be added to the business before its credit rating will probably be reduced. This information is useful for determining when to balance the corporate debt burden with the issuance of additional equity.

Timing of Changes to the Capital Structure

If an analysis of the capital structure reveals that a change is in order, this does not mean that such a change should be enacted at once. It is entirely possible that current market conditions are not optimal for the acquisition of new equity or debt funding. For example, there may be a bear market in which the price of equity securities are depressed, or a tight credit market in which the cost of debt is well above the historical average. If so, the most sensible approach may be to wait for conditions to improve, rather than taking any action that is not cost-effective for the business.

Summary

The capital structure of a business can be modeled using pro forma financial statements that show how changes in the amounts and relative proportions of debt and equity can impact a company's earnings, financial position, and risk. However, the large amount of qualitative decision making noted throughout this chapter should make it clear that the opinions of senior management and investors regarding the risk profile of the business should have a large bearing on the development of capital structure, rather than just using a rigid calculation that balances the cost of capital against the available use of funds.

The decision options explored in this chapter will likely result in a range of possible capital structure alternatives, all of which are acceptable ways to fund a business. As long as the actual capital structure does not stray beyond the boundaries of these alternatives, the structure can be considered satisfactory.

Chapter 3
Financial Planning

Introduction

In order to plan for fund raising and the deployment of funds, it is first necessary to have a cash prediction system in place. Over the short term, financial planning relies upon the cash forecast, which contains more precise information than the broader estimates found in a budget. The methods used to construct a cash forecast differ, depending upon the duration of the forecast. A short-term forecast relies upon actual cash payments and receipts, while a medium-term forecast relies more heavily upon the use of formulas. A master budget is used for long-term financial planning; this is a compilation of the lower-level department budgets and revenue plans that a business usually creates each year as part of its annual planning process. In this chapter, we cover the compilation of the short-term and medium-term cash forecast, as well as the development of the master budget.

> **Related Podcast Episode:** Episode 71 of the Accounting Best Practices Podcast discusses budget model improvements. The episode is available at: **accounting-tools.com/podcasts** or **iTunes**

The Cash Forecast

It is necessary to know the amount of cash that will probably be on hand in the near future, in order to make fund raising and investment decisions. This is accomplished with a cash forecast, which should be sufficiently detailed to warn of projected cash shortfalls and excess funds on at least a weekly basis. This section covers the details of how to create and fine-tune a cash forecast.

The cash forecast can be divided into two parts: near-term cash flows that are highly predictable (typically covering a one-month period) and medium-term cash flows that are largely based on revenues that have not yet occurred and supplier invoices that have not yet arrived. The first part of the forecast can be quite accurate, while the second part yields increasingly tenuous results after not much more than a month has passed. The following exhibit shows the severity of the decline in accuracy for short-term and medium-term forecasts. In particular, there is an immediate decline in accuracy as soon as the medium-term forecast replaces the short-term forecast, since less reliable information is used in the medium-term forecast.

Variability of Actual from Forecasted Cash Flow Information

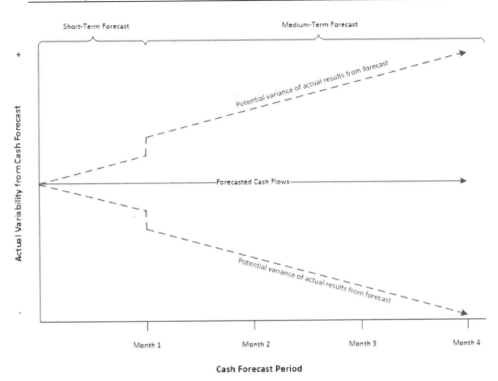

Cash Forecast Period

Through the remainder of this section, we will deal separately with how to construct the short-term and medium-term portions of the cash forecast.

The Short-Term Cash Forecast

The short-term cash forecast is based on a detailed accumulation of information from a variety of sources within the company. The bulk of this information comes from the accounts receivable, accounts payable, and payroll records, though other significant sources are the treasurer (for financing activities), the CFO (for acquisitions information) and even the corporate secretary (for scheduled dividend payments). Since this forecast is based on detailed itemizations of cash inflows and outflows, it is sometimes called the *receipts and disbursements method*.

The forecast needs to be sufficiently detailed to create an accurate cash forecast, but not so detailed that it requires an inordinate amount of labor to update. Consequently, include a detailed analysis of only the *largest* receipts and expenditures, and aggregate all other items. The detailed analysis involves the manual prediction of selected cash receipts and expenditures, while the aggregated results are scheduled based on average dates of receipt and payment (see the comments at the end of this section about the use of averaging).

> **Tip:** Use detailed analysis of cash items in the cash forecast for the 20% of items that comprise 80% of the cash flows, and use aggregation for the remaining 80% of items that comprise 20% of the cash flows.

The following table notes the treatment of the key line items in a cash forecast, including the level of detailed forecasting required.

Cash Forecast Line Items

+/-	Line Item	Discussion
+	Beginning cash	This is the current cash balance as of the creation date of the cash forecast, or, for subsequent weeks, it is the ending cash balance from the preceding week. Do not include restricted cash in this number, since it may not be available to pay for expenditures.
+	Accounts receivable	Do not attempt to duplicate the detail of the aged accounts receivable report in this section of the forecast. However, the largest receivables should be itemized, stating the period in which cash receipt is most likely to occur. All other receivables can be listed in aggregate.
+	Other receivables	Only include this line item if there are significant amounts of other receivables (such as customer advances) for which cash should be received within the forecast period.
-	Employee compensation	This is possibly the largest expense item, so be especially careful in estimating the amount. It is easiest to base the compensation expense on the amount paid in the preceding period, adjusted for any expected changes.
-	Payroll taxes	List this expense separately, since it is common to forget to include it when aggregated into the employee compensation line item.
-	Contractor compensation	If there are large payments to subcontractors, list them in one or more line items.
-	Key supplier payments	If there are large payments due to specific suppliers, itemize them separately. You may need to change the dates of these payments in the forecast in response to estimated cash positions.
-	Large recurring payments	There are usually large ongoing payments, such as rent and medical insurance, which can be itemized on separate lines of the forecast.
-	Debt payments	If there are significant principal or interest payments coming due, itemize them in the report.
-	Dividend payments	If dividend payments are scheduled, itemize them in the forecast; this tends to be a large expenditure.

+/-	Line Item	Discussion
-	Expense reports	If there are a large number of expense reports in each month, they are probably clustered near month-end. You can usually estimate the amount likely to be submitted.
=	Net cash position	This is the total of all the preceding line items.
+/-	Financing activities	Add any new debt, which increases cash flow, or the reduction of debt, which decreases cash flow. Also add any investments that mature during the period.
	Ending cash	This is the sum of the net cash position line item and the financing activities line item.

The following example illustrates a cash forecast, using the line items described in the preceding table.

EXAMPLE

The CFO of Suture Corporation constructs the following cash forecast for each week in the month of September.

+/-	Line Item	Sept. 1-7	Sept. 8-14	Sept. 15-22	Sept. 23-30
+	Beginning cash	$50,000	$30,000	$2,000	$0
+	Accounts receivable				
+	Alpha Pharmaceuticals	120,000		60,000	
+	St. Joseph's Burn Center		85,000		52,000
+	Third Degree Burn Center	29,000		109,000	
+	Other major receivables	160,000	25,000	48,000	60,000
+	Other receivables	10,000		5,000	
-	Employee compensation	140,000		145,000	
-	Payroll taxes	10,000		11,000	
-	Contractor compensation				
-	Bryce Contractors	8,000		8,000	
-	Johnson Contractors	14,000		12,000	
-	Key supplier payments				
-	Chico Biomedical	100,000		35,000	
-	Stanford Research	20,000	80,000	29,000	14,000
-	Other suppliers	35,000	40,000	30,000	48,000
-	Large recurring payments				
-	Medical insurance				43,000
-	Rent				49,000
-	Debt payments		18,000		

+/-	Line Item	Sept. 1-7	Sept. 8-14	Sept. 15-22	Sept. 23-30
-	Dividend payments			20,000	
-	Expense reports	12,000	0	0	21,000
=	Net cash position	$30,000	$2,000	-$66,000	-$63,000
+/-	Financing activities			66,000	63,000
=	Ending cash	$30,000	$2,000	$0	$0

The forecast reveals a cash shortfall beginning in the third week, which will require a cumulative total of $129,000 of additional financing if the company wants to meet its scheduled payment obligations.

The format is designed with the goal of giving sufficient visibility into cash flows to reveal the causes of unusual cash shortfalls or overages, without burying the reader in an excessive amount of detail. To meet this goal, note the use of the "Other receivables" and "Other suppliers" line items in the exhibit. They are used to aggregate smaller projected transactions that do not have a major impact on the forecast, but which would otherwise overwhelm the document with an excessive amount of detail if they were listed individually.

A possible addition to the cash forecast is the use of a *target balance*. This is essentially a "safety stock" of cash that is kept on hand to guard against unexpected cash requirements that were not planned for in the cash forecast. All excess cash above the target balance can be invested, while any shortfalls below the target balance should be funded. If a target balance had been incorporated into the preceding cash forecast example in the amount of $10,000, the amount would have been listed for the week of September 1-7 as a deduction from the ending cash position, leaving $20,000 of cash available for investment purposes.

The very short-term portion of the cash forecast may be subject to some tweaking, usually to delay a few supplier payments to adjust for liquidity problems expected to arise over the next few days. To incorporate these changes into the forecast, use a preliminary draft of the forecast to coordinate changes in the timing of payments with the controller, and then record the delays in the forecast before issuing the final version.

The Medium-Term Cash Forecast

The medium-term forecast begins one month into the future, which is the point at which the information used to compile the short-term forecast is no longer reliable. The components of the medium-term forecast are largely comprised of formulas, rather than the specific data inputs used for a short-term forecast. For example, if the sales manager were to contribute estimated revenue figures for each forecasting period, then the model could derive the following additional information:

- *Cash paid for cost of goods sold items.* Can be estimated as a percentage of sales, with a time lag based on the average supplier payment terms.

- *Cash paid for payroll.* Sales activity can be used to estimate changes in production headcount, which in turn can be used to derive payroll payments.
- *Cash receipts from customers.* A standard time lag between the billing date and payment date can be incorporated into the estimation of when cash will be received from customers.

The concept of a formula-filled cash forecast that automatically generates cash balance information breaks down in some parts of the forecast. In the following areas, it will be necessary to make manual updates to the forecast:

- *Fixed costs.* Some costs are entirely fixed, such as rent, and so will not vary with sales volume. Be aware of any contractually-mandated changes in these costs, and incorporate them into the forecast.
- *Step costs.* If revenues change significantly, the fixed costs just described may have to be altered by substantial amounts. For example, a certain sales level may mandate opening a new production facility. A more common step cost is having to hire an overhead staff position when certain sales levels are reached. Be aware of the activity levels at which these step costs will occur.
- *Seasonal / infrequent costs.* There may be expenditures that only arise at long intervals, such as for the company Christmas party. These amounts are manually added to the forecast.
- *Contractual items.* Both cash inflows and outflows may be linked to contract payments, as may be the case with service contracts. If so, the exact amount and timing of each periodic payment can be transferred from the contract directly into the cash forecast.

The methods used to construct a medium-term cash forecast are inherently less accurate than the much more precise information used to derive a short-term forecast. The problem is that much of the information is derived from the estimated revenue figure, which rapidly declines in accuracy just a few months into the future. Because of this inherent level of inaccuracy, do not extend the forecast over too long a time period. Instead, settle upon a time range that provides useful information for financial planning purposes.

The Use of Averages

There can be a temptation to use averages for estimated cash flows in the cash forecast. For example, it may seem reasonable to divide the average cash collections for receivables in a month by four, and then enter the resulting average cash receipts figure in each week of the forecast. This is not a good idea in the short-term portion of the forecast, since there are a number of timing differences that will make actual results differ markedly from average results. The following bullets contain several cash flow issues that can have sharp spikes and declines in comparison to the average:

- The receipt of payment for an unusually large invoice

- The designation of a large invoice as a bad debt
- Once-a-month payments, such as rent and medical insurance
- Sporadic payments, such as for dividends and property taxes

It is particularly dangerous to use averaging to estimate accounts receivable. In many companies, there is a disproportionate amount of invoicing at the end of each month, which means that there is a correspondingly large amount of cash receipts one month later (assuming 30-day payment terms). In short, it is quite common to have billing surges cause payment surges that vary wildly from average cash receipt numbers.

If one were to rely upon an averages-based cash forecast, there would be a high risk of routinely having cash shortfalls and overages. After all, it is necessary to ensure liquidity *every day*, not just on average. Thus, we strongly recommend against the use of averages when forecasting the larger items in a short-term cash forecast.

The situation is different in a medium-term forecast, since the time period is sufficiently far into the future to make it impossible to predict cash flows with any degree of precision. In this case, one can estimate based on averages, though with three enhancements:

- Insert specifically identifiable cash flows, such as contractually-mandated payments or receipts.
- Insert specific cash flows that have historically proven to be reliable. For example, if a customer has proven to be consistent in paying on a certain day of the month, assume that these payments will continue with the same timing.
- It may be possible to substitute actual cash flow information for averages in the least-distant time periods. This is particularly likely for cash outflows, such as payroll, where there is not a significant amount of change in the amount paid from period to period.

The Reliability of Cash Flow Information

After building cash forecasts for a few months, it will become apparent that certain information is highly reliable, while other types of information vary considerably from expectations. It is useful to identify which types of information are *least* reliable, so that the most time can be spent monitoring them. Highly reliable information can be copied forward into successive versions of the cash forecast with minimal cross-checking. The following table notes the reliability of different types of cash flow information.

Reliability of Cash Flow Information

Cash Flow Item	Reliability	Comments
Cash Inflows		
Credit sales	Average	If there are many small invoices, it should be possible to calculate the time periods within which certain proportions of all billed invoices will be paid. The situation is more dire if there are a few large invoices, since reliability is subject to the whims of a few customers. Timing is particularly problematic for payments coming from international customers, since there are more ways in which payments can be held up in transit.
Investments	Very high	If an investment has a specific maturity date, the related cash receipt can be scheduled with high confidence.
Cash Outflows		
Payroll	High	If a company uses a third party payroll supplier, the full amount of the payroll will be extracted from the company's account on a specific date. If payroll is handled in-house and especially with check payments, then the reliability of payments will be high within a period of a few days.
Suppliers	High	The dates for supplier payments are based on negotiated payment terms, which make the reliability of this information quite high. The reliability can be eroded if there are disputes with suppliers that delay payments.
Income tax payments	Varies	Quarterly income tax payments can be based on prior year payments, and so are very predictable. However, the final annual payment is based on annual net profits, which may be considerably less predictable.
Other tax payments	High	Sales tax remittances are usually compiled several weeks in advance, and can also be predicted as a percentage of sales.
Dividends	Very high	The amount and timing of dividends are determined several months in advance by the board of directors.
Debt payments	Very high	Debt repayment schedules are usually quite rigidly enforced. The lender may even use an ACH debit to extract debt payments from the company's bank account on specific dates.

The preceding table points out that the credit sales component of cash inflows can have the most problematic reliability. Thus, this is likely to be the area to focus on when developing a cash forecast.

The Impact of Special Events

There are a number of special events that can have a profound (and usually negative) impact on the cash forecast. From the perspective of financial planning, it is critical to identify these events and incorporate them into the cash forecast as early as possible. Doing so improves the likelihood that sudden cash shortages can be avoided. Here are several examples of special events that can impact cash flows:

- *Commodity price spikes.* The price of a key commodity suddenly increases, and the company is unable to pass the increase through to its customers. This will cause a significant jump in cash outflows in 30 days, when supplier invoices are due for payment. This will impact the transitional period in the cash forecast between the end of the short-term forecast and the start of the medium-term forecast.
- *Competing product introduction.* A competitor unexpectedly introduces an excellent competing product at a low price point, which immediately drives down the company's market share. This will impact the medium-term cash forecast, as sales drop and cash inflows decline.
- *Supply chain disruption.* A flood destroys a key supplier facility. It will take three months to mitigate the supply chain damage. In the meantime, existing buffer stocks of finished goods will be drawn down and sales will then terminate for all goods containing the parts provided by the supplier. This will not impact the short-range cash forecast, but may trigger a massive decline in cash inflows from customers over the medium term.
- *War.* An insurgency impacts deliveries into a key market in the Middle East, cutting off the company from its distributors. All sales are expected to cease until the insurgency can be put down. This will certainly impact the medium-term forecast, and may even roll into the short-term forecast, if the impacted distributors cannot make payments on outstanding invoices.

These examples of special events all impact the cash forecast to a major extent. It is entirely possible that a business may be subjected to at least one of these events every year or so. Given the reasonable probability of these occurrences, be sure to maintain strong lines of communication with everyone in the company who is most likely to be best informed about these events. This means having ongoing discussions with the purchasing manager to understand changes in the supply chain, as well as with the sales manager to learn firsthand what is happening with the company's products and distribution systems. This enhanced level of communication allows for the more rapid inclusion of special events in the cash forecast.

Tip: Include in the forecasting procedure a requirement to contact the purchasing and sales managers for updates on special events. Otherwise, this investigation will likely be forgotten.

The Master Budget

The master budget is the summary level document derived from the annual budgeting process. Its core documents are the budgeted income statement and the budgeted balance sheet, from which differing levels of financing information can be derived. In the following sub-sections, we make note of the contents and derivation of these planning documents, as well as the related financing budget.

The Budgeted Income Statement

The core of the master budget is the budgeted income statement. It is derived from nearly all of the revenue and departmental budgets, and looks quite a bit like a standard income statement. This is a sufficient summarization of the budget for many companies, because they are primarily concerned with financial performance. However, some companies may still have an interest in their projected financial position (especially cash), which is contained in the balance sheet. Since the balance sheet is more difficult to derive than the income statement, they may be content to use a rough calculation of ending cash position whose components are mostly derived from information already in the budget. The following sample income statement contains this rough estimation of the ending cash balance in each period.

Sample Budgeted Income Statement

	Quarter 1	Quarter 2	Quarter 3	Quarter 4
Revenue	$2,200,000	$2,425,000	$2,500,000	$2,545,000
Cost of goods sold:				
Direct labor expense	220,000	253,000	253,000	253,000
Direct materials expense	767,000	838,000	831,000	840,000
Manufacturing overhead	293,000	293,000	309,000	310,000
Total cost of goods sold	1,280,000	1,384,000	1,393,000	1,403,000
Gross margin	$920,000	$1,041,000	$1,107,000	$1,142,000
Sales and marketing	315,000	351,000	374,000	339,000
Administration	453,500	452,500	435,000	447,000
Research and development	50,000	52,000	54,000	55,500
Profits before taxes	$101,500	$185,500	$244,000	$300,500
Income taxes	35,500	65,000	85,500	105,000
Profits after taxes	$66,000	$120,500	$158,500	$195,500
Cash flow:				
Beginning cash	$50,000	-$52,500	$77,500	$7,000

	Quarter 1	Quarter 2	Quarter 3	Quarter 4
+ Net profit	66,000	120,500	158,500	195,500
+ Depreciation	19,500	17,500	18,000	18,000
- Capital expenditures	-38,000	-8,000	-47,000	-28,000
- Dividends	-150,000	0	-200,000	0
Ending cash	-$52,500	$77,500	$7,000	$192,500

The calculation of ending cash is appended to the budgeted income statement because it is partly derived from the net income figure located directly above it in the budget. Also, if a company does not intend to create a balance sheet, it is practical to include a cash calculation on the same page as the income statement.

The trouble with the ending cash measurement presented in the sample is that it is not complete. It does not incorporate any timing delays for when cash may be received or issued, and it also does not factor in the impact of changes in working capital. Thus, it can present inaccurate estimates of cash flow. For a more detailed derivation of ending cash, we need a balance sheet. The compilation of that document is discussed in the next sub-section.

Components of the Budgeted Balance Sheet

The balance sheet is difficult to derive as part of the budgeting process, because little of the information derived through the budgeting process is designed for it. Instead, a number of estimates must be made to approximate the amounts of various asset and liability line items as of the end of each budgeted reporting period. The key elements of the balance sheet that require estimation are:

- Accounts receivable
- Inventory
- Fixed assets
- Accounts payable

We will address the derivation of these items below.

Accounts Receivable

Accounts receivable is the amount of sales made on credit that have not yet been paid by customers. It is closely correlated with sales, with a delay measured using days sales outstanding (DSO). DSO is calculated as:

$$\frac{\text{Accounts receivable}}{\text{Annual sales} \div 365 \text{ days}}$$

The DSO figure is then applied to projected credit sales during the budget period to determine the amount of accounts receivable outstanding at any given time.

EXAMPLE

Quest Adventure Gear has a division whose annual sales are $10 million. Its accounts receivable balance at the end of the most recent month was $1,400,000. Its DSO is calculated as:

$$\frac{\$1,400,000 \text{ accounts receivable}}{\$10,000,000 \text{ annual sales} \div 365 \text{ days}}$$

$$= 51 \text{ days sales outstanding}$$

Thus, it takes an average of 51 days for Quest to collect an account receivable. In its balance sheet budget, Quest would record as accounts receivable the current month's sales plus 21/30ths of the sales budgeted in the immediately preceding month. Thus, Quest's budgeted receivables would be calculated as follows for a four-month sample period:

	December (prior year)	January	February	March
Credit sales	$790,000	$810,000	$815,000	$840,000
Receivables for month	--	810,000	815,000	840,000
Receivables from prior month	--	553,000	567,000	571,000
Total receivables in balance sheet	--	$1,363,000	$1,382,000	$1,411,000

An alternative approach for calculating the amount of accounts receivable is to calculate the percentage of credit sales that are collected within the month of sales and then within each of the next 30-day time buckets, and apply these layers of collections to a calculation of the ending accounts receivable in each budget period. The following example illustrates the concept.

EXAMPLE

The CFO of Quest Adventure Gear decides to use an alternative method for deriving the ending accounts receivable balance for the division described in the preceding example. The CFO finds that, historically, the following percentages of credit sales are paid within the stated time periods:

	Percent Paid	Percent Unpaid
In month of sale	10%	90%
In following month	65%	25%
In 2nd month	18%	7%
In 3rd month	5%	2%
In 4th month	2%	0%
Total	100%	

The CFO then uses the following table to derive the ending accounts receivable balance for the month of January, which is part of the budget period. The information from the preceding three months is needed to derive the ending accounts receivable balance in January.

	October (prior year)	November (prior year)	December (prior year)	January
Credit sales	$815,000	$820,000	$790,000	$810,000
90% of January sales				729,000
25% of December sales				198,000
7% of November sales				57,000
2% of October sales				16,000
Total ending accounts receivable				$1,000,000

A truly detailed model would assume an even longer collection period for some receivables, which may extend for twice the number of months shown in the model. If you choose to use this method, the increased accuracy from adding more months to the model does not appreciably improve the accuracy of the ending accounts receivable figure. Thus, restrict the accounts receivable layering to no more than three or four months.

The receivables layering method is clearly more labor intensive than the DSO method, though it may result in slightly more accurate results. In the interests of modeling efficiency, we prefer the DSO method. It requires much less space in the budget model, is easy to understand, and produces reasonably accurate results.

There are a number of concerns regarding the estimation of accounts receivable to be aware of. They are:

- *Credit policy.* If the company alters its credit policy, then estimate its impact on DSO. For example, if management wants to loosen credit in order to increase sales, expect DSO to increase. Conversely, a tighter credit policy should reduce the DSO figure.
- *Arbitrary DSO changes.* Do not arbitrarily alter the historical DSO rate used in the budget. A common practice by senior managers is to assume that cash flow can be improved with more aggressive collection practices, so they budget for a reduced amount of DSO. This does not happen in practice, because the collections staff is presumably already engaged in the optimum level of collection activities.
- *Large receivables.* If there will be large individual invoices outstanding during the budget period, the collection of these specific invoices can dramatically alter the DSO. If this will be the case, adjust the DSO for the company's historical collection experience with the customers who will owe the largest invoices.
- *General economic conditions.* Customers are subject to general economic conditions, so if there is a general worsening in the business environment,

expect *their* customers to pay late, which will cause your customers to pay late. The reverse is not necessarily true; if economic conditions improve and customers are flush with cash, they may be paying in accordance with an internal payment policy, and so will *not* pay any sooner.

In general, our recommendation is to maintain the historical DSO through the budget period; it is rarely good practice to assume a reduction in DSO. If anything, DSO is more likely to increase.

Inventory

There should be a relatively constant relationship between the level of sales and the amount of inventory on hand. Thus, if you can calculate the historical number of days of inventory on hand and then match it against the budgeted amount of cost of goods sold through the budget period, you can estimate the amount of inventory that should be on hand at the end of each budget period. The calculation of the days of inventory on hand is:

$$\frac{\text{Inventory}}{\text{Annual cost of goods sold} \div 365 \text{ days}}$$

Or, if inventory levels vary by quarter, divide the quarterly cost of goods sold by the number of days in the quarter. The calculation is:

$$\frac{\text{Inventory}}{\text{Quarterly cost of goods sold} \div 91 \text{ days}}$$

The estimation concept is shown in the following example.

EXAMPLE

Quest Adventure Gear has a division that manufactures sleeping bags. It maintains a substantial amount of raw materials in the form of premium goose down, polyester fill, rip stop nylon, and zippers, as well as finished goods. The company calculates the days of inventory on hand for the preceding quarter as follows:

$$\frac{\$1,000,000 \text{ ending inventory}}{\$1,875,000 \text{ quarterly cost of goods sold} \div 91 \text{ days}}$$

$$= 49 \text{ days of inventory on hand}$$

Quest expects that the division will continue to have roughly the same proportion of inventory to sales throughout the budget period, so it uses the same days of inventory on hand calculation to derive the ending inventory for each budget period as follows:

	Quarter 1	Quarter 2	Quarter 3	Quarter 4
Cost of goods sold (quarterly)	$1,875,000	$2,000,000	$2,100,000	$1,900,000
Cost of goods sold (monthly)	625,000	667,000	700,000	633,000
Days of inventory assumption	49 days	49 days	49 days	49 days
Ending inventory*	$1,021,000	$1,089,000	$1,143,000	$1,034,000

* Calculated as monthly cost of goods sold × (49 days ÷ 30 days)

The calculation reduces the quarterly cost of goods sold to a monthly figure, so that it can more easily be compared to the days of inventory on hand.

The ending inventory calculation can be thrown off by a number of factors. Consider the following issues, and adjust the calculation as needed:

- *Distant sourcing.* If the company begins to purchase goods from more distant locations, it will likely need to maintain larger amounts of safety stock to guard against any disruptions in deliveries.
- *Distribution system.* If the company alters its warehousing system, this will likely impact the amount of inventory required to keep the distribution pipeline full.
- *Manufacturing system.* If the company plans to change to a material requirements planning or just-in-time system during the budget period, this will likely reduce the amount of inventory on hand.
- *Materials mix.* The mix of materials, labor, and overhead is assumed to remain the same in the cost of goods sold. A higher mix of materials would call for a higher days of inventory assumption, and vice versa.
- *Obsolescence.* If a company's products are subject to rapid obsolescence, this makes it more likely that the obsolete items will remain in stock, thereby increasing the number of inventory days on hand.
- *Production change.* If the duration of the production process increases, as may be caused by a reconfiguration of the shop floor, then the amount of inventory held in work-in-process will also increase, and vice versa.
- *Stockpiling.* If management believes that some materials will be in short supply during the budget period, it may authorize the stockpiling of those materials in greater than normal quantities.

Finally, it is possible that there is a history of seasonal changes in the days of inventory measurement. If these changes are significant, consider using a different days of inventory measurement for each budgeted accounting period, based on the historical days of inventory measurement for each period.

Capital Expenditures

The amount and timing of expenditures for fixed assets come from the capital budgeting process, and are easily transferred into a fixed asset table that can be used as a source document for the budgeted balance sheet. Further, it may be useful to include in the schedule a standard amount of capital expenditures for each new employee hired; this typically includes the cost of office furniture and computer equipment. Finally, consider including a reserve in the schedule for as-yet unspecified fixed assets. There will always be unforeseen asset purchases, so be sure to reserve some funds for them. The following example illustrates the concepts of scheduling fixed assets.

EXAMPLE

Quest Adventure Gear plans to hire 10 administrative staff into one of its divisions during the budget year, and also plans to buy a variety of fixed assets. The following schedule itemizes the major types of fixed assets and the timing of their acquisition.

	Quarter 1	Quarter 2	Quarter 3	Quarter 4
Fixed asset purchases:				
Furniture and fixtures	$28,000	$0	$0	$32,000
Office equipment	0	40,000	0	0
Production equipment	100,000	25,000	80,000	0
Vehicles	32,000	0	32,000	0
Unspecified purchases	15,000	15,000	15,000	15,000
Subtotal	$175,000	$80,000	$127,000	$47,000
Purchases for new hires:				
Headcount additions	3	2	1	4
$6,000 × New hires	$18,000	$12,000	$6,000	$24,000
Total fixed asset purchases	$193,000	$92,000	$133,000	$71,000

Accounts Payable

A significant short-term liability listed in the balance sheet is accounts payable. It can be estimated with a reasonable amount of precision, because there is usually a constant relationship between the level of credit purchases from suppliers and the amount of unpaid accounts payable. Thus, if you can calculate the days of accounts payable that are usually on hand, then you can relate it to the estimated amount of credit purchases per accounting period and derive the ending accounts payable balance. The formula for accounts payable days is:

$$\frac{\text{Accounts payable}}{\text{Annual credit purchases} \div 365}$$

Or, if the days of accounts payable changes by quarter, divide the quarterly credit purchases by the number of days in the quarter. The calculation is:

$$\frac{\text{Accounts payable}}{\text{Quarterly credit purchases} \div 91}$$

The estimation concept is illustrated in the following example.

EXAMPLE

Quest Adventure Gear has a division whose annual purchases on credit in the past year were $4,250,000. Its average accounts payable balance during that period was $410,000. The calculation of its accounts payable days is:

$$\frac{\$410,000 \text{ accounts payable}}{\$4,250,000 \text{ annual credit purchases} \div 365}$$

= 35 accounts payable days

Quest expects that the division will continue to have roughly the same proportion of credit terms with its suppliers through the budget period, so it uses the same accounts payable days amount to derive the ending accounts payable for each budget period as follows:

	Quarter 1	Quarter 2	Quarter 3	Quarter 4
Purchases on credit (monthly)	$350,000	$380,000	$390,000	$400,000
Accounts payable days assumption	35 days	35 days	35 days	35 days
Ending accounts payable*	$408,000	$443,000	$455,000	$467,000

* Calculated as monthly purchases on credit × (35 days ÷ 30 days)

The problem with the calculation of accounts payable is where to find the information about credit purchases. To calculate the amount of these purchases, start with the total expenses for the measurement period and subtract from it all payroll and payroll tax expenses, as well as depreciation and amortization. There are other adjusting factors, such as expense accruals and payments made in cash, but this simple calculation should approximate the amount of purchases on credit.

Additional Estimation Elements

There are a few other line items in the balance sheet that require estimation for the budget period. These items are usually adjusted manually, rather than through the use of any formulas. They are:

- *Prepaid expenses.* This line item includes expenses that were paid in advance, and which therefore may be charged to expense at some point during or after the budget period. Examples of prepaid expenses are prepaid rent and insurance. These items may not change in proportion to the level of general corporate activity, so it is best to track them on a separate spreadsheet and manually determine when there will be additions to and deletions from the account.

- *Other assets.* There are likely to be a smorgasbord of stray assets on a company's books that are aggregated into this account. Examples of other assets are rent deposits, payroll advances, and accounts receivable from company officers. As was the case with prepaid expenses, these items may not change in proportion to the level of corporate activity, so track them separately and manually adjust the budget for any changes in them.

- *Income taxes payable.* If a company is earning a taxable profit, then it must make estimated tax payments on the 15th days of April, June, September, and December. You can either schedule these payments to equal the tax paid in the previous year, or a proportion of the actual tax liability in the budget year. Budgeting for this liability based on the tax paid in the previous year is quite simple. If you choose to instead budget for a liability equal to a proportion of the actual tax liability in the budget year, then use the effective tax rate expected for the entire year.

  If you are budgeting for this liability based on the net income in the budget year, it can be difficult to estimate. You may be using accelerated depreciation for the calculation of taxable income, as well as other deferred tax recognition strategies that cause a difference between taxable and actual net income. If such is the case, track these differences in a supporting budget schedule.

- *Accrued liabilities.* There may be a variety of accrued liabilities, such as unpaid vacation time, unpaid wages, and unpaid property taxes. In some cases, such as property taxes, the liability is unlikely to vary unless the company alters its property ownership, and so can be safely extended through the budget period with no alterations. In other cases, such as unpaid vacation time and unpaid wages, there is a direct correlation between the general level of corporate activity (such as headcount) and the amount of the liability. In these cases, use a formula to adjust the liability based on the appropriate underlying measure of activity.

- *Notes payable.* This can encompass loans and leases. Most of these items are on fixed repayment schedules, so a simple repayment table is usually sufficient for tracking the gradual reduction of notes payable. Also, the amount of each periodic debt repayment should be deducted from the amount of cash on hand. Additions to the notes payable line are addressed in the financing budget.

- *Equity*. The equity section of the balance sheet is composed of a beginning balance that is simply rolled forward from the previous period, a retained earnings balance into which is incorporated any gains and losses as the budget period progresses over time, and various equity-related financing issues that are addressed in the financing budget.

There are a number of line items shown here, so be prepared to maintain a number of supporting schedules to keep track of the ending balances for them.

The Cash Line Item

After filling in all other parts of the balance sheet, the cash line item becomes the "plug" entry to make the statement balance. Just because an amount is entered in the cash line item does not mean that the company will necessarily generate that amount of cash. An early iteration of a budgeted balance sheet has a strange way of revealing an astonishing surplus of cash! Instead, once the initial version of the balance sheet has been created, test it to see if all of the line items are reasonable. Use the following techniques to do so:

- *Growth impact*. If the company is planning on substantial growth, this means that the investment in accounts receivable and inventory should grow significantly, which will consume cash. Conversely, if the company plans to shrink in size, it should be converting these same items into cash. Thus, if the proposed balance sheet appears to be retaining a consistent amount of working capital through the budget period, irrespective of the sales level, the working capital line items should probably be revised.
- *Historical comparison*. Compare all line items in the proposed balance sheet to the same line items in the balance sheet for various periods in the preceding year. Are the numbers about the same, or are they approximately in the same proportions to each other? If not, investigate why there are differences.
- *Turnover analysis*. Compare the amount of accounts receivable, inventory, and accounts payable turnover in the proposed budget to the actual turnover ratios for these items in the preceding year. Unless significant structural changes are being made in the business, it is likely that the same turnover ratios should apply to the budget period.

The following table shows the impact on cash of turnover changes in the balance sheet. In particular, note the changes in the "Caused By" column that are required to alter turnover levels. If management does not take any of these actions, then do not budget for a change in turnover – instead, the business will likely experience the same turnover as last year.

Turnover Table

Type of Turnover	Cash Impact	Caused By
Accounts receivable turnover - Increase	Cash increases	More aggressive collection activity, tighter credit policy
Accounts receivable turnover - Decrease	Cash decreases	Less collection activity, looser credit policy
Inventory turnover – Increase	Cash increases	Reduce safety stock levels, use just-in-time deliveries, reduce number of product options
Inventory turnover – Decrease	Cash decreases	Increase safety stock levels, engage in bulk purchases
Accounts payable turnover - Increase	Cash decreases	Pay suppliers quicker, take early payment discounts, use suppliers with shorter payment terms
Accounts payable turnover - Decrease	Cash increases	Pay suppliers more slowly, stop taking early payment discounts, use suppliers with longer payment terms

If you are satisfied that the budgeted balance sheet appears reasonable after these tests, then the cash line item may also be considered achievable.

The Budgeted Balance Sheet

The budgeted balance sheet is derived from all of the preceding discussions in this section about the components of the balance sheet. The balance sheet should be compiled in two parts: a detailed compilation that contains a variety of calculations, and a summary-level version that is indistinguishable from a normal balance sheet. The following sample of a detailed balance sheet compilation includes a discussion of each line item. The numbers in the sample are irrelevant – we are only trying to show how the balance sheet is constructed.

Sample Detailed Balance Sheet Compilation

Line Item	Source	Amount
Assets		
Cash	The amount needed to equalize both sides of the balance sheet	$225,000
Accounts receivable	Based on sales by period and days receivables outstanding	450,000
Inventory	Based on cost of goods sold by period and days of inventory on hand	520,000
Prepaid expenses	Based on beginning balance and adjusted for specific changes	55,000
Fixed assets	Based on beginning balance and changes in the capital budget	1,490,000
Accumulated depreciation	Based on beginning balance and changes in the capital budget	-230,000
Other assets	Based on beginning balance and adjusted for specific changes	38,000
Total assets		**$2,548,000**
Liabilities		
Accounts payable	Based on credit purchases and days of accounts payable	$182,000
Accrued liabilities	Based on schedule of specific liabilities or based on corporate activity	99,000
Income taxes payable	Based on either the tax paid in the previous year or a proportion of the actual tax liability in the current year	75,000
Notes payable	Based on the beginning balance	720,000
- Debt repayments	Based on a schedule of required repayments	-120,000
+ New debt	From the financing budget	90,000
Total liabilities		$1,046,000
Equity		
Retained earnings	Based on the beginning balance	802,000
- Dividends	As per management instructions	-75,000
- Treasury stock purchases	As per management instructions	-50,000
+ Profit/loss	From the budgeted income statement	475,000
+ Stock sales	From the financing budget	350,000
Total equity		$1,502,000
Total liabilities and equity		**$2,548,000**

For the purposes of the budgeted balance sheet, we are not overly concerned with whether an asset or liability is classified as short-term or long-term. Given the inevitable inaccuracies inherent in a budgeted balance sheet, there is little point in making this designation.

The Financing Budget

Once a first draft of the budget has been prepared and a preliminary balance sheet constructed, you will get an idea of the cash requirements of the business, and can then construct a financing budget.

This budget addresses the need of a business for *more* cash. A financing budget can be constructed that addresses this need by including either debt or equity financing. In addition to these solutions, also consider going back into the main budget and making one or more of the following changes, thereby altering the amount of cash needed by the business:

- *Cost reduction.* There may be some parts of the business where expenses can be pruned in order to fund more activities elsewhere. Across-the-board reductions are usually a bad idea, since some parts of the business may already be running at a minimal expenditure level, and further reductions would cut into their performance.
- *Discretionary items.* If there are discretionary expenditures in the budget whose absence will not have an immediate impact on the business, consider reducing or eliminating them or changing the date on which they are purchased.
- *Dividends.* If there are dividends planned that have not yet been authorized by the board of directors, then consider either reducing them or delaying the payment date.
- *Sales growth.* If the budgeted level of sales is creating a significant requirement for more working capital and capital expenditures, consider reducing the amount of planned growth to meet the amount of financing that is available.
- *Sell assets.* If there is a strong need for cash that is driven by an excellent business opportunity, it may be time to sell off assets in lower-performance parts of the business and invest the funds in the new opportunity.

Once all of the preceding adjustments have been made, construct the financing budget. It should contain an itemization of the cash position as stated in the budgeted balance sheet, after which it itemizes the various types of financing needed to ensure that the company maintains a positive cash balance at all times. In addition, there should be a section that derives from the balance sheet the total amount that the company can potentially borrow against its assets (the borrowing base); this establishes an upper limit on the amount of borrowing. The following example illustrates the concept of the financing budget.

EXAMPLE

Quest Adventure Gear has completed a first draft of its budget, and finds that there are several cash shortfalls during the budget period. The CFO constructs the following financing budget to address the problem.

	Quarter 1	Quarter 2	Quarter 3	Quarter 4
Available borrowing base:				
Ending inventory	$1,200,000	$1,280,000	$1,310,000	$1,350,000
Ending trade receivables	1,800,000	1,850,000	1,920,000	1,980,000
Allowable inventory (60%)	720,000	768,000	786,000	810,000
Allowable receivables (80%)	1,440,000	1,480,000	1,536,000	1,584,000
Total borrowing base	$2,160,000	$2,248,000	$2,322,000	$2,394,000
Preliminary ending cash balance	-$320,000	-$480,000	-$600,000	-$680,000
Debt Funding:				
Beginning loan balance	$2,000,000			
Available debt*	160,000	88,000	74,000	72,000
Adjusted ending cash balance	-$160,000	-$232,000	-$278,000	-$286,000
Equity Funding:				
Stock issuance	$400,000	0	0	0
Final ending cash balance	$240,000	$168,000	$122,000	$114,000

* Calculated as the total borrowing base minus existing debt

The financing budget reveals that Quest has already used most of the debt available under its loan agreement, and is only able to incrementally borrow in each quarter as the amount of underlying assets gradually increases. To fund the remaining cash shortfall, Quest plans to sell $400,000 of stock to investors in the first quarter. This not only provides enough cash to cover the projected shortfall, but also leaves a small residual cash buffer.

If the financing budget includes a provision for more debt, then also include a line item in the budgeted income statement to address the associated incremental increase in interest expense. This means that there is a feedback loop between the financing budget and the balance sheet from which it draws its beginning cash balance; financing solutions may impact the beginning cash balance upon which the financing budget is based, which in turn may impact the amount of financing needed.

Summary

The information on which financial planning is based can be quite accurate in the near term, since it is usually based on the short-term cash forecast. If constructed properly, the information in this forecast should be reliable, with only minor variations from actual cash balances. This level of reliability is increasingly *not* the case when the medium-term cash forecast and especially the annual budget are used as the basis for financial planning. The increasing level of planning difficulty over time means that corporate finance becomes less of a science and more of an art form, where it is necessary to build substantial planning buffers into the funding requirements and investment opportunities of a business.

Chapter 4
Early-Stage Financing

Introduction

For the founders of startup companies, obtaining funding can be a struggle, especially when there is little more than a proof of concept to show to potential investors. In this chapter, we make note of two possible methods of obtaining early-stage funding. Angel investors are willing to provide initial funding when a business is just starting out, while venture capital funds provide somewhat larger blocks of cash to assist with the rapid expansion of promising businesses.

Angel Investors

When a business is in its initial conceptual phase, the owners have created a product prototype. The device may not even be functional yet, but at least demonstrates the general concept that the organization is intending to pursue. To develop the concept further requires cash to hire employees, as well as office space in which to house them.

A possible source of early-stage financing that may be willing to invest funds at this stage is the angel investor. An angel investor is a wealthy individual who usually invests between $25,000 and $1,000,000 in a business in exchange for a significant minority ownership position. This is an extremely risky investment for the investor, since the business is unproven and could quite possibly fail. Given the high risk, expect to issue a disproportionate number of shares for this investment.

The knowledge and experience of angel investors can vary widely. Some are in the "friends and family" category, and simply invest because they know the company founders. Other angels specialize in specific industry categories, and so have a better understanding of the product category in which the startup will be competing. This latter group of investors is more likely to have a larger group of active investments that are roughly clustered around their areas of interest, and may be more amenable to discussions about making an investment.

Venture Capital

After a business has developed a proof of concept, or has perhaps issued its first products or services, it may again be in need of cash to ramp up its rate of growth. The cash requirement at this point will be larger, so funding from angel investors will no longer be sufficient. Instead, a venture capital fund (VC) is a possible source of capital. A VC is a corporate entity that pools the cash contributions of multiple investors for investments in startup companies. A VC is usually organized as a limited partnership, with institutional investors and wealthy individuals making investments for which placement decisions are made by a general partner. Larger companies may also set up in-house venture capital businesses; these operations are usually interested in making investments in areas similar to those currently being addressed by their corporate parents. Typical investments made by a VC are in the range of $500,000 to $5,000,000. The amount available for investment increases as a startup works through the development of its concept, proves that a market exists, and demonstrates initial sales. Thus, late-stage financing is usually for significantly larger amounts than early-stage financing.

It can be quite difficult to obtain funding from VCs, since they are looking for those few companies that have the potential for an extremely high rate of growth. Their basic business model is to invest in a number of companies that have superstar potential, knowing that most will fail or become substandard investments, while a few will have stratospheric returns that offset the losses in the rest of their portfolios. They also prefer to invest in certain industries where there is a greater chance of experiencing a high rate of growth, such as the technology and medical sectors. A startup operating outside of these growth areas may have an exceptionally difficult time attracting the attention of a VC.

To obtain funding from a VC, create a short presentation and business plan, and present it to a VC partner. This presentation is critical, since venture funds see an enormous number of proposals every year, and only select a few for investment. It can be quite difficult to even obtain this initial meeting, since many VC firms prefer to only examine proposals forwarded to them through a network of lawyers, accountants, and bankers who pre-screen candidate firms. When presenting to a VC, be aware that the VC gives a higher rating to those who have a calm demeanor, appear trustworthy, and are receptive to feedback.

If the VC partner is interested, expect a detailed due diligence investigation before any funding offer is made.

Venture firms want a certain amount of control over their investments. This nearly always involves one or more seats on the board of directors of the business. In many cases, a VC might insist on obtaining preferred stock, which would give them certain preferential rights in regard to future payouts in the event of a liquidation or sale of the entity. A VC may also insist on having a *liquidation preference*, where the VC has the right, when the business is sold, to recoup its investment before the founder is paid anything. This clause protects the VC's investment. The VC may go further, insisting on a multiple of its original investment as its liquidation preference, allowing the VC to be paid quite a substantial amount of the final sale price of the business.

If the founders of a business find themselves in the rare situation of having multiple VC firms pursuing them to make an investment, the question will be how to judge between their offers. The most quantitatively obvious selection criterion is to take the offer that provides the highest valuation for the business, so that the smallest number of shares is issued in exchange for a certain amount of funding. However, this approach ignores the level of expertise that certain VC firms can bring to a business. VC partners are very experienced and extremely well connected, and so can provide valuable advice to the firm, as well as bring in just the right advisors and employee candidates. This expertise can be of great value, since the founders do not necessarily have a high level of business expertise. Consequently, the potential qualitative value that a VC can bring to a startup company should be considered more valuable than the valuation being offered.

Dangers of Venture Capital

A strong case can be made that most businesses should not even attempt to gain VC funding. A VC firm will push a company to expand extremely rapidly in order to increase its valuation as quickly as possible. This rapid approach is needed by the VC in order to maximize its potential gains from the investment, which the VC needs to eventually pay back its investors. For example, if a VC firm has attracted capital for a startup fund, it may have committed to investing the funds and then liquidating the investments over a five-year period. If so, the VC has a five-year window within which to maximize its investment opportunity.

An excessively rapid pace of growth can severely damage a company and increase its long-term risk of failure. For example, a rapid growth rate may not leave sufficient time to polish a product, thereby increasing the risk of product failures in the field and a very public level of customer annoyance with the company. Also, a market may be slow to develop, perhaps because customer acceptance or the level of technology needed is just not there yet. If so, trying to sell into the market will likely yield a low sales level.

Another issue is that an additional entity is now a partial owner of the business. This can create strains among the owners. If the VC feels that one of the founders is not helping the business, it may exert pressure to move that person into a less pivotal role, and to bring in more professional managers. While these changes may be for the best in terms of the organization's future growth, it can also result in a group of frustrated founders who feel that their contributions are being marginalized.

Finally, the VC will eventually pressure the founders to sell the company or take it public, so that the shares held by the VC can be converted to cash. This means that the founders may eventually see their business taken over by a third party or at least shared with the general public. While this end game may result in a notable boost in their personal wealth, losing the company may not be what they want. Instead, some founders prefer to continue their ownership, quietly running the business for a much longer period of time.

For these reasons, it may make more sense to adopt a slower-growth stance with more traditional forms of equity and debt funding, or by bootstrapping with the owners' funds. This approach eliminates the pressure to grow at a fast pace.

Summary

Realistically, venture capital is not an option for most new businesses. The required growth rates for this type of funding are not achievable for the vast majority of startup companies. Instead, it will be necessary to take the slower path of gradually expanding the business with internally-generated funds, modest stock sales to investors, loans from friends and family, and many of the other financing methods discussed elsewhere in this book. Even if a business will qualify for a VC investment, the founders should be skeptical about the impact on their fledgling organization; sales could possibly take off like a jet aircraft, or the extra money might simply result in new products that find no traction in the marketplace. In addition, accepting VC money will likely lead to the eventual sale of the business. In short, the use of VC funding is usually not an option, and even if such funding is available, it might not be the right choice.

Chapter 5
The Initial Public Offering

Introduction

When the owners of an organization want to sell shares to the public, they must first prepare for and undergo the initial public offering (IPO) process, which is an expensive and time-consuming ordeal. This chapter contains a high-level review of the IPO, and also notes the reasons both in favor of and against engaging in this process.

Related Podcast Episode: Episode 69 of the Accounting Best Practices Podcast discusses listing on a stock exchange. The episode is available at: **accounting-tools.com/podcasts** or **iTunes**

Reasons for and Against an IPO

There are several reasons why the owners of a business may want to take it public through an IPO. The first is the perception that the owners can more easily sell their shares, or at least have the option to do so through a stock exchange. Second, being publicly held makes it easier to raise funds with which to operate the business or pay for acquisitions. Third, the absence of restrictions on the sale of shares tends to increase their price. Fourth, the increased ease with which a company can sell shares tends to reduce its proportion of debt to equity, which can reduce the risk of its financial structure. Another reason is prestige – taking a company public is considered by some to be the capstone of one's professional career. Also, the awarding of stock options has more meaning in a public company, since they can eventually be sold on a stock exchange. Finally, there is some evidence that the management team of a public company receives higher compensation than they would in a similar private company, so managers tend to be in favor of going public.

While these reasons may seem compelling, there are a number of other excellent reasons for *not* going public. The first issue is the very high cost associated with raising funds in this manner. The following costs will be incurred:

- *Underwriting discount.* This is the difference between the price paid by the underwriter to the company and the price at which the underwriter sells the company's shares to investors. This can be in the range of 7% of the total share placement, and so is the single largest cost of the IPO.
- *Auditing fees.* Outside auditors must audit the company's accounting records for the past few years and generate a full set of audited financial statements for the periods covered. In addition, the auditors will charge additional fees to examine the company's system of controls. The auditors will also spend a

large amount of time reviewing the company's initial registration filing with the Securities and Exchange Commission (SEC). Further, these fees are ongoing, since the auditors will henceforth engage in quarterly reviews and annual audits of the company's financial statements, and review its ongoing filings with the SEC.

- *Control systems.* A likely result of the auditors' review of the company's control systems is that the controls will need to be enhanced, which may call for system modifications, employee training, and further testing to ensure that the new controls are working as intended.
- *Legal fees.* Securities attorneys are needed to construct the registration filing with the SEC. They will also be needed to examine all future filings with the SEC.
- *In-house support.* It will probably be necessary to hire additional employees to support the company's new activities as a public company. This may include additional accounting staff, a controls analyst, an internal audit team, and investor relations personnel.
- *Insurance.* The cost of directors and officers liability insurance will increase, possibly by several multiples of the prior expense. This is because of the heightened risk of investor lawsuits once the number of shareholders increases as a result of the IPO.
- *Stock exchange listing.* The company will likely want to list its shares on a stock exchange, since investors need an exchange to more easily buy and sell the company's shares. The initial and ongoing stock listing fees can be considerable, depending on the exchange and the number of shares to be listed.
- *Management time.* A significant cost is the amount of management time that will be diverted toward public company activities. These activities include attendance at shareholder meetings, analyst meetings, earnings calls, and road shows.

Another negative issue is that the new owners of the business may demand that the company focus more attention on the immediate generation of profits, rather than the pursuit of longer-term goals. Also, there is a risk that required public disclosures might shift some competitive advantage to other players in the industry.

Yet another issue is the risk that the original owner will be forced out as part of an unfriendly takeover, which would have been impossible if the company had remained private.

In addition to the problems just pointed out, smaller firms may also suffer from stock manipulation. When there are few registered shares outstanding, it is relatively easy for dishonest shareholders to create transactions that rapidly alter the stock price and allow them to sell out at a profit.

In short, there are a number of arguments both in favor of and against going public. Smaller companies will likely find that the cost of compliance with securities laws will erase a large part of their profits, and so may elect to remain private. A larger firm with more revenues will probably find that these costs only reduce profits by a relatively small amount, so that the overall benefits of being public outweigh those of being private.

Preparation for the IPO

A company should be preparing for an IPO several years before the actual event takes place. By doing so, the organization will have the appropriate system of controls and proper governance structures demanded by auditors, stock exchanges, the SEC, and the investment community. It may also be necessary to alter the asset base of the business, as well as to strip away low-growth or unprofitable business segments. The necessary changes are outlined in the following bullet points:

- *Auditors.* The company's auditors must be registered with the Public Company Accounting Oversight Board (PCAOB). Many auditors choose not to pay the fees or engage in the extra compliance activities required by the PCAOB, so it is entirely likely that the company will have to switch auditors. This also means that the fees paid for the annual audit will increase, since the larger and more sophisticated audit firms are the only ones registered with the PCAOB.
- *Advisors.* The company's advisors in many areas may not be accustomed to the demands of the public markets. This could mean that new advisors must be found to assist with risk management, taxes, controls, and other functional areas. In particular, the company's audit firm must maintain a high level of independence from the company in a public environment, and so can no longer provide certain services to the company, such as preparing tax provisions and assisting with the development of internal controls.
- *Asset reduction.* The investment community rewards companies that can operate lean, with a minimal asset base. Otherwise, a company needs more equity to fund its assets, which means that it must sell more shares, which in turn reduces the earnings per share that it generates. Reducing assets can require many actions, such as outsourcing manufacturing to eliminate fixed assets, tightening the credit policy to minimize accounts receivable, and having employees work from home in order to reduce facility investments.
- *Board of directors.* The existing board of directors may be comprised of company managers or friends of the owners. A higher level of governance can be achieved by replacing this group with a set of more independent directors who are willing to place the interests of investors ahead of the requirements of the managers. It can be useful to invest in a high-profile group of directors who sit on a number of boards, and so are experienced in public company governance.
- *Closing speed.* A publicly-held company is required to file financial reports with the SEC within a relatively short time period following the end of each fiscal quarter and year. If the accounting department is accustomed to a leisurely closing process, it may be necessary to impose a more regimented closing process that mandates specific release dates for the financial state-

ments, along with the completion of disclosures to be included with the quarterly financial statements. This process includes having the necessary schedules prepared for the auditors, so that they can conduct their quarterly reviews and year-end audits.

- *Committees.* Part of the IPO process involves being listed on a stock exchange, which can greatly increase the amount of trading in a company's shares. Each stock exchange imposes its own governance requirements on those entities trading their shares on the exchange. This typically means that there must be an audit committee and compensation committee; both must meet regularly and record meeting minutes.

- *Growth focus.* Investors are much more willing to pay a high price for the shares of a company when it has a proven record of achieving a high rate of growth, year after year. Ideally, the growth should be concentrated in areas where the market has been rewarding other companies with high price/earnings multiples. To achieve this growth rate, review the various components of the business several years in advance of the IPO and eliminate those parts that have declining or tepid growth. Also, invest heavily in those parts of the business with the highest growth prospects. This can be a difficult task, especially if the owners are attached to the original core part of the business, which may no longer be growing.

- *Legal review.* The legal structure of the company, its contracts, and board minutes could all contain issues that could derail an IPO at the last minute. To ensure that all legal issues are discovered and corrected well in advance, hire a high-quality securities law firm well in advance of the IPO, and have them conduct a thorough investigation.

- *Management team.* The management team of a publicly-held business is expected to behave in a professional manner, create and adhere to a coherent strategic plan, and generally operate the business to benefit its shareholders. It is entirely possible that some members of the management team cannot meet these expectations, and so should be replaced. If so, conduct replacements far enough in advance of the IPO that the new managers are fully settled into their jobs.

- *Personal transactions.* In a closely-held business, the owners commonly mix their personal affairs with those of the business. For example, they may run personal vacation spending though the accounts payable system, or require the business to guarantee the loans of other businesses that are separately run by the owners. All of these personal transactions must be stripped away from the company well before the IPO, so that they do not appear in the financial statements for the two preceding years that must be presented to investors as part of the IPO.

- *Profitability.* It is not always possible for a high-growth business to report outsized profits, since it may be necessary to spend an inordinate amount supporting the high rate of growth – on new product development, new staff additions, product rollouts in new regions, and so forth. Nonetheless, there must still be a certain amount of attention to the bottom line, to keep prospective investors from believing that the company is suffering from runaway expenses. This means there should be a strong system of cost controls in place, perhaps supported by periodic consulting or benchmarking reviews to locate any areas in which costs can be further reduced.

- *Research and development (R&D).* If the company is competing based on its products, be sure to invest in a strong R&D group several years in advance. By doing so, there is a greater chance that the business will have a broader product line by the IPO date that is clearly differentiated from other products in the marketplace. This is a major concern. If a company has only developed a single unique product, and especially one with a limited lifespan, the organization cannot present a valid case to investors for why they should purchase its shares in an IPO.

- *Revenue threshold.* It is much easier to sell shares in an IPO to a small number of large investors, such as pension funds. These institutional investors will only buy shares if the company is sufficiently large to foster an active market for its stock. This means that the management team needs to grow the business to the point where its expected market capitalization will be at least $100 million. This is not an easy feat, and will likely require years of concentrated effort to achieve.

- *Stock options.* A review of the company's system of compensation may reveal a need to create a pool of stock options for future distribution to the staff. If so, it is easier to gain approval to set aside these options before the company goes public.

The multitude of requirements noted here should make it abundantly clear that several years (or more) of preparation are needed before a business is sufficiently ready to attempt an IPO.

The Initial Public Offering

The following discussion of the IPO process represents the *approximate* flow of activities. In reality, there is some timing overlap between events. We have also clustered together some actions to improve the narrative flow. The intent is to give a sense of how the process works, rather than an exact series of perfectly sequenced steps.

When the board of directors believes that a company is ready to make the step from being a private company to a public company, it hires one or more underwriters to assist the entity in going public. An underwriter uses its contacts within the investment community to sell the company's shares to investors.

The choice of which investment bank to use as an underwriter depends upon a number of factors, such as the prestige of the bank, whether it has prior experience in the company's industry, the size of its contacts within the investor community, and its fee. A larger and more prestigious firm usually charges a higher fee, but also has a greater ability to sell the entire amount of a company's offering of securities.

> **Tip:** Obtain references from candidate underwriters and call the CFOs of those companies to obtain an understanding of the actual level of support that each candidate provides, as well as its expertise and willingness to continue to support the company.

The selected underwriter may enroll the efforts of additional underwriters to assist it in selling shares. This is more likely to be the case for a larger IPO, where it is more difficult to place all the shares that the company wants to sell.

> **Tip:** It is better to hire the services of an underwriter that has previously been a *managing underwriter*, which means that it has experience in managing the IPO process. If a bank has only been part of an underwriting syndicate, it may lack the requisite amount of experience.

The company negotiates the terms of a letter of intent with its preferred underwriter. The following are among the key elements of the letter of intent:

- *Fee.* The primary fee of the underwriter is a percentage of the total amount of funds collected. In addition, there are a variety of legal, accounting, travel, and other costs that it may pass through to the company for reimbursement.
- *Funding arrangement.* The underwriter will agree to one of several possible ways in which the company's shares will be sold. The variations are:
  - *Firm commitment.* Under a firm commitment deal, the underwriter agrees to buy a certain number of shares from the company, irrespective of its ability to sell those shares to third parties. This is preferable if the company is targeting raising a certain amount of cash. This arrangement places the risk of selling the shares on the underwriter. In firm commitment deals, it is common for the underwriter to form a syndicate with several other investment banks, in order to sell the shares to the largest possible group of investors. Doing so reduces the risk that some shares will not be sold. The underwriter can sell the shares to investors at any price it can obtain, and then pockets the difference between the ultimate sale price and the price paid to the company. This difference is called the *underwriting discount.*
  - *Best efforts.* Under a best efforts deal, the underwriter takes a commission on as many shares as it can sell. If an underwriter insists on a best efforts deal, it indicates that there is some risk of not being able to sell the targeted number of shares. If the underwriter cannot sell shares at the offering price, the entire issuance may be withdrawn.
  - *Dutch auction.* The underwriter conducts an auction among prospective purchasers to determine the maximum share price that in-

vestors are willing to pay for a given number of shares. The share price is derived from the bids submitted by investors. Though commonly used for the sale of bonds, this is a rarely-used technique in an IPO.

EXAMPLE

The owners of Aquifers International want to sell 100,000 shares to the public through a Dutch auction. The company's investment banker receives the following five bids from prospective investors:

Bidder	Share Quantity	Bid Price
A	10,000	$20.00
B	20,000	18.00
C	50,000	16.00
D	60,000	14.00
E	90,000	12.00

The table reveals that, predictably enough, the number of shares that can be sold increases as the price declines. To achieve the targeted number of shares to be sold, the owners should sell at a $14.00 price. Note that Bidders A, B, and C will pay less than their bid prices, since the auction process establishes a uniform price of $14.00 at which the entire block of 100,000 shares will be sold. Bidder E will receive no shares, since his bid was below the final price point.

An additional issue is that those bidders bidding at least $14.00 per share indicated a willingness to buy a total of 140,000 shares, but the owners are only planning to sell 100,000 shares. The company issues shares to them based on an allotment process, using the ratio of shares bid to shares available. This results in an allocation ratio of 0.71x, which is computed as follows:

$$100{,}000 \text{ Shares available} \div 140{,}000 \text{ Shares bid} = 0.71x$$

Thus, Bidder B, who offered to purchase 20,000 shares at a price of $18.00 each, will be sold 14,200 shares at a price of $14.00 each.

- *Overallotment.* The underwriter may want the option to purchase additional shares from the company at a certain price within a set time period after the IPO date, which it can then sell to investors at a profit.

The underwriter will first engage in a detailed due diligence review of the company. The intent of this review is to ensure that the company is correctly representing itself to the investment community. The underwriter team will examine the company's financial statements and accounting records, contact business partners, investigate the backgrounds of the management team, and a great deal more. This level of investigation is needed to ensure that the information later presented in the company's filings with the SEC is correct. If a material point is missed, the underwriter could be liable, so this investigation is quite detailed. The underwriter may ask the company's auditors for a *comfort letter*, which declares that there is no indication of false or misleading information in the company's financial statements, and that the presented information is in compliance with the applicable accounting standards.

A legal firm is then hired that specializes in SEC filings to complete a registration statement. As noted in the preceding section, this firm may have been hired several years earlier, to prepare the company for its IPO.

The registration statement is mandated by the SEC, and contains a detailed review of the company's financial and operational condition, risk factors, and any other items that it believes investors should be aware of before they buy the company's stock. The primary categories of information in a registration statement are:

- Summary information and risk factors
- Use of proceeds
- Description of the business
- Financial statements
- Management's discussion and analysis of the business
- Compensation of key parties
- Related party transactions

There are a large number of additional categories of information, as well. As a result, the registration statement can be a massive document. Since the company's auditors and attorneys must review it several times and in great detail, it is also a very expensive document to create.

Once the SEC receives the registration statement, its staff has 30 days in which to review the document – which it will, and in excruciating detail. The SEC's in-house accountants and attorneys look for inconsistencies and errors in the registration statement as well as unclear or overblown statements, and summarize these points in a comment letter, which it sends to the company. Some of the comments made by the SEC involve substantive issues, such as the nature of the revenue recognition methodology used by the company, and which may call for a restatement of the company's financial statements. Other comments may note minor typographical issues, such as a missing middle initial in the name of a board member. The SEC does not impose a materiality convention on its staff for reviews – *all* parts of the registration statement are subject to review, no matter how minor the resulting changes may be.

The company responds to all of the SEC's questions and updates its registration statement as well, and then sends back the documents via an amended filing for another review. The SEC is allowed 30 days for each iteration of its review process. The SEC staff is in absolutely no hurry to assist a company with its IPO; consequently, this question-and-answer process may require a number of iterations and more months than the management team would believe possible.

> **Tip:** High-end securities attorneys are extremely expensive, and totally worth the money, since they can minimize the number of question-and-answer iterations with the SEC, thereby accelerating the process of going public.

The underwriter supervises the creation of a road show presentation, in which the senior management team is expected to present a summary of the company and its investment prospects to prospective investors. These investors are likely to be mostly institutional investors, such as the managers of pension funds. The bankers and management team will go through a number of iterations to polish the presentation.

The management team and its investment bank advisors embark on a road show, which spans several weeks and takes them to a number of cities to meet with investors. If investors are interested in buying the company's stock, they tell the bankers how many shares they want to buy, and at what price. This process of obtaining purchasing information from investors is called *book building*.

> **Tip:** Do not sell fewer than one million shares during the initial public offering. Otherwise, there will not be a sufficient number of shares available to create an active market. Also, most stock exchanges require that at least one million registered shares be outstanding.

At this time, the company also files an application with the stock exchange on which it wants its stock to be listed. The stock exchange verifies that the company meets its listing requirements and then assigns it a ticker symbol. In addition, if it does not already have one, the company hires a stock transfer agent to handle the transfer of shares between parties. The company's legal staff will also submit filings to the securities agencies of those states in which the company anticipates selling shares (see the following Blue Sky Laws section).

From the period when the company files a registration statement with the SEC to the date when the SEC declares the registration statement effective, the federal securities laws limit the amount of information that the company can release to the public. This is known as the *quiet period*, and the intent is to keep from overheating investor expectations prior to sale of the stock, which could lead to an unwarranted bubble in the stock price. During the quiet period, no information should be released that would cause investors to change their stock holdings. For example, the following topics should be avoided in any releases to the public:

- Progress toward achieving company goals
- New sales made or contracts signed
- Major new product offerings
- Major new partnership deals
- Changes in the management team

This does not mean that all information is suppressed. A company can continue to publish factual business information that it has already been releasing on a regular basis, as long as the information is intended for recipients other than in their capacity as investors.

Tip: The safest approach to dealing with information releases during the quiet period is to have corporate counsel give final approval of all information releases during this time period.

When the SEC is satisfied with the latest draft of the registration statement, it declares the filing to be "effective." The management team and its bankers then decide upon the price at which the company will sell its shares. A key determinant is the price at which institutional investors are most likely to buy shares, since they usually comprise a large part of the initial block of shares sold. Underwriters want to set the initial share price slightly low, so that there is more likely to be a run-up in the first trading day that they can publicize. Also, a slightly low price makes it easier to create an active aftermarket in the stock, since other investors will be interested in obtaining and holding the stock to realize additional gains. Further, an excessively high initial price may cause a withdrawal of orders, so that the entire offering must be withdrawn.

Tip: The underpricing of shares is most common in an IPO. If management wants to obtain the highest price per share, consider selling fewer shares during the IPO and more shares in a secondary offering, when the amount of underpricing is less extensive.

The underwriter traditionally likes to set the initial price of a share at somewhere between $10 and $20. Doing so may require a stock split or reverse stock split, depending on the number of shares currently outstanding. For example:

- A company has an initial valuation of $100 million, and has one million shares outstanding. To offer shares at an initial price of $20, there must be a five-for-one stock split that brings the number of shares outstanding to five million shares. Thus, a $100 million valuation divided by five million shares equals $20 per share.
- A company has an initial valuation of $80 million, and has 20 million shares outstanding. To offer shares at an initial price of $16, there must be a four-for-one reverse stock split that brings the number of shares outstanding to five million. Thus, an $80 million valuation divided by five million shares equals $16 per share.

The company then sends the registration statement to a financial printer. The printer puts the final stock price in the document, and uploads it to the SEC.

In those cases where there is more demand for shares than are to be sold, the underwriter is forced to allocate shares among its customers. The bankers will likely allocate more shares to their best customers, and may be somewhat more inclined to reduce allocations to those customers who are less likely to hold the stock for a reasonable period of time.

The underwriter sells the shares to the investors that it has lined up. The underwriter collects cash from the investors, takes out its underwriting discount, and pays the remaining proceeds to the company at a closing meeting.

In some cases, the share price trends downward immediately after shares are made available for sale. If so, the underwriter may buy shares on the open market. This action is intended to stabilize the share price over the short-term, after which the underwriter no longer provides this support.

The company is now listed on a stock exchange, has registered shares that are being traded among investors, and has presumably just received a large amount of cash for its efforts.

Share Lockup Period

A typical part of any IPO process is a requirement that the existing shareholders continue to hold their shares for at least 180 days following the date of the IPO. This is known as a *lockup period*, and is intended to force shareholders to have a continuing economic interest in the business for a half-year period. The lockup requirement tends to have the following effects:

- *Risk of price decline.* If the current owners suspect there is a high risk of a decline in the stock price during the 180-day period, they may be more inclined to cash out by some other means in the short term, thereby locking in the best possible price.
- *Performance boost.* The current owners will be more inclined to push employees to report the best possible results during the first half-year of the company's existence as a public company, in order to run up the stock price before the insiders can sell their shares.
- *Over supply.* There may be an inordinate number of insiders planning to sell their shares as soon as the 180-day limitation expires, which can force down the market price of the stock following the expiration date.

Blue Sky Laws

The state governments individually enacted blue sky laws to prevent securities dealers from committing fraud through the sale of fake securities to investors. The "blue sky" name is derived from being able to "sell the sky" to an investor without the restrictions of any regulations.

In essence, blue sky laws mandate that securities being offered for sale for the first time be qualified by the state regulatory commission, and registered with the state. Further, the terms and prices of the securities must follow the statutory guidelines imposed by the state. These guidelines are usually modeled on the Uniform Securities Act of 1956, for which the main provisions are:

- *Reason for existence.* The securities issuer is engaged in business. It is not bankrupt or in an organizational state, nor is it a blind pool, blank check, or shell company that has no purpose for being in existence.
- *Price.* The security is priced at a reasonable level in comparison to its current market price.
- *Unsold allotment.* The security is not related to any unsold allotments given to a securities dealer who has underwritten the security.
- *Asset base.* The issuer owns a minimum amount of assets.

Consequently, it is not possible for a securities dealer to market a company's stock for sale, unless the stock conforms to both state and SEC regulations. If a security is sold that does not conform to state blue sky laws, the following comment applies (as taken from section 410(a) of the 1956 Act):

> "Any person who offers or sells a security is liable to the person buying the security from him, who may sue… to recover the consideration paid for the security, together with interest at six percent per year from date of payment, [court] costs, and reasonable attorney's fees, less the amount of income received on the security, upon tender of the security, or for damages if he no longer owns the security."

The onerous penalties of the 1956 Act are a major concern for securities dealers, since its provisions may require them to buy securities back from investors. Since a buy back would only happen if securities had lost some or all of their value, the buyback could bankrupt a securities dealer. Given the ramifications of this penalty, securities dealers are very careful to ensure that blue sky laws are always followed.

An issuing entity is exempt from the blue sky laws if its securities are listed on a national stock exchange, such as the NASDAQ or New York Stock Exchange. For businesses listed in this manner, states issue a "manual exemption," which (despite the name) automatically allows securities to be sold within their borders. This exemption was initiated under the National Securities Markets Improvement Act of 1996.

The exemption is not so clear if an issuer's securities are only available for sale in the over the counter (OTC) market. If an issuer registers with one of the credit rating agencies and renews the registration each year, the majority of state governments will allow a registration exemption. This registration is a lengthy filing that includes the issuer's financial statements, the names of the executive officers of the business, and a description of what the entity does. Despite the presence of this registration facility, some states continue to require registration directly with them; these states are Alabama, California, Georgia, Illinois, Kentucky, Louisiana, New York, Pennsylvania, Tennessee, Virginia, and Wisconsin.

The content of blue sky laws vary by state. Consequently, if a company intends to sell its securities in a specific state, it should obtain legal advice in that state, to ensure that the local regulations are being followed. Also, anyone participating in a road show should be able to answer questions about the company's blue sky status, since this question is commonly asked by investors and brokers.

Summary

The requirements for going public are not especially onerous for a larger organization, but can be profoundly expensive and time-consuming for a smaller business. This means that the owners of smaller entities are well advised to delay the IPO process until their organizations have increased in size, and so can more easily absorb the requirements of an IPO while still operating the core functions of the business.

This chapter has described the process involved in having an initial set of shares registered with the SEC. This is only the first step on the long road of being a publicly-held entity, which also involves dealing with a stock exchange, managing the expectations of the investment community, and maximizing the stock float of the business. For more information about these additional activities, see the author's *Investor Relations Guidebook*.

Chapter 6
Other Capital Raising Alternatives

Introduction

In the two preceding chapters, we covered one possible approach to raising capital, which might be considered the "classic" path. A startup company initially obtains angel financing, then proceeds to venture capital funding, and then raises capital through an initial public offering. Unfortunately, the vast majority of organizations do not raise capital by any of these three methods. Instead, they must find alternative approaches to selling shares. In this chapter, we describe several possible methods, including Regulation A and Regulation D stock sales, as well as crowdfunding. Another alternative for a business that has successfully followed the classic capital raising path is the seasoned equity offering, which is described near the end of the chapter. Several related topics are also covered, including accredited investors, the rights offering, and dilution.

Regulation D Stock Sales

The requirements for registering shares are so onerous that a company may want to explore other alternatives that can bring in needed funds with less effort. One option is the sale of restricted stock under Regulation D to accredited investors. This approach is commonly used by businesses not willing to go public just yet, but can also be employed by organizations that have already gone public.

Related Podcast Episode: Episode 89 of the Accounting Best Practices Podcast discusses Regulation D stock sales. The episode is available at: **accounting-tools.com/podcasts** or **iTunes**

Regulation D provides an exemption from the normal stock registration requirement. This is an exceedingly useful exemption, since unregistered shares can be sold to investors with a minimal amount of reporting to the SEC. Thus, the administrative aspects of registering shares are almost entirely eliminated.

Regulation D Rules

The detailed aspects of Regulation D are described in the SEC's Rules 504, 505, and 506. In general, to sell shares under Regulation D, a company must follow these rules:

- Only sell shares to accredited investors (as described in a later section).
- Investors cannot be contacted through a general solicitation, such as advertising or free seminars open to the public.

- If shares are sold over a long time period, prove that all sales are covered by Regulation D (rather than being separate offerings). This can be done by documenting a financing plan, selling the same type of stock to all investors, showing that all shares are sold for the same type of consideration, *and* by proving that the sales are being made for the same general purpose.

Regulation D Process Flow

Because of the inability to advertise a stock sale, companies usually turn to investment bankers, who contact their clients to see who is interested in buying shares. The bankers impose a fee for this service, which is a percentage of the amount of funds generated.

If a prospective investor is interested in buying shares, the company sends them a boilerplate questionnaire to fill out, in which they state that they are accredited investors. This form provides the company with legal protection, in case the SEC questions whether the stock issuance is protected by Regulation D. The questions posed by this questionnaire typically include the following:

- *Knowledge and experience.* The investor has sufficient knowledge of and experience in financial matters to be able to properly evaluate the merits and risks of the stock offering.
- *Restricted nature of shares.* The investor understands that the securities are restricted, and so cannot be sold until they have been registered.
- *Ability to invest.* The investor affirms that his/her total commitment to unregistered investments is not out of proportion to his/her net worth. Further, the investor has sufficient liquidity to provide for personal needs, and does not expect a change in liquidity that will require the sale of these securities at a later date.
- *Personal ownership.* The investor will hold the securities for his/her personal account, not with the intent of selling them to a third party.
- *Questions asked.* The investor affirms that he/she can question the company concerning the securities prior to purchasing them, and that these questions have been asked prior to the purchase.
- *Completeness of information.* The investor affirms that the information he/she provides in this questionnaire is complete and accurate.
- *Accredited investor qualifications.* The questionnaire also includes yes/no affirmations of each line item in the definition of an accredited investor, as described in a following section. This information is used to determine whether a prospective investor falls within the definition of an accredited investor, and so can purchase shares from the company under Regulation D.

Investors then send their money to an escrow account that is maintained by a third party, until such time as the total amount of funding meets the minimum requirement set by the company. The investment banker extracts its fee from the escrowed funds, the company collects its cash, and the company's stock transfer agent sends stock certificates to the investors.

Shares issued under Regulation D are not initially registered, which means that a restriction statement appears on the back of each certificate. This statement essentially prohibits the shareholder from selling to a third party. A sample statement is:

> The shares represented by this certificate have been acquired for investment and have not been registered under the Securities Act of 1933. Such shares may not be sold or transferred or pledged in the absence of such registration unless the company receives an opinion of counsel reasonably acceptable to the company stating that such sale or transfer is exempt from the registration and prospectus delivery requirements of said Act.

This restriction on the resale of stock is usually a major concern for all but the most long-term investors. Accordingly, investors like to see one or more of the following guarantees being offered by a company:

- *Piggyback rights.* The company promises to include their shares in any stock registration statement that it may eventually file with the SEC. This is a near-universal inclusion in a Regulation D offering, since it does not impose an immediate obligation on the company.
- *Registration promise.* The company promises to file a registration statement with the SEC by a certain date. If the company is currently privately held, this promise essentially requires it to become publicly-held, along with the various ongoing SEC filing requirements that are part of being a public company. A more onerous agreement will even require the company to issue additional stock if it does not obtain SEC approval of the registration statement by a certain date.

The downside of using a Registration D stock sale is that investors typically want something extra in exchange for buying unregistered stock. This may take the form of a reduced price per share. In addition, investors may demand warrants, which are a formal right to buy additional company stock at a certain exercise price.

EXAMPLE

Hegemony Toy Company sells 10,000 shares of its common stock for $10.00, along with 10,000 warrants to buy additional shares of the company for the next three years at $10.00 per share. The price of the company's stock later rises to $17.00, at which point the investor uses his warrant privileges to buy an additional 10,000 shares at $10.00 each. If he can then have the shares registered and sells them at the $17.00 market price, he will pocket a profit of $70,000 on his exercise of the warrants.

A company is paying a steep price if it issues warrants and then experiences a sharp increase in its stock price, since the recipient of the warrants will eventually buy shares from the company at what will then be an inordinately low price. If the company had not issued warrants, it would instead be able to later sell shares at the full market price.

If an investor wants one warrant for every share purchased, this is called 100% warrant coverage. If an investor agrees to one warrant for every two shares purchased, this is called 50% warrant coverage. These are the two most common warrant issuance terms, though any proportion of warrants to shares purchased may be agreed to.

An even more serious downside of using Regulation D is when prospective investors insist upon buying preferred stock, rather than common stock. Preferred stock may include a number of oppressive terms, such as favorable conversion rights into common stock, the payment of dividends, and perhaps even override voting privileges concerning the sale of the company or other matters.

Given the number of rights that investors may demand in a Regulation D stock sale, it is best to only use this approach when the company is operating from a position of strength, where it does not have an immediate need for cash.

The Form D Filing

An organization that sells shares under the provisions of Regulation D must file a report with the SEC concerning the sale. This is the Form D, which must be filed by the securities issuer no later than 15 calendar days after the date on which securities were first sold. This date is considered to be when the first investor is irrevocably contractually committed to invest. Examples of first sale dates are:

- When the entity receives a stock subscription agreement from an investor
- When the entity receives a check from an investor to pay for shares

An amendment to this form must be filed annually, if the entity is continuing to sell shares under the offering contained within the original notification. An amendment is also needed if there is a material mistake of fact or error in the preceding filing, or if there is a change in the information provided (with certain exceptions). The main types of information to be described on the Form D are:

- *Identity*. The name and type of entity of the issuer.
- *Contact information*. The location and contact information for the issuer.
- *Related persons*. The executive officer, directors, and promoter of the issuer, as well as their contact information.
- *Industry type*. The industry group in which the issuer is situated.
- *Issuer size*. The revenue range or aggregate net asset value range of the issuer.
- *Exemptions*. The federal exemptions or exclusions claimed, under which the shares are being sold.
- *Investment*. The minimum investment amount to be accepted from investors.
- *Sales compensation*. The identification of anyone receiving compensation as part of the stock sales, and the states in which solicitations are being made.

- *Offering and sales amounts*. The total offering amount, the amount sold, and the amount remaining to be sold.
- *Expenses*. The amounts of any sales commissions and finder's fees to be paid as part of the offering.
- *Use of proceeds*. The uses to which the resulting funds are to be put.

The amount of information required by the Form D is relatively small, compared to the much more comprehensive requirements of a formal securities registration document.

Rule 506(c)

One of the exemptions from the SEC's registration requirements is located in Rule 506(c) of the SEC's Regulation D. Under this Rule, the amount of funding that can be raised is unlimited and sales are restricted to accredited investors. The downside of limiting investors in this manner is that the pool of potential investors will be relatively small. Further, the fundraising entity must verify that investors actually qualify as accredited investors. Prior to this Rule, the burden of proof was on the investor, who would usually fill out a form in which they certified that they were accredited. Now, the issuer must take reasonable steps to verify that all investors are properly classified as being accredited. The SEC offers two ways in which this verification can be accomplished. They are:

- *Principles-based approach*. The issuer uses its judgment to decide whether an investor is accredited. This means looking at the nature of the investor, the type of accredited investor the individual purports to be, the kind of information on hand about the investor, how the investor was reached, and the terms of the offering. The problem here is that the SEC may decide that the issuer's judgment was flawed, which could result in the loss of its 506(c) exemption.
- *Formal verification*. The issuer determines an investor's accredited status based on "hard" documentation, which is the safer approach for verifying accredited status. This can include the following:
  - Review the investor's tax returns to verify income over the past two years.
  - Obtain a written statement from the investor regarding income expectations for the current year.
  - Review the investor's consumer credit report, bank statements, brokerage statements, and/or real estate appraisals to estimate net worth.
  - Obtain a written confirmation from a registered or licensed professional, such as a certified public accountant or a securities attorney, that the investor is verified as being accredited.

Despite these issues, Rule 506(c) actually represents a favorable regulatory environment for fund raising. Those websites that usually assist in raising funds already have procedures in place to satisfy the accreditation requirement. For example, a fundraising portal may require prospective investors to provide substantiation of their income or net worth. This pre-existing base of accredited investors is quite useful, for a business is allowed under the Rule to advertise their fundraising activities. By combining advertising with a base of accredited investors that is already available through a fundraising portal, a business may be able to reach a wider audience of investors. Further, there is no ceiling on the amount of funds that can be raised under this Rule.

In short, Rule 506(c) provides one of the most cost-effective ways to raise money through a restricted form of crowdfunding. This is especially the case when a business does not already have relationships with entities that might be interested in investing.

The Accredited Investor

An accredited investor qualifies under SEC rules as being financially sophisticated. The SEC definition of an accredited investor is:

1. A bank, insurance company, registered investment company, business development company, or small business investment company;
2. An employee benefit plan, within the meaning of the Employee Retirement Income Security Act, if a bank, insurance company, or registered investment adviser makes the investment decisions, or if the plan has total assets in excess of $5 million;
3. A charitable organization, corporation, or partnership with assets exceeding $5 million;
4. A director, executive officer, or general partner of the company selling the securities;
5. A business in which all the equity owners are accredited investors;
6. A natural person who has individual net worth, or joint net worth with the person's spouse, that exceeds $1 million at the time of the purchase, excluding the value of the primary residence of such person;
7. A natural person with income exceeding $200,000 in each of the two most recent years or joint income with a spouse exceeding $300,000 for those years and a reasonable expectation of the same income level in the current year; or
8. A trust with assets in excess of $5 million, not formed to acquire the securities offered, whose purchases a sophisticated person makes.

This definition comes from Rule 501 of the SEC's Regulation D.

A questionnaire is used to ascertain whether a prospective investor is accredited; elements of this questionnaire were noted earlier in the Regulation D Stock Sales section. The company should go to some lengths to ensure that all investors who intend to buy shares under Regulation D have completed and signed the questionnaire, since this represents the company's only evidence that it has sold shares to accredited investors.

Regulation A+ Overview

The preceding discussion of Regulation D was oriented toward stock sales to accredited investors. What if a company does not have access to this group of wealthy investors, or cannot find any who are willing to invest? An alternative is available under the Regulation A+ exemption.

Under Regulation A+, a company can issue securities under two tiers. The more essential requirements associated with each tier are noted in the following table.

Regulation A+ Tiers

	Tier 1	Tier 2
Amount raised per year	$20 million maximum	$50 million maximum
Investment limitations	None	For non-accredited investors, 10% of the greater of income or net worth, per offering
Non-accredited investors allowed	Yes	Yes
Audited financials required	No	Yes
Registration required with SEC	Yes	Yes
Shares freely tradable	Yes	Yes
Ongoing reporting requirements	No	Yes (semi-annual)

The Regulation A+ exemption is not available to a number of types of companies. They are investment companies, foreign companies, oil and gas companies, public companies, and companies selling asset-backed securities.

If a company qualifies for this exemption, the basic process flow is to issue an SEC-reviewed offering circular to attract investors, then file a Form 1-A with the SEC, then sell shares, and then file a Form 1-Z to document the termination or completion of the offering. If the company is in Tier 2, it must then file a Form 1-K annual report that includes audited financial statements, a discussion of its financial results, and information about its business and management, related-party transactions, and share ownership. The Form 1-K is estimated to require 600 hours to complete. A Tier 2 company must also file a Form 1-SA semi-annual report that includes interim unaudited financial statements, as well as a discussion of the company's financial results. The Form 1-SA is estimated to require 187 hours to complete. Finally, a Tier 2 company must file a Form 1-U within four business days of certain events, such as a bankruptcy, change in accountant, or change in control.

A key feature of Regulation A+ stock sales is that shares are freely tradable. This might initially appear to be an exceedingly valuable feature for investors. However, because the shares are not being traded on a public exchange, it still may be difficult for investors to sell their shares.

In short, Regulation A+ can be considered a miniature version of an initial public offering. It allows a business to raise a fairly significant amount of money, but incurs significant reporting burdens in exchange.

Private Investments in Public Equity

When a publicly-held company's equity is sold to accredited private investors, this is referred to as a private investment in public equity (PIPE). Private investors are usually willing to engage in such a transaction when they are offered a discount from the market price of a company's stock, typically in the range of a 10% to 25% discount. The sale of securities under a PIPE can be structured in a number of ways, including the following:

- Common stock sold at a specific price point
- Common stock sold with warrants having fixed exercise prices
- Common stock sold with warrants having resettable exercise prices
- Common stock sold at a variable price point
- Convertible preferred stock
- Convertible debt

A major advantage of a PIPE is that it is considered a private investment by the SEC under Regulation D, so the shares do not have to be immediately registered with the SEC. Since no registration is required, the offering can be completed quickly and with minimal administrative hassles. A further advantage for the issuing company is that shares are typically sold in large blocks under a PIPE transaction to longer-term and more knowledgeable investors.

However, there are some disadvantages to entering into a PIPE transaction, from the perspective of the company. Consider the following issues:

- *Additional shares.* The company may have to guarantee the issuance of additional shares to PIPE investors if the market price of the shares subsequently falls below a threshold amount.
- *Rapid sell-off.* Unless the company is careful about which investors are allowed to buy shares in a PIPE deal, it may find that the investors sell off their shares as soon as possible after the shares have been registered, thereby driving down the market price of the stock.
- *Registration obligation.* The company is typically obligated to file a registration statement with the SEC shortly after the sale is completed, so that the investors can eventually have the restrictions removed from their stock certificates and can then sell their shares.
- *Short seller manipulation.* If the company is obligated to issue more shares to investors if the stock price declines, short sellers could take advantage of the situation by continually driving down the stock price, which triggers the issuance of more and more shares. This *death spiral PIPE* can even result in majority ownership of the company by the PIPE investors. The scenario can

be avoided by specifying a minimum stock price below which no additional compensatory shares will be issued.

- *Warrants*. Investors may demand that they also be granted warrants, so that they can participate in any upside growth in the price of the company's stock.

Crowdfunding

The JOBS Act was passed in 2012, with the intent of making it easier for companies to raise small amounts of capital, both by opening up stock sales to the general public and by reducing the reporting requirements of businesses.

Related Podcast Episode: Episode 242 of the Accounting Best Practices Podcast discusses crowdfunding. The episode is available at: **accountingtools.com/podcasts** or **iTunes**

When Congress passed the JOBS Act, it required the SEC to create a regulation that embodied the requirements of the Act. Accordingly, the SEC issued Regulation Crowdfunding in 2016. The key provisions of this regulation are noted in the following sub-sections.

Requirements

An organization can only use the crowdfunding exemption if it meets all of the following requirements, where monetary amounts have been adjusted for inflation as of 2017:

- *Aggregate limitation.* The firm is limited to raising a maximum amount of $1,070,000 in a 12-month period. This limit includes the amount it has already sold during the preceding 12-month period and the amount it intends to raise in this offering. This total does not include other exempt (non-crowdfunding) offerings during the period. We discuss these exemptions in the next chapter.
- *Investor limitations.* The aggregate amount that can be sold to any single investor cannot exceed:
    - The greater of $2,200 or five percent of the annual income or net worth of the investor, if the annual income or net worth of the investor is less than $107,000; and
    - Ten percent of the annual income or net worth of the investor, not to exceed a maximum aggregate amount sold of $107,000, if either the annual income or net worth of the investor is equal to or greater than $107,000.

EXAMPLE

An investor has annual income of $150,000 and a net worth of $80,000. The individual can invest the greater of $2,200 or 5% of $80,000. Therefore, the maximum possible investment is $4,000.

An investor has annual income of $200,000 and a net worth of $900,000. The individual can invest 10% of the $200,000 income, which is a $20,000 investment.

- *Intermediary.* An entity acting as an intermediary in a crowdfunding sale of securities must register with the SEC and FINRA[1] as a broker-dealer or a funding portal, that will provide investors with investor-education information, affirm that investors understand that they are risking the loss of their entire investments, and take steps to reduce the risk of fraud with respect to these transactions. Fraud reduction includes obtaining a background and securities history check on each officer, director, and person holding more than 20 percent of the outstanding equity of the issuing entity. No later than 21 days prior to the first day on which securities will be sold by an issuer, the intermediary must make available to the SEC and to potential investors any information provided by the issuer. Also, the entity can only forward funds to the issuer when the aggregate capital raised from all investors equals or exceeds the target offering amount.
- *Ineligible entities.* The following types of organizations are not eligible to use the Regulation Crowdfunding exemption:
  - Non-U.S. companies
  - Companies already subject to the reporting requirements of the Exchange Act
  - Certain types of investment companies
  - Companies that are disqualified under the Regulation's disqualification rules (see the following Bad Actor Disqualification sub-section)
  - Companies that have not met the Regulation's annual reporting requirements during the preceding two years
  - Companies that have no specific business plan
  - Companies that plan to engage in unidentified mergers or acquisitions

Disclosures

When an organization plans to conduct an offering under the Regulation, it must electronically file its offering statement on Form C, via the SEC's EDGAR[2] system, as well as with the entity that is acting as the intermediary in the offering. The Form

---

[1] The Financial Industry Regulatory Authority
[2] EDGAR is short for the Electronic Data Gathering, Analysis and Retrieval System

C is essentially an abbreviated version of the much longer filing required when a firm wants to register shares with the SEC for a public offering. The Form C is estimated to require about 50 hours to complete. Its main information requirements are:

- Information about the firm's officers, directors, and owners of 20% or more of its shares
- A description of the business
- A description of how the proceeds from the offering will be used
- The price at which the shares will be offered, or the method used to determine the price
- The target offering amount
- The deadline by which the offering amount must be reached
- Whether the firm will accept investments in excess of the target amount
- A description of certain related-party transactions
- A discussion of the firm's financial condition and financial statements

If the firm plans to raise $107,000 or less, it must provide its income tax return for the most recently completed year, and its financial statements (to be certified by the principal executive officer). However, if the firm has either audited or reviewed financial statements, it must provide these statements instead.

If the firm plans to raise more than $107,000 but not more than $535,000, it must provide financial statements that have been reviewed by an independent public accountant. However, if the firm has audited financial statements, it must provide these statements instead.

If the firm plans to raise more than $535,000 and it is a first-time user of the Regulation Crowdfunding exemption, it must provide financial statements that have been reviewed by an independent public accountant. However, if the firm has audited financial statements, it must provide these statements instead.

If the firm plans to raise more than $535,000 and it has previously used the Regulation Crowdfunding exemption, it must provide financial statements that have been audited by an independent public accountant.

There may be cases in which an organization has material updates to the information it has provided to the SEC. If these changes occur while an offering is not yet complete, the firm should include the changes in a Form C/A. Also, the firm must reconfirm any outstanding investment commitments within five business days, or else the commitment will be considered cancelled.

The firm must provide periodic updates to the SEC on the Form C-U. This report must be filed within five business days of reaching 50% of the targeted funding amount, as well as when the 100% threshold has been reached. If the firm accepts proceeds in excess of the target amount, it must file yet another Form C-U that states the total amount of securities sold in the offering.

When a firm sells securities under the Regulation Crowdfunding exemption, it must provide an annual report to the SEC, using the Form C-AR. This report must be filed no later than 120 days after the end of the firm's fiscal year. The firm must also post the completed Form on its website. The content of this Form is similar to what was required for the Form C, though there is no requirement to have the firm's financial statements audited or reviewed. These annual report filings must continue into the future until one of the following happens:

- The firm is required to file reports under Exchange Act sections 13(a) or 15(d)
- The firm has filed at least one annual report and has fewer than 300 holders of record
- The issuer has filed at least three annual reports and has total assets of not greater than $10 million
- The firm or another party purchases or repurchases all of the securities, including any payment in full of debt securities or any complete redemption of redeemable securities
- The firm liquidates itself

When a firm is terminating its annual reporting obligation, it must file a Form C-TR with the SEC, stating that it will no longer be providing annual reports.

Limits on Advertising and Promoters

An issuer is not allowed to advertise the terms of a Regulation Crowdfunding offering, except to issue a statement that sends investors to the intermediary's platform. This statement can only include the following information:

a) A statement that the issuer is conducting an offering pursuant to Section 4(a)(6) of the Securities Act, the name of the intermediary through which the offering is being conducted, and a link directing the potential investor to the intermediary's platform;
b) The terms of the offering, which means the amount of securities offered, the nature of the securities, their price, and the closing date of the offering period; and
c) Factual information about the legal identity and business location of the issuer, which is limited to the name of the issuer, its address, phone number, and website, the e-mail address of a representative of the issuer, and a brief description of its business.

It is allowable for the issuer to communicate with investors about the terms of the offering through communication channels provided on the intermediary's platform.

An issuer is allowed to compensate third parties to promote its crowdfunding offerings through communication channels provided by the intermediary, but only if the issuer ensures that the promoter discloses the compensation in each communication made.

Restrictions on Resale

When securities are sold in a crowdfunding transaction, they cannot be resold for one year. The only exceptions are when the securities are transferred to the issuer, or an accredited investor, or as part of an offering registered with the SEC, or to a member of the family of the purchaser or to a trust controlled by the purchaser.

Exemption from Section 12(g)

Section 12(g) of the Exchange Act states that an issuer having total assets of more than $10 million and a class of securities held by either 2,000 persons or 500 persons who are not accredited investors must register those securities with the SEC. However, securities issued under Regulation Crowdfunding are exempt from this requirement, as long as the following conditions are met:

- The issuer is current in its ongoing reporting requirements to the SEC; and
- The issuer has assets as of the end of its last fiscal year of $25 million or less; and
- The issuer has engaged the services of a transfer agent that is registered with the SEC.

If these requirements are not met, the issuer has a two-year transition period in which to register its securities with the SEC, as long as it continues to file all required reports with the SEC in a timely manner.

Bad Actor Disqualification

The SEC will disqualify an offering if the issuer or other covered persons have experienced a disqualifying event. Issuers must conduct an inquiry to determine whether any covered person has had a disqualifying event. Covered persons include the following:

- The issuer
- The issuer's directors, officers, general partners, or managing members
- Beneficial owners of 20% or more of the issuer's outstanding voting equity securities
- Promoters associated with the issuer
- Persons compensated for soliciting investors

These disqualifying events must have occurred after May 16, 2016, and include the following:

- Certain criminal convictions
- Certain court injunctions and restraining orders
- Certain final orders of state and federal regulators
- Certain SEC disciplinary orders
- Certain SEC cease and desist orders

- Suspension or expulsion from membership in a self-regulatory organization, such as FINRA
- SEC stop orders and orders suspending the Regulation A+ exemption
- U.S. Postal Service false representation orders

The regulation contains an exemption from disqualification when the issuer can demonstrate that it did not know, and could not have known that a covered person with a disqualifying event had participated in an offering.

Seasoned Equity Offerings

A follow up to the initial public offering discussed in the preceding chapter is the seasoned equity offering (SEO). This refers to any issuance of securities where the securities have been previously issued. Publicly-held companies tend to be cautious about issuing new SEOs, since the investment community tends to take the stance that more shares will water down their existing holdings, and so will bid down the price of the company's stock. A company may gain back this initial loss over time, if it can use the proceeds from the SEO to create a disproportionate increase in earnings (see the Dilution section later in this chapter).

Despite the possible short-term negative effect of an SEO, this is a more cost-effective approach to raising capital than the initial public offering. The company is already in compliance with the various mandates of the SEC, and so will incur no additional internal labor costs as a result of the SEO. Also, the company is presumably already listed on a stock exchange, so the incremental listing cost associated with the additional shares will be relatively small. Further, investment bankers usually charge a somewhat smaller fee than the hefty underwriting discount that they charge for an initial public offering. Consequently, if a public company continues to require additional funds that it does not want to obtain through more debt, an ongoing series of SEOs can be a reasonable way to obtain the funds.

A common method followed for an SEO is to use a *shelf registration*. This is a new issuance of securities registered with the SEC, where the issuance is to be made sometime during the next three years. This approach means that a business has pre-registered securities in hand, which it can issue on short notice. The CFO can maximize the funds raised from an equity shelf registration by waiting until the company's stock price is at a high point, and selling shares to investors at that point. This approach is easiest for a well-known seasoned issuer (WKSI), for which the shares associated with a shelf registration are declared effective as soon as the registration document is filed with the SEC. An organization qualifies as a WKSI if the market value of its stock owned by non-affiliates is at least $700 million, or it has issued at least $1 billion of non-convertible debt securities during the last three years.

The Rights Offering

The articles of incorporation of an organization may mandate that any new issuance of shares first be offered to existing shareholders. This requirement is designed to concentrate ownership among the existing shareholders, rather than watering down their investments as new investors acquire shares in the business.

An issuance of shares to existing shareholders is called a *rights offering*. In essence, a rights offering is an option to purchase shares. Under the terms of this option, a shareholder can purchase a certain number of shares at a designated price. The option expires on a specific date, after which the company can sell shares to outside investors. An option is exercised when a shareholder sends the required payment to the subscription agent handling the offering on behalf of the company.

EXAMPLE

Eskimo Construction, maker of energy-efficient homes, has 5,000,000 shares of common stock outstanding. These shares are currently selling on a stock exchange at $11 per share, which implies a market value for the company of $55 million. Management plans to use a rights offering to raise an additional $10 million.

Eskimo sets the price of the offering at $10. Doing so attracts the attention of the current investors, since they can buy at a price that is $1 below the market rate. Since management wants to raise $10 million at a price of $10 per share, it will be necessary to sell an additional 1,000,000 shares. To raise this sum, Eskimo will need to issue 1,000,000 rights.

A rights offering has value, since it typically allows the holder to buy shares at a below-market price. In the preceding example, a $1 discount per share was available to each rights holder. However, this advantage is only available until the termination date of the rights offering. This means that someone purchasing a company's shares should pay more for those shares up until the rights termination date, in order to account for the increased value associated with the attached rights offering. The price of the stock should decline immediately thereafter, to reflect the termination of the rights offering.

A company that engages in a rights offering usually sets the price sufficiently low that any declines in the market price of the stock during the offering period will not fall below the subscription price. Doing so essentially ensures that the rights will be used by shareholders, so that the company receives the full amount of proceeds from the offering. A business can guarantee its receipt of the expected funds by entering into a standby underwriting arrangement with an underwriter, which will commit to purchase all unsubscribed shares for a fee. The fee charged for this service is essentially a form of insurance against the loss of funds.

Dilution

When raising capital, the existing shareholders may be concerned that their ownership interest in the business will be diluted, since shares will now be sold to a new set of shareholders. This inherent level of dilution can be avoided with a rights offering, where the current investors are first given the opportunity to purchase additional shares.

EXAMPLE

Mr. Smith is one of the founding shareholders of Blitz Communications, maker of office phones. He originally purchased 10,000 shares, which represented a 10% share of the total number of shares outstanding.

The management of Blitz needs to raise capital, and proposes selling an additional 100,000 shares to the public. If Mr. Smith does not purchase any of these new shares, his ownership interest in the company will decline to 5%, which is calculated as follows:

10,000 Shares held ÷ 200,000 Total shares outstanding = 5% Ownership interest

The company elects to initiate a rights offering arrangement, where the existing shareholders are given the opportunity to purchase shares at a rate of one new share for each share currently held. Mr. Smith elects to purchase his full allotment of 10,000 additional shares. His ownership interest in the company is now 10%, which is calculated as follows:

20,000 Shares held ÷ 200,000 Total shares outstanding = 10% Ownership interest

---

A valid concern may be raised that shareholders will suffer a reduction in the value of their shares if new shares are sold. There are numerous factors that influence the market price of a share, but certainly among the more crucial factors are earnings per share and cash flow per share. If a company sells shares to raise capital and then invests the new funds in activities that generate a lower incremental level of earnings or cash flow, then investors will likely be less inclined to invest in the shares, and their market price will decline.

EXAMPLE

Creekside Industrial currently has 5,000,000 shares of common stock outstanding, which sell on a national stock exchange for $20 per share. The company currently produces income of $25,000,000, which is $5.00/share. This means that investors are buying the stock at a 4x multiple of the earnings per share.

The management team believes that there is a golden opportunity to manufacture batteries for hybrid cars, and needs $10,000,000 of capital to construct a battery production facility for this purpose. Accordingly, the board of directors authorizes the sale of 500,000 shares of common stock to raise the required amount of capital. The money is raised, and is invested in the facility. However, the company finds that foreign competition is driving down the price of hybrid car batteries, so the new facility can only break even.

The result is no change in company income, which remains at $25,000,000. However, there are now 5,500,000 shares of common stock outstanding, so the earnings per share figure has declined to $4.55. Assuming that investors are still assigning a 4x multiple to the earnings per share figure, this means that the market value of the company's stock has now declined to $18.20.

Stock price dilution is a particular concern among investors when shares are being sold to pay for an acquisition. The majority of acquisitions do not achieve initial expectations, so the additional shares issued are not likely to trigger an increase in earnings per share or cash flow per share. Consequently, it is not uncommon to see a market price decline for the shares of the acquirer, even before an acquisition has been completed – investors are simply making their expectations known by fleeing the stock.

Summary

The capital raising alternatives described in this chapter all have flaws or restrictions that limit their use. For example:

- *Regulation A*. The fatal flaw in Regulation A from the perspective of the issuer is that the organization is still required to produce a considerable amount of information for the Form 1-A, and yet can only obtain a maximum of $50 million for all of this effort. From the perspective of investors, they will obtain unrestricted stock, but the issuer is likely so small that there is not much of a market for the shares, making them difficult to sell.
- *Regulation D*. The Regulation D option does not result in registered stock, so investors cannot easily sell their shares. A common outcome is that the issuer must offer one or more enticements to prospective investors in order to convince them to buy shares. These enticements could be quite expensive, or force the issuer to take itself public at a later date.
- *Crowdfunding*. The annual crowdfunding limitation for a business is so small that it is likely to be a viable alternative only for the smallest startup companies. Further, a prospective issuer will likely compare the amount of money to be gained to the level of required information reporting, and conclude that the trade-off is not a reasonable one.
- *Seasoned equity offerings*. This is a fine, lower-cost approach to raising capital, but is only available to businesses that have already gone public. Consequently, an SEO is only a viable option for a small number of businesses.

Chapter 7
Debt Financing

Introduction

A business may not be able to obtain additional funding through the issuance of equity, or its owners may be reluctant to do so. If this is the case, a common alternative is to instead obtain debt financing. In this chapter, we review the different types of debt. The bulk of the debt alternatives available are based upon the assets of a business, which imposes a limitation on the total amount of debt that can be obtained. A smaller number of unsecured financing choices are available to businesses that have more robust financial results. These options are described in the following sections.

> **Related Podcast Episodes:** Episodes 124 and 125 of the Accounting Best Practices Podcast discuss lender relations and refinancing debt, respectively. The episodes are available at: **accountingtools.com/podcasts** or **iTunes**

Overview of Debt Financing

If a business cannot meet its funding requirements by internally generating cash or selling shares, then the best remaining option is to obtain debt funding. There are several types of debt financing, which fall into these categories:

- *Asset-based financing.* Company assets are used as collateral for this type of debt. Examples are the line of credit, invoice discounting, factoring, receivables securitization, inventory financing, loan stock, purchase order financing, hard money loans, mezzanine financing, and leases.
- *Unsecured financing.* No company assets are used as collateral. Instead, lenders rely upon the cash flows of the business to obtain repayment. Examples are long-term loans and bonds.
- *Guaranteed financing.* A third party guarantees debt payments by the company. Government entities, such as the Export-Import Bank, usually provide these guarantees.

Examples of these types of debt financing are noted through the remainder of this chapter. Lease financing is addressed separately in the Leasing chapter.

If a company obtains financing, it must pay interest on the amount borrowed. The interest percentage may be variable, with the rate adjusting in accordance with a benchmark rate at regular intervals. If the rate is variable and may rise suddenly, a company is at some risk of incurring much higher interest expenses. These costs are mitigated by the tax deductibility of interest expense. For example, if a company incurs $100,000 of interest expense and is in the 35% incremental income tax bracket, it can use the $100,000 interest deduction to reduce its income tax liability (if any) by $35,000.

There may also be a fee for an annual audit of the company's books by a bank-designated auditor, as well as an annual facility fee for keeping open a line of credit.

When reviewing the following types of debt, take note of any administrative charges that may also be billed to the company. This is a particularly large issue for financings involving accounts receivable or inventory as collateral, and can noticeably increase the total borrowing cost.

The Line of Credit

A line of credit is a commitment from a lender to pay a company whenever it needs cash, up to a pre-set maximum limit. A line of credit is generally secured by company assets, which the lender can take if the company is unable to pay back the line of credit. The lender will not allow a drawdown against a line of credit if the total amount lent will then exceed the amount of assets pledged as collateral against the line (known as the *borrowing base*). Any debt made available under a line of credit can be accessed multiple times over the course of the debt agreement. The lender may also block out a portion of a line of credit for letter of credit transactions where the borrower is committing to pay a supplier a predetermined amount on a future date. A line of credit is a highly useful form of financing for a business that does not have sufficient cash reserves to fund its day-to-day needs.

A larger and more credit-worthy business may be able to avoid any collateral; if so, the lender is relying on the general credit quality of the company. The usual agreement under which a line of credit is granted requires the company to pay an annual fee in exchange for the lender's commitment to keep a certain amount of debt available for the company's use; this is called a *committed* line of credit. It is also possible to have a less formal arrangement at a lower cost, where the lender is not obligated to make funds available to the company. This latter arrangement is called an *uncommitted* line of credit, and is useful for rare lending needs when a company has several sources of funds from which to choose.

When a bank offers a line of credit, it is typically under the agreement that the bank will also handle the company's other banking business, such as its checking accounts and lockboxes. This arrangement can be useful, since the staff can monitor cash balances and routinely transfer borrowed funds back to the bank through an inexpensive intrabank transfer transaction. Doing so on a frequent basis minimizes the interest cost of the line of credit.

When entering into a line of credit arrangement, be sure to also obtain separate debt funding to handle all of the company's long-term debt needs. The reason is that a line of credit is intended to be a source of short-term funding *only*, which means that the line of credit balance is expected to drop to zero at some point each year. Otherwise, it will appear that the company is using the line as part of its long-term borrowing arrangements.

The Borrowing Base

A borrowing base is the total amount of collateral against which a lender will lend funds to a business. This typically involves multiplying a discount factor by each type of asset used as collateral. For example:

- *Accounts receivable.* 60% to 80% of accounts receivable less than 90 days old may be accepted as a borrowing base. Receivables from related parties and foreign entities are excluded.
- *Inventory.* A smaller percentage of finished goods inventory may be accepted as a borrowing base. Raw materials and work-in-process, as well as custom-made goods and slow-moving finished goods are usually not allowed, since they are more difficult to liquidate.

It is also common for a lender to only use the accounts receivable of a borrower as collateral - it may not accept *any* inventory as part of the borrowing base.

If the business is a small one, the lender issuing a line of credit will probably also want a personal guarantee from the owner of the business, in addition to the underlying collateral.

A business that borrows money under a borrowing base arrangement usually fills out a *borrowing base certificate* at regular intervals, in which it calculates the applicable borrowing base. A company officer signs the certificate and submits it to the lender, which retains it as proof of the available amount of collateral. If the borrowing base stated on the certificate is less than the amount that the company is currently borrowing from the lender, then the company must pay the difference to the lender at once.

EXAMPLE

Hammer Industries enters into a line of credit arrangement that has a maximum lending limit of $6 million. The amount of the accounts receivable to be used in the borrowing base is limited to 80% of all trade receivables less than 90 days old. The amount of the inventory to be used is limited to finished goods. The amount of finished goods to be used in the borrowing base is limited to 65%.

At the end of March, there are $4.8 million of accounts receivable outstanding, of which $200,000 are more than 90 days old. Hammer also has $6.5 million of inventory on hand, of which $3.5 million is finished goods. The amount of debt that has been drawn down on the line of credit is $5 million. Based on this information, the CFO of Hammer constructs the following borrowing base certificate:

Hammer Industries	
Borrowing Base Certificate	as of 3/31/20x3
Total accounts receivable	$4,800,000
Less: Receivables > 90 days old	-200,000
Eligible accounts receivable	$4,600,000
× Advance rate	80%
= Collateral value of accounts receivable	$3,680,000
Total finished goods inventory	$3,500,000
× Advance rate	65%
= Collateral value of finished goods inventory	$2,275,000
Total collateral	$5,955,000
Total debt outstanding	5,000,000
Excess collateral	$955,000

A lender may want to protect its borrowing base by requiring the borrower to obtain credit insurance for all of its outstanding accounts receivable. The cost of this insurance is essentially an additional borrowing cost for the borrower.

Careful monitoring of the borrowing base is of particular importance in seasonal businesses, since the inventory portion of the base gradually builds prior to the selling season, followed by a sharp increase in the receivable asset during the selling season, and then a rapid decline in all assets immediately after the season has been completed. It is necessary to balance loan drawdowns and repayments against these rapid changes in the borrowing base to ensure that a company does not violate its loan agreement.

Invoice Discounting

Invoice discounting is the practice of using a company's unpaid accounts receivable as collateral for a loan, which is issued by a finance company. Invoice discounting essentially accelerates cash flow from customers, so that instead of waiting for customers to pay within their normal credit terms, cash is received almost as soon as an invoice is issued.

This is an extremely short-term form of borrowing, since the finance company can alter the amount of debt outstanding as soon as the amount of accounts receivable collateral changes. The amount of debt issued by the finance company is less than the total amount of outstanding receivables (typically 80% of all invoices less than 90 days old).

The finance company earns money both from the interest rate it charges on the loan (which is well above the prime rate), and a monthly fee to maintain the arrangement. The amount of interest that it charges the borrower is based on the amount of funds loaned, not the amount of funds available to be loaned.

Invoice discounting is impossible if another lender already has blanket title to all company assets as collateral on a different loan. In such cases, the other lender needs to waive its right to the accounts receivable collateral, and instead take a junior position behind the finance company.

From an operational perspective, the borrower sends an accounts receivable report to the finance company at least once a month, aggregating receivables into the categories required by the finance company. The finance company uses this information to adjust the amount of debt that it is willing to loan the borrower. The borrower retains control over the accounts receivable, which means that it is responsible for extending credit to customers, invoicing them, and collecting from them. There is no need to notify customers of the discounting arrangement.

Invoice discounting works best for companies with relatively high profit margins, since they can readily absorb the higher interest charges associated with this form of financing. It is especially common in high-profit businesses that are growing at a rapid rate, and need the cash flow to fund additional growth. Conversely, this is not a good form of financing for low-margin businesses, since the interest on the debt may eliminate any prospect of earning a profit.

Invoice discounting tends to be a financing source of last resort, because of the substantial fees associated with it. It would normally be used only after most other forms of financing have been attempted.

Factoring

Another type of asset-based lending is factoring. A company that engages in factoring sells its accounts receivable to a third party, known as the *factor*. As was the case with invoice discounting, factoring is only an option if a company has not allowed other parties to attach its receivables as collateral on other loans. The pricing arrangement for a factoring deal includes the following components:

- *Advance*. This is a proportion of the face amount of the invoices that the factor pays to the company at the point of sale.
- *Reserve*. This is the remaining proportion of the face amount of the invoices, which the factor retains until collections have been completed.
- *Fee*. This is the cost of the factoring arrangement, which is deducted from the reserve payment.

Once the factor owns a company's receivables, customers are notified to send their payments to a lockbox controlled by the factor. Payments made into the lockbox are retained by the factor. If the factoring arrangement is *with recourse*, the factor can pursue the company for any unpaid customer invoices. If the arrangement is *without recourse*, the factor absorbs any bad debt losses. A without recourse arrangement is more expensive, to compensate the factor for bad debt losses.

The total amount of fees associated with a factoring arrangement can be substantial, so this is generally considered a fund-raising arrangement of last resort.

Receivables Securitization

A larger organization can convert its accounts receivable into cash at once by securitizing the receivables. This means that individual receivables are aggregated into a new security, which is then sold as an investment instrument. A securitization can result in an extremely low interest rate for the issuing entity, since the securities are backed by a liquid form of collateral (i.e., receivables). In essence, a receivables securitization is accomplished with these steps:

1. Create a special purpose entity (SPE). An SPE is designed to acquire and finance specific assets, while separating the risk associated with those assets from any risks associated with the parent entity.
2. Transfer selected accounts receivable into the SPE.
3. Have the SPE sell the receivables to a bank conduit.
4. Have the bank conduit pool the company's receivables with those from other companies, and issue commercial paper backed by the receivables to investors.
5. Pay investors back based on cash receipts from the accounts receivable.

These process steps indicate that the securitization of accounts receivable is complex, and so is reserved for larger companies that can attend to the many steps. Also, the receivables included in a pool should be widely differentiated (so there are many customers), with a low historical record of customer defaults. Despite the complexity, securitization is tempting for the following reasons:

- *Interest cost.* The cost to the issuer is low, because the use of the SPE isolates the receivables from any other risks associated with the company, typically resulting in a high credit rating for the SPE. This credit rating must be assigned by a rating agency, which will take into account such factors as the historical performance of the receivables in the pool, unusually large debtor concentrations in the pool, and the conservatism of the issuing company's credit and collection policies.
- *Non-recordation.* The debt incurred by the company is not recorded on its balance sheet, since the debt is passing through an SPE.
- *Liquidity.* The flow of cash into the business can be accelerated, rather than waiting for customers to pay their bills.

The low interest cost of a receivables securitization can only be achieved and maintained if there is considerable separation between the SPE and the company. This is accomplished by designating the transfer of receivables to the SPE as a nonrecourse sale, where creditors of the company cannot access the transferred receivables. In short, the company cannot be allowed to regain control over any transferred receivables.

Inventory Financing

The preceding Invoice Discounting and Factoring sections discussed how to use accounts receivable as collateral for different types of loan arrangements. The same approach can be applied to inventory. To make this arrangement work to the satisfaction of the lender, the inventory being used as collateral is placed in a controlled area and under the supervision of a third party that only releases inventory with the approval of the lender. The lender is paid from the proceeds of inventory sales. Under a less controlled environment, the lender may agree to periodic inventory reports by the borrower, with occasional inspections of the inventory to ensure that the counted amounts match the borrower's reports.

There must be a sufficient amount of insurance in place to ensure that the lender will be paid back if the inventory is destroyed or damaged. Also, depending on state laws, it may be necessary to post notices around the collateralized inventory, stating that a lien has been imposed on the inventory. Further, the inventory cannot be used as collateral on any other loans, unless they are subordinate to the arrangement with the inventory financing company.

If the amount of inventory being used as collateral drops below the amount of the loan associated with it, the borrower must immediately pay the lender the difference.

Because of the cost of third party monitoring, inventory financing is one of the more expensive forms of financing available and can also be quite intrusive, so it is used only after less-expensive alternatives have been explored. The sole advantage of this form of financing is that the lender relies exclusively on the inventory asset to ensure that it is repaid; it does not impose covenants on the borrower.

Floor planning is a method of financing inventory purchases, where a lender pays for assets that have been ordered by a distributor or retailer, and is paid back from the proceeds from the sale of these items. The arrangement is most commonly used when large assets, such as automobiles or household appliances, are involved.

The entity at risk in this arrangement is the lender, who is relying upon the sale of the underlying assets in order to be repaid. Accordingly, the lender may demand the following:

- That all assets acquired under the floor planning arrangement be sold at a price that is no lower than its original purchase price.
- That the inventory of assets in stock is regularly counted and matched against the records of the lender.
- That the lender be repaid at once if there is any shortfall in the inventory count.
- That the loan be paid back no later than a certain date, thereby avoiding the risk of product obsolescence.

Floor planning may be a valid option when the seller of the goods does not have adequate financing to use other options.

Loan Stock

Loan stock is shares in a business that have been pledged as collateral for a loan. The lender may require that it retain physical control of the shares for the duration of the loan, and will return the shares to their owner once the loan has been paid off. If the borrower defaults on the loan, the lender can then retain the shares. This type of collateral is most valuable for a lender when the shares are publicly traded on a stock exchange and are unrestricted, so that the shares can be easily sold for cash. This arrangement is of less use when a business is privately held, since the lender cannot easily sell the shares.

Loan stock can be a problem from a corporate control perspective, since a loan default means that the lender acquires the shares, and therefore the related ownership percentage in the business, along with all associated voting rights.

A loan stock arrangement can be risky for the lender, since the market value of the shares being used as collateral may decline. If a portion of the loan principal is being paid back on an ongoing basis, this is less of a problem, since the loan balance will be declining over time. If the loan is being paid off incrementally, there may be a clause in the lending agreement under which some portion of the shares are returned to the borrower before the end of the lending arrangement.

Purchase Order Financing

Purchase order financing is applicable when a company receives an order from a customer that it cannot process with its existing working capital. A lender accepts the purchase order as collateral, which allows the borrower to obtain sufficient funds to buy the materials and labor required to complete the order. This arrangement is risky for the lender, since the borrower must perform under the contract in order to receive payment from the customer. Given the extra risk, the borrowing cost is much higher for purchase order financing.

Hard Money Loans

A hard money loan is a short-term, high-interest rate loan. This type of loan is typically extended to businesses whose financial situations are poor, and so cannot qualify for lower-cost forms of debt. A hard money loan typically has the following characteristics:

- *High interest rate.* The rate may be several multiples of the prime rate, and is intended to cover the much higher risk that the lender takes on in this type of arrangement.
- *Short term.* The intent of the loan is to keep the borrower solvent for a short period of time. In essence, this is a bridge loan.
- *Collateral.* The lender typically bases repayment on the assets of the borrower, rather than the borrower's cash flow. This means the lender is willing to shut down the borrower's organization and liquidate its assets in order to obtain repayment of the loan and any outstanding interest.

Banks do not engage in hard money lending, since these loan characteristics go well beyond the normal borrowing rules of a bank. Instead, this type of loan is more likely to be offered by wealthy individuals or smaller firms that are willing to accept a high degree of risk. Given their high fee structures, these lenders are more likely to compete based on the rapid turnaround of loan applications than to offer lower interest rates.

A borrower must have substantial assets in order to take on a hard money loan. Otherwise, a prospective lender will see no obvious way to be repaid. Consequently, this type of financing arrangement is rare in the services industries, which are traditionally light on assets. These loans are more commonly found in the real estate industry, which is asset intensive.

Mezzanine Financing

Mezzanine financing is positioned partway between the equity and debt financings used by a business. It is designed to provide cash to an existing business that requires the funds to grow, or for a leveraged buyout, or a corporate restructuring. The borrower in a mezzanine financing situation is usually not publicly-held, and so does not have access to the public markets as a more ready source of cash. This type of financing is usually obtained from smaller lenders who specialize in mezzanine financing, rather than from more traditional banking institutions. Mezzanine financing is typically structured as:

- Convertible debt that can be swapped by the lender for company stock if the price of the stock rises.
- Debt with a significant number of attached warrants that allow the lender to acquire company stock if the price of the stock rises.
- Preferred stock that earns a dividend, and which may have special voting rights, the ability to convert to common stock, or other special features.

Mezzanine financing, if structured as debt, is usually junior to the debt of a company's more traditional lenders, such as the bank that issues its line of credit or any long-term loans. This means that, in the event of company cash flow troubles, the holders of senior debt are paid first from available cash, while those in a junior position are paid only from any residual cash available once the claims of all senior lenders and creditors have been satisfied.

Given the increased riskiness of being in a junior position, the lender of mezzanine financing wants to earn an unusually high return that is usually in the range of 20% to 30% per year. The lender may also charge a large up-front arrangement fee. A borrower may not be in a position to make ongoing interest payments in the 20% to 30% range on an ongoing basis, which is why the use of warrants and conversion features are heavily used to give the lender an alternative method for achieving its return on investment goal. This also means that principal is not scheduled to be repaid until the end of the loan period, and may be paid back with company stock, if the lender can realize an adequate return from taking this form of payment.

Mezzanine financing can also be used in a leveraged buyout situation, where it is used as a stopgap measure to provide short-term financing until a lower-cost and longer-term arrangement can be made.

Though mezzanine financing can provide a significant amount of cash, it has a number of downsides. First, the lender may impose a number of restrictive covenants to protect its investment. Second, the lender may end up being a large shareholder in the business, and so is in a position to influence decisions made by the company. Third, it is one of the most expensive forms of financing available. And finally, mezzanine financing is only available after a prolonged investigation by a prospective lender.

The Long-Term Loan

When a company finds that it is unable to draw its line of credit down to zero at any point during the year, this means that its funding needs have become more long-term. If so, it should apply to a lender for a long-term loan that will be paid off over a number of years.

The following points may clarify whether it is even possible to obtain such a loan, and whether one would want to do so:

- *Banking services*. The provider of a long-term loan may insist on providing a complete package of banking services, to maximize its profits. If so, expect to shift all bank accounts, lines of credit, lockboxes, and other services to the lender.
- *Cash flow*. The lender is particularly sensitive to the historical and projected performance of the business, since the loan must be repaid from continuing cash flows. If positive cash flows have been a rare event, it will be very difficult to obtain a long-term loan. The lender may also want to see a budget for at least the next year.
- *Covenants*. The lender will probably impose covenants on the company that are designed to keep it from disbursing cash outside of the normal course of business. In particular, dividends may be restricted.
- *Creditor positioning*. A lender willing to commit to a long-term loan will certainly want to be designated as having the senior position among all creditors of the company, so that it will be more likely to be paid back in the event of a loan default. This positioning is necessary, because the lender is committing a large amount of funds over a long period of time, during which the company's financial results may change dramatically.
- *Personal guarantee*. In a smaller business where there are few owners, and especially where historical cash flow has been uncertain, the lender may insist on personal guarantees that allow the lender to pursue the owners for repayment.

A long-term loan can be configured as a series of fixed payments, or as interest-only payments with a large balloon payment due at the end of the loan. While the balloon payment option may appear tempting from a short-term cash flow perspective, it introduces the risk that credit conditions may have changed by the time it is due for payment, making it difficult to refinance.

The conditions associated with a long-term loan might leave management less inclined to pursue this option. However, a long-term loan allows a business to lock in debt for an extended period of time, without having to worry about the vagaries of the short-term credit markets. Thus, it can make sense to assign a portion of a company's debt to longer-term loans.

Bonds

When a business sells a fixed obligation to investors, this is generally described as a *bond*. The typical bond has a face value of $1,000, which means that the issuer is obligated to pay the investor $1,000 on the maturity date of the bond. If investors feel that the stated interest rate on a bond is too low, they will only agree to buy the bond at a price lower than its stated amount, thereby increasing the effective interest rate that they will earn on the investment. Conversely, a high stated interest rate can lead investors to pay a premium for a bond.

When a bond is registered, the issuer is maintaining a list of which investors own its bonds. The issuer then sends periodic interest payments directly to these investors. When the issuer does not maintain a list of investors who own its bonds, the bonds are considered to be *coupon bonds*. A coupon bond contains attached coupons that investors send to the issuer; these coupons obligate the company to issue interest payments to the holders of the bonds. A coupon bond is easier to transfer between investors, but it is also more difficult to establish ownership of the bonds.

There are many types of bonds. The following list represents a sampling of the more common types:

- *Collateral trust bond.* This bond includes the investment holdings of the issuer as collateral.
- *Convertible bond.* This bond can be converted into the common stock of the issuer at a predetermined conversion ratio. See the Debt for Equity Swaps section.
- *Debenture.* This bond has no collateral associated with it. A variation is the subordinated debenture, which has junior rights to collateral.
- *Deferred interest bond.* This bond offers little or no interest at the start of the bond term, and more interest near the end. The format is useful for businesses currently having little cash with which to pay interest.
- *Income bond.* The issuer is only obligated to make interest payments to bond holders if the issuer or a specific project earns a profit. If the bond terms allow for cumulative interest, then the unpaid interest will accumulate until such time as there is sufficient income to pay the amounts owed.
- *Mortgage bond.* This bond is backed by real estate or equipment owned by the issuer.

- *Serial bond.* This bond is gradually paid off in each successive year, so the total amount of debt outstanding is gradually reduced.
- *Variable rate bond.* The interest rate paid on this bond varies with a baseline indicator, such as the London Interbank Offered Rate (LIBOR).
- *Zero coupon bond.* No interest is paid on this type of bond. Instead, investors buy the bonds at large discounts to their face values in order to earn an effective interest rate.
- *Zero coupon convertible bond.* This variation on the zero coupon bond allows investors to convert their bond holdings into the common stock of the issuer. This allows investors to take advantage of a run-up in the price of a company's stock. The conversion option can increase the price that investors are willing to pay for this type of bond.

Additional features can be added to a bond to make it easier to sell to investors at a higher price. These features can include:

- *Sinking fund.* The issuer creates a sinking fund to which cash is periodically added, and which is used to ensure that bonds are eventually paid off.
- *Conversion feature.* Bond holders have the option to convert their bonds into the stock of the issuer at a predetermined conversion rate.
- *Guarantees.* The repayment of a bond may be guaranteed by a third party.

The following additional bond features favor the issuer, and so may reduce the price at which investors are willing to purchase bonds:

- *Call feature.* The issuer has the right to buy back bonds earlier than the stated maturity date.
- *Subordination.* Bond holders are positioned after more senior debt holders to be paid back from issuer assets in the event of a default.

Agency Financing

When a company needs to finance the export or import of goods, this can constitute a large surge in borrowings that cannot be supported by its line of credit. A good alternative is to use agency-backed financing for these transactions. An "agency" is a government-sponsored export credit agency, such as the Export-Import Bank (Ex-Im Bank) of the United States. These agencies provide financial packages for the export or import of goods. A typical financing arrangement is for a commercial bank to supply credit to the borrowing entity, with the agency providing a credit guarantee to the bank. Alternatively, an agency may directly provide credit, thereby eliminating the need for an intermediary bank.

Agencies are not in the business of losing money on their financing packages, so minimum standards apply to all applications. For example, a first-time applicant to the Ex-Im Bank of the United States must meet the following criteria:

- Has been in the same line of business for at least three years

- Has at least one year of exporting experience
- Had an operating profit in the most recent fiscal year
- Has a Dun & Bradstreet Paydex score of at least 50, as well as no derogatory information
- Has signed financial statements for the last fiscal year that show positive net worth
- Has no material adverse issues

In addition, the Ex-Im Bank may require corporate guarantees, personal guarantees, and/or collateral. Thus, agencies do not gratuitously give away funds; a company must qualify for financing under specific standards, and may be turned down. Nonetheless, this is a viable alternative when other sources of funds are not available.

Debt for Equity Swaps

In some cases, it may be possible to swap company shares for outstanding company debt securities. This is most common when a company issues convertible bonds that allow bond holders to convert their bonds into company stock at certain predefined exchange ratios. This option is only available to publicly-held companies.

In a privately-held company, a debt for equity swap usually occurs only when a company is in such dire financial straits that it is unable to repay its debt. If so, taking an equity interest in the company may be the only option remaining to the lender, other than writing off the debt as being uncollectible. This conversion to equity is more likely when the lender is an individual, rather than a bank, since banks may be constrained by their own lending rules from engaging in debt for equity swaps. A company that succeeds in converting debt to equity under these difficult financial circumstances may find that it can issue stock at such a low valuation that it is required by the accounting standards to book a profit on the conversion of debt to equity.

When a large public company issues convertible debt, any resulting conversions to equity are unlikely to be large enough to alter the debt-equity ratio of the business to a significant extent. The reverse is the case when a private company succeeds in converting debt to equity; it may be eliminating much of its debt, and had such little equity to begin with that it switches from having a dangerously unbalanced debt-equity ratio to one that gives the appearance of being solidly well-funded. Of course, the operational profitability of such a company is still questionable, but the debt for equity swap can repair its balance sheet.

Summary

Most of the forms of debt financing noted in this chapter can only be accessed in limited amounts that are defined by the amount of collateral, after which lenders will be extremely unwilling to advance additional funds. For really high debt levels, it will be necessary to obtain personal guarantees from the company owners, or the sale of stock to increase the amount of equity on hand.

If a business has extremely variable earnings, it may not make sense to have *any* debt, since it may be difficult to pay back the lender. In such a situation, it makes more sense to stockpile cash during periods when the company is flush with cash, or to rely primarily on the sale of stock to raise cash.

Chapter 8
Leasing

Introduction

One source of funding is the lease, which is tied to the use of a specific asset. A business may find that lease arrangements are an indispensable source of funds under certain circumstances, or could cause significant issues in other situations. In this chapter, we describe the leasing concept, the lease or buy decision, and the advantages and disadvantages of using lease financing.

The Lease Arrangement

A lease is an arrangement where the lessor agrees to allow the lessee to use an asset for a stated period of time in exchange for a series of fixed payments. The lessor may be the original manufacturer of the asset being leased, or an independent entity that provides financing. In the latter case, the independent entity buys the asset from the manufacturer, and then leases the asset to the lessee.

The arrangement typically requires that the asset be returned after a stated interval, though the lessee may have the option to extend the lease or buy the asset at the end of the lease term. The first scenario works best for a business that is more concerned with using an asset for a certain period of time, rather than with owning it outright.

A variation on the basic leasing concept is the sale and leaseback. Under this arrangement, an organization that owns an asset sells it to the lessor, and then leases the asset back from the lessor. For example, a company could sell its corporate headquarters building to a lessor, and then lease the facility from the lessor. This arrangement is designed to give the seller access to a large amount of up-front cash in exchange for a long-term stream of payments.

Leases are especially useful under the following circumstances:

- *Cash flow*. Lease payments are spread out over the term of a lease, thereby keeping a business from having to deal with large one-time cash outflows to purchase assets.
- *Covenants*. A lessor does not impose any covenants on a company as a whole, since it is only concerned with the specific asset it is leasing to the company. Thus, a company wanting to avoid covenants should consider leases.
- *Residual value uncertainty*. A business that is risk-averse will not want to buy assets, since it does not know what the residual value of the purchased assets will be when it is time to dispose of them. A lease shifts this uncertainty to the lessor, who owns the assets.

- *Specific collateralization.* When a company has pledged its other assets under a blanket collateralization agreement for another loan, a lease essentially segregates a single asset as collateral for a new loan (the lease).

The Lease or Buy Decision

When an organization needs to acquire an asset, it can either lease or buy the asset. The decision could be based on the lease payment terms being offered. However, there are a multitude of factors that a lessor includes in the formulation of the monthly rate that it charges, such as the down payment, the residual value of the asset at the end of the lease, and the interest rate; the number of factors involved makes it difficult to break out and examine each element of the lease. Instead, it is much easier to create separate net present value tables for the lease and buy alternatives, and then compare the results of the two tables to see which alternative is better from a cash flow perspective (see the Discounted Cash Flows chapter for more information about net present value). The following example illustrates the use of net present value for this analysis.

EXAMPLE

Milford Sound is contemplating the purchase of an asset for $500,000. It can buy the asset outright, or do so with a lease. Its cost of capital is 8%, and its incremental income tax rate is 35%. The following two tables show the net present values of both options.

Buy Option

Year	Depreciation	Income Tax Savings (35%)	Discount Factor (8%)	Net Present Value
0				-$500,000
1	$100,000	$35,000	0.9259	32,407
2	100,000	35,000	0.8573	30,006
3	100,000	35,000	0.7938	27,783
4	100,000	35,000	0.7350	25,725
5	100,000	35,000	0.6806	23,821
Totals	$500,000	$175,000		$360,258

Lease Option

Year	Pretax Lease Payments	Income Tax Savings (35%)	After-Tax Lease Cost	Discount Factor (8%)	Net Present Value
1	$135,000	$47,250	$87,750	0.9259	$81,248
2	135,000	47,250	87,750	0.8573	75,228
3	135,000	47,250	87,750	0.7938	69,656
4	135,000	47,250	87,750	0.7350	64,496
5	135,000	47,250	87,750	0.6806	59,723
Totals	$675,000	$236,250	$438,750		$350,351

Thus, the net purchase cost of the buy option is $360,258, while the net purchase cost of the lease option is $350,351. The lease option involves the lowest cash outflow for Milford, and so is the better option.

In the example, the income tax savings is lower for the buy option than for the lease option. This is because the lessee can only deduct depreciation expense from its taxable income when buying an asset, whereas it can deduct the full amount of all lease payments under the lease option.

Leasing Concerns

There is an undeniable attraction to acquiring assets with a lease, since it replaces a large up-front cash outflow with a series of monthly payments. However, before signing a lease agreement, be aware of the following issues that can increase the cost of the arrangement:

- *Buyout price*. Many leases include an end-of-lease buyout price that is inordinately high. If the lessee wants to continue using a leased asset, the buyout price may be so outrageous that the only realistic alternative is to continue making lease payments, which generates outsized profits for the lessor. Therefore, always negotiate the size of the buyout payment before signing a lease agreement. If the buyout is stated as the "fair market value" of the asset at the end of the lease term, the amount can be subject to interpretation, so include a clause that allows for arbitration to determine the amount of fair market value.
- *Deposit*. The lessor may require that an inordinately large deposit be made at the beginning of the lease term, from which the lessor can then earn interest over the term of the lease.
- *Deposit usage*. The terms of a lease may allow the lessor to charge any number of fees against the up-front deposit made by the lessee, resulting in little of the deposit being returned at the end of the lease.
- *Lease fee*. The lessor may charge a lease fee, which is essentially a paperwork charge to originate the lease. It may be possible to reduce or eliminate this fee.
- *Rate changes*. The lessor may offer a low lease rate during the beginning periods of a lease, and then escalate the rates later in the lease term. Be sure to calculate the average lease rate to see if the implicit interest rate is reasonable. In these sorts of arrangements, a rate ramp-up usually indicates an average interest rate that is too high.
- *Return fees*. When the lease term is over, the lessor may require that the leased asset be shipped at the lessee's cost to a distant location, and sometimes even in the original packaging.
- *Termination notification*. The lease agreement may require the lessee to notify the lessor in writing that it intends to terminate the lease as of the termination date stated in the contract. If the lessee does not issue this noti-

fication in a timely manner, it is obligated to continue leasing the asset, or to pay a large termination fee. Whenever this clause appears in a lease agreement, always negotiate it down to the smallest possible termination notification period.

- *Wear-and-tear standards.* A lease agreement may contain unreasonable standards for assigning a high rate of wear-and-tear to leased assets when they have been returned to the lessor, resulting in additional fees being charged to the lessee.

In short, many lessors rely upon obfuscation of the lease terms to generate a profit, so it makes sense to delve into every clause in a lease agreement and to be willing to bargain hard for changes to the terms. Also, have a well-managed system in place for retaining lease agreements and monitoring when the key dates associated with each lease will arise. Finally, conduct a cost review after each lease agreement has been terminated, to determine the total out-of-pocket cost and implicit interest rate; the result may be the discovery that certain lessors routinely gouge the company, and should not be used again.

In addition to the issues just noted, the lessee also loses access to any favorable changes in the residual value of leased assets, since the lessor usually retains ownership of the assets.

The list of concerns with leasing arrangements may appear formidable. However, they also have a number of advantages, as explained in the next section.

Leasing Advantages

The leasing concerns just described should introduce a note of caution into dealings with lessors, since a careful analysis of lease terms may reveal an inordinately high cost. However, there are also a number of advantages to leasing, which include:

- *Asset servicing.* The lessor may have a sophisticated asset servicing capability. Though the cost of this servicing may be high, it can result in fast servicing intervals and therefore extremely high equipment usage levels. In some cases, the presence of a servicing capability may be the main attraction of a leasing deal.
- *Competitive lease rates.* A lessor can offer quite competitive lease rates. This situation arises when a lessor buys assets in such high volumes that it can obtain volume purchase discounts from suppliers, some of which it may pass along to lessees. The lessor may also be able to borrow funds at a lower rate than the lessee, and can share some of the cost differential.
- *Financing accessibility.* A lessor is more likely to enter into a leasing arrangement with a company that is experiencing low profitability than a traditional lender. This is because the leased asset is collateral for the lessor, which can take the asset back if the lessee is unable to continue making timely lease payments. Conversely, a traditional lender might have a consid-

erably more difficult time accessing company assets, and so would be less inclined to lend funds for the purchase of assets.

- *New technology.* A non-monetary advantage of leasing is that a company is continually swapping out old equipment for newer and more technologically advanced equipment. This can present a competitive advantage in those cases where the equipment is being used within a core function, or used to enhance products or services.
- *Off-balance sheet transaction.* Depending on the terms of a leasing arrangement, it may be possible for a lessee to avoid having to state its remaining lease payment liabilities on its balance sheet. By doing so, the balance sheet shows the company as having fewer obligations than is really the case, and so the business appears more solvent. However, it may still be necessary to reveal the annual amount of future lease payments in the accompanying financial statement disclosures.
- *Reserve available debt.* The company can reserve room on its existing line of credit by instead using a lease to buy an asset.
- *Short-term usage.* A leasing arrangement can be an effective alternative for those assets that are expected to have little value by the end of their lease terms, or for which the company expects to install a replacement asset at about the time of the lease termination.

Summary

We have spent a large proportion of this chapter addressing the ways in which a lease can turn sour, due to terms that may be hidden deep within a lease agreement. Though the result can be an inordinately high financing cost, leasing can still prove to be an excellent alternative to buying assets outright. The keys to a successful leasing deal are to be aware of the situations in which leasing makes the most sense, reviewing lease terms with great care before signing an agreement, and complying with all lease terms.

Chapter 9
The Cost of Capital

Introduction

When a company makes a decision about how to invest its funds in various assets, part of the evaluation is based on the cost of those funds. This cost is known as the cost of capital. It is important to be as precise as possible in deriving the cost of capital, since an incorrect measurement could lead to investments that yield excessively low returns, or foregone investments that would have generated returns in excess of the real cost of capital. In this chapter, we describe how the cost of capital is calculated and the ways in which the result can be skewed.

Cost of Capital Derivation

The cost of capital is the cost of funds for a business. Any investment of those funds must equal or exceed the cost of capital, or else investors in the business will experience a negative return on their investment, and the business may eventually fail.

The cost of capital is comprised of the cost of a company's debt, preferred stock, and common stock, which are then combined into a weighted average cost of capital. We will address the calculation of the cost of each of these components in this section at a simplified level, and then develop the concept in the following sections.

Cost of Debt

The cost of a company's debt is not just the average interest rate that it pays for all outstanding debt. Interest expense is tax-deductible, so reduce the interest rate by its tax impact. The calculation of the cost of debt is:

$$\frac{\text{Interest expense} \times (1 - \text{tax rate})}{\text{Amount of debt}} = \text{After-tax interest rate}$$

For example, if a company has \$1,000,000 of outstanding debt at an interest rate of 6%, and its income tax rate is 35%, then its after-tax interest rate is:

$$\frac{\$60,000 \text{ interest expense} \times (1 - 35\% \text{ tax rate})}{\$1,000,000 \text{ of debt}} = 3.9\% \text{ after-tax interest rate}$$

> **Tip:** If there are additional costs associated with debt, such as a placement fee, include this amount in the calculation of the interest rate being paid on the debt. The result will be a slight increase in the interest rate.

Cost of Preferred Stock

Preferred stock is the next component of the cost of capital. It is a form of equity that does not have to be repaid to the investor, but for which a dividend must be paid each year. This dividend is not tax-deductible to the company, so preferred stock is essentially a more expensive form of debt. The calculation of the cost of preferred stock is:

$$\frac{\text{Dividend expenditure}}{\text{Amount of preferred stock}} = \text{Preferred stock dividend rate}$$

For example, if a company has $2,000,000 of preferred stock that requires an annual dividend payment of $180,000, then the cost of the stock on a percentage basis is:

$$\frac{\$180,000 \text{ dividend expenditure}}{\$2,000,000 \text{ of preferred stock}} = 9\% \text{ preferred stock dividend rate}$$

Cost of Common Stock

The final component of the cost of capital is common stock, which is a more difficult calculation. The best way to calculate this cost is through the capital asset pricing model (CAPM). The CAPM is comprised of the following three elements:

1. The risk-free rate of return, which is usually considered to be the return on a U.S. government security.
2. The return on a group of securities considered to have an average risk level, such as the Standard & Poor's 500 or the Dow Jones Industrials. This is considered to be the premium that investors demand above the risk-free rate to invest in the stock market.
3. The beta of the company's stock, which defines the amount by which its stock returns vary from the returns of stocks having an average level of risk. A beta of 1.0 indicates average risk, while a higher figure indicates increased risk and a lower figure indicates reduced risk. A highly cyclical business is more likely to have a high beta, since its returns are unusually positive during an expansion of the business cycle, and unusually poor during a contraction. Sellers of expensive retail goods tend to have high betas, while utilities generally have low betas. Beta is available from a variety of research firms for most publicly-held companies.

The preceding component parts then plug into the following calculation of the cost of common stock:

$$\text{Risk-free return} + (\text{beta} \times (\text{average stock return} - \text{risk-free return})) = \text{Cost of common stock}$$

For example, if the risk-free return is 2%, the return on the Standard & Poor's 500 is 9%, and a company's beta is 1.2, the cost of its common stock would be:

$$2\% \text{ risk-free return} + (1.2 \text{ beta} \times (9\% \text{ average stock return} - 2\% \text{ risk-free return})) = 10.4\% \text{ cost of common stock}$$

If a company is privately-held, there will be no beta information for it. Instead, select a publicly-held firm that is operationally and financially similar to the company, and use the beta for this proxy firm. Better yet, use an average of the betas for several similar publicly-held firms, thereby avoiding the risk of using a comparative beta that represents an outlier value.

Weighted Average Cost of Capital

After the cost of each element of the cost of capital has been determined, calculate the weighted average cost of capital (WACC), which is based on the amount of common stock, preferred stock, and debt outstanding at the end of the most recent reporting period. The following table shows how to conduct the calculation. Note that the weighted average of the various elements of the cost of capital in the sample calculation is 12%, which would then be used for the analysis of proposed investments.

Sample Cost of Capital Calculation

	Outstanding Amount	Interest Rate	Cost
Common stock	$10,000,000	15%	$1,500,000
Preferred stock	2,000,000	8%	160,000
Debt	4,500,000	7%	315,000
Totals	$16,500,000	12%	$1,975,000

This section has described the calculation of the WACC at a simplistic level. In the following two sections, we will describe how the inputs to the model can vary, and how the cost of capital can be adjusted for different situations.

Variations in the Cost of Capital

It can be quite difficult to derive an accurate cost of capital. This is not a minor issue, since the cost of capital is used to create discounted cash flow analyses for capital budgeting decisions. If the cost of capital is incorrect by even a small amount, this can alter management's decision to invest in a project. There are a number of ways in which the cost of capital may be incorrectly derived. For example, the following are all methods used to derive the cost of debt in the cost of capital formula:

- *The forecasted interest rate on the next new debt issuance.* This is the cost of the debt needed to fund the next round of capital projects, and so is the most relevant interest rate to include in the WACC formula.

- *The current average rate on debt outstanding.* This is the cost of debt needed to fund the *last* round of capital projects, which may not be applicable if interest rates have changed markedly in the meantime.

- *The historical rate of interest.* This may be the cost of debt that has been retired, and which may not have been applicable for the last few years.

There could be a particularly large difference between the historical and forecasted interest rate, which can result in a significant error in the derivation of the cost of capital. In most cases, the forecasted interest rate (which is the incremental rate) should be used.

A further error arises if the incorrect tax rate is used to derive the net cost of debt. The tax rate that should be used is the company's marginal tax rate that will apply to the specific investment transaction being contemplated. However, some organizations are more inclined to use their average tax rate, which could be significantly different.

The most difficult component of the cost of capital to calculate is the cost of equity, which means that this cost is the most likely to be wrong. Consider the following points:

- *Risk-free rate.* The risk-free rate is an input used to derive the cost of equity; but what is the risk-free rate? Most organizations use the interest rate on U.S. Treasury bonds as a proxy for the risk-free rate, but there is no agreement on which bond. The instruments chosen typically vary from the 90-day bill to the 30-year bond, which presents a wide range of interest rates. Further, some organizations derive an *average* rate from instruments having different maturities, while others may choose to use a *forecasted* U.S. Treasury rate. There may also be inconsistency in using different U.S. Treasury instruments over time.

- *Stock market premium.* The additional return over the risk-free rate that investors demand in order to invest in the stock market is also used to derive the cost of equity. There is a wide range in the assumed amount of this return. Once selected, companies are not in the habit of adjusting the rate, even though there may be changes over time in the comparative level of turmoil in the financial markets that would warrant an adjustment.

- *Beta.* Beta is the amount of variability in the value of a company's stock in comparison to the market. The level of beta will change over time, so there is an issue with the historical time period over which beta should be calculated. A short-duration calculation period may happen to include a radical swing in a company's stock price, which would trigger a high beta. However, a very long-term time horizon would tend to downplay any recent stock price volatility. Thus, the time period covered by the calculation can cause major differences in a company's beta, and therefore in its cost of capital.

We have thus far identified a variety of ways to modify the outcome of the components of the cost of capital. In addition, the assumptions used to assemble these components into a weighted average cost of capital can also result in different outcomes. The most common basis for deriving the WACC is to weight the components based on the book values of debt and equity. However, some organizations elect to derive the weighting based on one of these other methods:

- The targeted amounts of debt and equity that will be on the books as of a later date
- The current market values of debt and equity
- The current market value of debt and the book value of equity
- The book value of debt and the current market value of equity

Ideally, the current market values of debt and equity should be used to derive the WACC, since this most accurately reflects the current expectations of investors regarding the funding mix that the company employs. If management expects that the current round of funding will notably alter the mix of debt and equity, then it can incorporate these changes into its use of the current market values of debt and equity.

It may be acceptable to derive the WACC using the book value of debt, if the company is not expecting to obtain additional debt financing. In this case, the amount recorded on the books is indeed the company's actual cost of debt. The same cannot be said for the cost of equity, which is constantly changing as investors bid the price of a company's stock up or down in accordance with their current expectations for a return on investment.

The method chosen can lead to major differences in the weighting of the debt and equity components of the cost of capital. The problem is especially apparent when a business is in financial difficulties and at least one element of the weighting is based on market value, since the market value is likely to be far less than book value. The following example illustrates the issue.

EXAMPLE

Creekside Industrial issued debt and stock to the public five years ago, after which it has reported reduced financial results that have led investors to believe that the company will have difficulty surviving as an independent business. The result has been a significant decline in the market value of its debt and equity. However, since the bonds payable are classified as senior debt, investors have a reasonable chance of obtaining repayment, so the bonds have retained their value better than the components of equity.

Creekside's CFO is now engaged in a review of the company's cost of capital. She creates the following table, which reveals the book value and market value of its funding sources, as well as their relative proportions:

(000s)	Book Value	Proportion of Total	Market Value	Proportion of Total
Bonds payable	$23,000	30%	$19,000	63%
Preferred stock	11,000	15%	3,000	10%
Common stock	42,000	55%	8,000	27%
Totals	$76,000	100%	$30,000	100%

Based on this information, the CFO derives the following weighted average cost of capital, based separately on book value and market value, which shows a significant 1.9% difference when the market values of debt and equity are employed.

	Book Value Weighting			Market Value Weighting		
	Cost	Weighting	Extended	Cost	Weighting	Extended
Bonds payable	6.0%	30%	1.8%	6.0%	63%	3.8%
Preferred stock	9.5%	15%	1.4%	9.5%	10%	1.0%
Common stock	12.5%	55%	6.9%	12.5%	27%	3.4%
Totals		100%	**10.1%**		100%	**8.2%**

The points made in this section should make it clear that achieving a precise cost of capital is difficult, given the extent to which assumptions can skew the measure. Consequently, it is important to clarify the assumptions used in the derivation of the cost of capital and to update the calculation on a regular basis. Otherwise, an incorrect cost of capital will likely lead to non-optimal investment decisions.

Adjustments to the Cost of Capital

Even after the cost of capital has been derived, questions may be raised concerning when to use it, and when to adjust it. Consider the following situations:

- *Multi-unit business.* A larger corporation may have a number of operating units, each of which operates in environments with different risk characteristics. It may be tempting to derive a separate cost of capital for each of these units, but the calculation requires that each one acquire its own debt and have its shares publicly traded, which is rarely the case for a subsidiary. An alternative is to estimate what the cost of capital would be, based on a mix of comparable companies that are publicly-held, and which operate primarily in the same markets as the subsidiary. The result will not be precise, but could yield a better indication of the real cost of capital than the corporate rate.

- *Single investment.* What if funding is being obtained for a specific investment? For example, a utility issues bonds specifically to build a power plant. In this case, the after-tax cost of the debt used to buy the power plant should be considered the cost of capital for the purpose of making an investment decision about that specific project, rather than the weighted average cost of capital for the entire business.
- *Foreign investment.* What if a multi-national company wants to make an investment in a foreign location? One option is to use the cost of capital for the entire company, since a multi-national is comprised of a portfolio of investments (subsidiaries), which result in an aggregated portfolio risk that can be applied to investments everywhere. If this approach is used, it may be necessary to adjust the cost of capital for any relative difference in the inflation rate between the home and foreign currencies. Another option is to derive a local cost of capital, on the grounds that each country has its own environmental factors, such as political risks and tax policy that can strongly influence the rate of return within that country. A third option is to apply a risk premium to the corporate cost of capital that is based on the risk factors in the foreign market. This risk premium is considered to be the interest rate on bonds issued by the foreign government, minus the interest rate on a risk-free bond issued by the home government, adjusted for the difference in the inflation rates of the home and foreign currencies.
- *Lending inefficiencies.* There may be times when it is difficult to obtain funds from a lender at a reasonable rate of interest, no matter how excellent a company's credit history may be. If so and there is variable-rate debt outstanding, the cost of capital should include the most recent interest rate, since that is the rate being charged to the company. Even if there is an expectation of a later decline in the interest rate, the only factual representation of the interest rate is the current inflated rate, which will apply to investments made in the near future.
- *Future expectations.* The beta component of the cost of equity is based on the historical results of a business. Management may feel that this beta figure is not valid, since it expects different results for the company in the future. However, the expectations of management do not always translate into actual results. Also, the market may continue to assign roughly the same beta to the company, simply because of the industry in which it is located. For these reasons, it is better to continue to use the existing beta, perhaps with a weighting that favors the most recent beta for the past year.

Cost of Capital as a Threshold Value

The primary use of the cost of capital is, as the name implies, to establish a cost for the funds that a business employs. Thus, if management is considering the acquisition of a fixed asset, it can judge the acquisition by comparing its projected return on investment to the cost of capital. If the projected return is less than the cost of capital, then the acquisition should be rejected, on the grounds that the cost of the funds required to buy the asset will exceed the return expected from the investment.

Given the variability in the calculation of the cost of capital, as noted earlier, some managers are reluctant to rely upon the cost of capital as a decision threshold. Instead, they may arbitrarily add several percentage points onto the cost of capital and use the result as the threshold for investment decisions. The reasons for doing so include:

- The higher rate allows for any errors that may have been incorporated into the cost of capital.
- The higher rate allows for any errors in the derivation of the capital budgeting proposals being judged.
- The higher rate acknowledges the existence of some investments that have no return at all (such as to meet regulatory requirements), so that other investments must generate a higher return in order to arrive at an average return for all investments that exceeds the cost of capital.

However, arbitrarily adding a few percentage points to the cost of capital reduces the level of quantitative rigor used to evaluate an investment. A better approach is to recognize what the upper and lower boundaries of the cost of capital may be, and to review investment proposals based on these two values.

The cost of capital may also be adjusted based on the perceived risk of a proposed investment. For example, the threshold value may be the cost of capital when a proposed investment pertains to an existing product line, but the threshold is increased by 5% if the investment is for an entirely new product in an untested market. This approach can be used to incorporate a high level of conservatism into the evaluation of riskier projects. However, at some point management must consciously invest in the strategic direction of the business, rather than relying upon quantitative measures to tell it where to spend money. For such strategic decisions, many other factors than the cost of capital must be considered, including the level of competition, government regulations, technology issues, and the perceived duration of any market opportunities.

Summary

This chapter showed how easy it is to derive a cost of capital that is excessively high or low, depending on the assumptions used in the calculation. The cost of capital is a key component of the decision making processes described in several of the following chapters, so be sure to spend as much time as possible questioning every aspect of the derived cost of capital. Hopefully, a rigorous review will yield a value that requires minimal inflation to guard against a mistake. Also, it is entirely possible that only a range of values can be derived for the cost of capital, rather than a single figure. If so, it may be necessary to use this range of values when examining investment alternatives, which may make it difficult to reach a purely quantitative decision.

Chapter 10
Discounted Cash Flows

Introduction

When evaluating investments, it is critical to understand the time value of money, and how it relates to corporate finance. In this chapter, we address the time value of money concept and describe present and future value tables, followed by descriptions of two discounted cash flow techniques – net present value and the internal rate of return. We also make note of terminal value and the types of information that should be included in a cash flow analysis.

> **Related Podcast Episode:** Episodes 147 and 214 of the Accounting Best Practices Podcast discuss net present value analysis and discounted cash flows, respectively. The episodes are available at: **accountingtools.com/podcasts** or **iTunes**

Time Value of Money

The foundation of discounted cash flow analysis is the concept that cash received today is more valuable than cash received at some point in the future. The reason is that someone who agrees to receive payment at a later date foregoes the ability to invest that cash right now. The only way for someone to agree to a delayed payment is to pay them for the privilege, which is known as interest income.

For example, if a person owns $10,000 now and invests it at an interest rate of 10%, then she will have earned $1,000 by having use of the money for one year. If she were instead to *not* have access to that cash for one year, then she would lose the $1,000 of interest income. The interest income in this example represents the time value of money.

To extend the example, what is the current payout of cash at which the person would be indifferent to receiving cash now or in one year? In essence, what is the amount that, when invested at 10%, will equal $10,000 in one year? The general formula used to answer this question, known as the *present value of 1 due in N periods*, is:

$$\frac{1}{(1 + \text{Interest rate})^{\text{Number of years}}}$$

The calculation for the example is:

$$\frac{\$10,000}{(1 + 10\%)^{1 \text{ year}}}$$

$$= \$9,090.91$$

In essence, if the person receives $9,090.91 now and invests it at a 10% interest rate, her cash balance will have increased to $10,000 in one year.

The effect of the present value formula becomes more pronounced if the receipt of cash is delayed to a date even further in the future, because the period during which the recipient of the cash cannot invest the cash is prolonged.

The concept of the time value of money also works in reverse, for expenditures. There is a monetary value associated with delaying the payment of cash, which is known as the *future amount of 1 due in N periods*. The general formula used to address this situation is:

$$\text{Amount deferred} \times (1 + \text{Interest rate})^{\text{Number of years}}$$

For example, if a person could delay the expenditure of $10,000 for one year and could invest the funds during that year at a 10% interest rate, the value of the deferred expenditure would be $11,000 in one year.

One of the common uses of the time value of money is to derive the present value of an annuity. An annuity is a series of payments that occur in the same amounts and at the same intervals over a period of time. An annuity is a common feature of a capital budgeting analysis, where a consistent stream of cash flows is expected for multiple years if a fixed asset is purchased. For example, a company is contemplating the purchase of a production line for $3,000,000, which will generate net positive cash flows of $1,000,000 per year for the next five years. This stream of incoming cash flows is an annuity. The formula used to derive the present value of an *ordinary annuity of 1 per period* is:

$$\frac{1 - \dfrac{1}{(1 + \text{Interest rate})^{\text{Number of years}}}}{\text{Interest rate}}$$

The preceding formula is for an *ordinary annuity*, which is an annuity where payments are made at the end of each period. If cash were instead received at the beginning of each period, the annuity would be called an *annuity due*, and would be formulated somewhat differently.

Present and Future Value Tables

In the last section, we discussed the general concept of the time value of money, and how this value can be translated into the present value formula. The concept is most commonly employed in an electronic spreadsheet. For example, the present value formula in Excel is:

$$(1/(1+\text{Interest rate})^{\wedge}\text{Number of years})$$

As an example, if the discount rate is 10% and you want to determine the discount for cash flows that will occur three years in the future, the Excel calculation is:

$$(1/(1+0.1)^{\wedge}3) = 0.75131$$

The easiest way to calculate present value is to use the preceding formula in Excel for the monetary amount and time period in question. However, what if an electronic spreadsheet is not available? The present value discount factor can also be derived from a present value table, which is commonly available in textbooks and on the Internet. The following present value table states the discount factors for the present value of 1 due in N periods for a common range of interest rates.

Present Value Factors for 1 Due in N Periods

Number of Years	6%	7%	8%	9%	10%	11%	12%
1	0.9434	0.9346	0.9259	0.9174	0.9091	0.9009	0.8929
2	0.8900	0.8734	0.8573	0.8417	0.8265	0.8116	0.7972
3	0.8396	0.8163	0.7938	0.7722	0.7513	0.7312	0.7118
4	0.7921	0.7629	0.7350	0.7084	0.6830	0.6587	0.6355
5	0.7473	0.7130	0.6806	0.6499	0.6209	0.5935	0.5674
6	0.7050	0.6663	0.6302	0.5963	0.5645	0.5346	0.5066
7	0.6651	0.6228	0.5835	0.5470	0.5132	0.4817	0.4524
8	0.6274	0.5820	0.5403	0.5019	0.4665	0.4339	0.4039
9	0.5919	0.5439	0.5003	0.4604	0.4241	0.3909	0.3606
10	0.5584	0.5084	0.4632	0.4224	0.3855	0.3522	0.3220
11	0.5268	0.4751	0.4289	0.3875	0.3505	0.3173	0.2875
12	0.4970	0.4440	0.3971	0.3555	0.3186	0.2858	0.2567
13	0.4688	0.4150	0.3677	0.3262	0.2897	0.2575	0.2292
14	0.4423	0.3878	0.3405	0.2993	0.2633	0.2320	0.2046
15	0.4173	0.3625	0.3152	0.2745	0.2394	0.2090	0.1827

To use the table, move to the column representing the relevant interest rate, and move down to the "number of years" row indicating the discount rate to apply to the applicable year of cash flow. Thus, if an analysis were to indicate $100,000 of cash flow in the fourth year, and the interest rate were 10%, you would multiply the $100,000 by 0.6830 to arrive at a present value of $68,300 for those cash flows.

The same type of table format is available for determining the future amount of 1 due in N periods. This table is used to derive the amount that you would accept on a future date in exchange for delaying the receipt of cash. The multipliers for this calculation are noted in the following table.

Future Value Factors for 1 Due in N Periods

Number of Years	6%	7%	8%	9%	10%	11%	12%
1	1.0600	1.0700	1.0800	1.0900	1.1000	1.1100	1.1200
2	1.1236	1.1449	1.1664	1.1881	1.2100	1.2321	1.2544
3	1.1910	1.2250	1.2597	1.2950	1.3310	1.3676	1.4049
4	1.2625	1.3108	1.3605	1.4116	1.4641	1.5181	1.5735
5	1.3382	1.4026	1.4693	1.5386	1.6105	1.6851	1.7623
6	1.4185	1.5007	1.5869	1.6771	1.7716	1.8704	1.9738
7	1.5036	1.6058	1.7138	1.8280	1.9487	2.0762	2.2109
8	1.5939	1.7182	1.8509	1.9926	2.1436	2.3045	2.4760
9	1.6895	1.8385	1.9990	2.1719	2.3580	2.5580	2.7731
10	1.7909	1.9672	2.1589	2.3674	2.5937	2.8394	3.1059
11	1.8983	2.1049	2.3316	2.5804	2.8531	3.1518	3.4786
12	2.0122	2.2522	2.5182	2.8127	3.1384	3.4985	3.8960
13	2.1329	2.4099	2.7196	3.0658	3.4523	3.8833	4.3635
14	2.2609	2.5785	2.9372	3.3417	3.7975	4.3104	4.8871
15	2.3966	2.7590	3.1722	3.6425	4.1773	4.7860	5.4736

To use the table, move to the column representing the relevant interest rate, and move down to the "number of years" row indicating the multiplier to apply to the applicable year of cash flow. Thus, if the option were available to delay the receipt of $10,000 for five years, and the funds could be invested at 8% in the meantime, you would multiply the $10,000 by 1.4693 to arrive at a future value of $14,693 for those cash flows.

The same table format is also available for determining the present value of an ordinary annuity of 1 per period. This table is used to derive the present value of a series of annuity payments. The multipliers for this calculation are noted in the following table.

Present Value Factors for Ordinary Annuity of 1 per Period

Number of Years	6%	7%	8%	9%	10%	11%	12%
1	0.9434	0.9346	0.9259	0.9174	0.9091	0.9009	0.8929
2	1.8334	1.8080	1.7833	1.7591	1.7355	1.7125	1.6901
3	2.6730	2.6243	2.5771	2.5313	2.4869	2.4437	2.4018
4	3.4651	3.3872	3.3121	3.2397	3.1699	3.1024	3.0373
5	4.2124	4.1002	3.9927	3.8897	3.7908	3.6959	3.6048
6	4.9173	4.7665	4.6229	4.4859	4.3553	4.2305	4.1114
7	5.5824	5.3893	5.2064	5.0330	4.8684	4.7122	4.5638
8	6.2098	5.9713	5.7466	5.5348	5.3349	5.1461	4.9676
9	6.8017	6.5152	6.2469	5.9952	5.7590	5.5370	5.3282
10	7.3601	7.0236	6.7101	6.4177	6.1446	5.8892	5.6502
11	7.8869	7.4987	7.1390	6.8052	6.4951	6.2065	5.9377
12	8.3838	7.9427	7.5361	7.1607	6.8137	6.4924	6.1944
13	8.8527	8.3577	7.9038	7.4869	7.1034	6.7499	6.4235
14	9.2950	8.7455	8.2442	7.7862	7.3667	6.9819	6.6282
15	9.7122	9.1079	8.5595	8.0607	7.6061	7.1909	6.8109

The annuity table contains a multiplier specific to the number of payments over which you expect to receive a series of equal payments and at a certain discount rate. When this factor is multiplied by one of the payments, you arrive at the present value of the stream of payments. For example, if you expect to receive five payments of $10,000 each and use a discount rate of 8%, then the factor would be 3.9927 (as noted in the preceding table in the intersection of the 8% column and the row for five years). You would then multiply the 3.9927 factor by $10,000 to arrive at a present value of the annuity of $39,927.

Net Present Value

Net present value (NPV) analysis is useful for determining the current value of a stream of cash flows that extend out into the future. It can also be used to compare several such cash flows to decide which has the largest present value. NPV is commonly used in the analysis of capital purchasing requests, to see if an initial payment for fixed assets and other expenditures will generate net positive cash flows.

To calculate net present value, we use the following formula:

$$NPV = X \times [(1+r)^n - 1]/[r \times (1+r)^n]$$

Where:

    X = The amount received per period
    n = The number of periods
    r = The rate of return

It is not that difficult to estimate the amount of cash received per period, as well as the number of periods over which cash will be received. The difficult inclusion in the formula is the rate of return. This is generally considered to be a company's average cost of capital (as described in the Cost of Capital chapter), but can also be considered its incremental cost of capital, or a risk-adjusted cost of capital. In the latter case, this means that several extra percentage points are added to the corporate cost of capital for those cash flow situations considered to be unusually risky.

EXAMPLE

The CFO of Franklin Drilling is interested in the NPV associated with a production facility that the CEO wants to acquire. In exchange for an initial $10 million payment, Franklin should receive payments of $1.2 million at the end of each of the next 15 years. Franklin has a corporate cost of capital of 9%. To calculate the NPV, we insert the cash flow information into the NPV formula:

$$1,200,000 \times ((1+0.09)^{\wedge}15\text{-}1)/(0.09 \times (1+0.09)^{\wedge}15) = \$9,672,826$$

The present value of the cash flows associated with the investment is $327,174 lower than the initial investment in the facility, so Franklin should not proceed with the investment.

The NPV calculation can be massively more complicated than the simplified example just shown. In reality, you may need to include the present values of the cash flows related to the following additional items:

- Ongoing expenditures related to the investment
- Variable amounts of cash flow being received over time, rather than the same amount every time
- Variable timing for the receipt of cash, rather than the consistent receipt of a payment on the same date
- The amount of working capital required for the project, as well as the release of working capital at the end of the project
- The amount at which the investment can be resold at the end of its useful life
- The tax value of depreciation on the fixed asset that was purchased

All of the preceding factors should be considered when evaluating NPV for an investment proposal. In addition, consider generating several models to account for the worst case, most likely, and best case scenarios for cash flows.

Internal Rate of Return

The internal rate of return (IRR) is the rate of return at which the present value of a series of future cash flows equals the present value of all associated costs. IRR is commonly used in capital budgeting to discern the rate of return on the estimated cash flows arising from an expected investment. The project having the highest IRR is selected for investment purposes.

The easiest way to calculate the internal rate of return is to open Microsoft Excel and then follow these steps:

1. Enter in any cell a negative figure that is the amount of cash outflow in the first period. This is normal when acquiring fixed assets, since there is an initial expenditure to acquire and install the asset.
2. Enter the subsequent cash flows for each period following the initial expenditure in the cells immediately below the cell where the initial cash outflow figure was entered.
3. Access the IRR function and specify the cell range into which you just made entries. The internal rate of return will be calculated automatically. It may be useful to use the Increase Decimal function to increase the number of decimal places appearing in the calculated internal rate of return.

As an example, a company is reviewing a possible investment for which there is an initial expected investment of $20,000 in the first year, followed by incoming cash flows of $12,000, $7,000 and $4,000 in the next three years. If you input this information into the Excel IRR function, it returns an IRR of 8.965%.

The IRR formula in Excel is extremely useful for quickly deriving a possible rate of return. However, it can be used for a less ethical purpose, which is to artificially model the correct amounts and timing of cash flows to produce an IRR that meets a company's capital budgeting guidelines. In this case, a manager is fudging the results in his or her cash flow model in order to gain acceptance of a project, despite knowing that it may not be possible to achieve those cash flows.

Incremental Internal Rate of Return

The incremental internal rate of return is an analysis of the financial returns where there are two competing investment opportunities involving different amounts of investment. The analysis is applied to the difference between the costs of the two investments. Thus, subtract the cash flows associated with the less expensive alternative from the cash flows associated with the more expensive alternative to arrive at the cash flows applicable to the difference between the two alternatives, and then conduct an internal rate of return analysis on this difference.

Based just on quantitative analysis, select the more expensive investment opportunity if it has an incremental internal rate of return higher than the minimum return considered acceptable. However, there are qualitative issues to consider as well, such as whether there is an incremental increase in risk associated with the more expensive investment.

If there is additional risk associated with the more expensive investment opportunity, then adjust for this risk by increasing the minimum return considered acceptable. For example, the minimum rate of return threshold for a low-risk investment might be 5%, while the threshold might be 10% for a high-risk investment.

EXAMPLE

Hassle Corporation is considering obtaining a color copier, and it can do so either with a lease or an outright purchase. The lease involves a series of payments over the three-year useful life of the copier, while the purchase option involves more cash up-front and some continuing maintenance, but it also has a resale value at the end of its useful life. The following analysis of the incremental differences in the cash flows between the two alternatives reveals that there is a positive incremental internal rate of return for the purchasing option. Barring any other issues (such as available cash to buy the copier), the purchasing option therefore appears to be the better alternative.

Year	Lease	Buy	Difference
0	-$7,000	-$29,000	-$22,000
1	-7,000	-1,500	5,500
2	-7,000	-1,500	5,500
3	-7,000	-1,500	5,500
Resale		+15,000	15,000
		Incremental IRR	13.3%

Terminal Value

The cash flows associated with an analysis may not have a discernible time horizon – that is, there is no expectation that they will end. In this case, it is customary to derive a terminal value, which is the aggregation of all cash flows beyond the date range for which cash flows are being predicted. Terminal value can be calculated with the *perpetuity formula*, which employs the following steps:

1. Estimate the cash flows associated with the final year of projections, and eliminate from this amount any unusual items that are not expected to occur again in later years.
2. Estimate a reasonable growth rate for this adjusted cash flow figure for later years. The amount should approximate the rate of growth for the entire economy. The rate of sustainable growth should be quite small, and may even be zero or a negative figure.
3. Subtract this growth rate from the company's weighted-average cost of capital (WACC), as derived in the Cost of Capital chapter, and divide the result into the adjusted cash flows for the final year. The formula is:

$$\frac{\text{Adjusted final year cash flow}}{\text{WACC} - \text{Growth rate}} = \text{Terminal value}$$

EXAMPLE

Glow Atomic is reviewing the projected income stream from a new type of fusion plant that could generate electricity in perpetuity. The analysis is broken into annual cash flows for the first 20 years, followed by a terminal value. The expected cash flow for the 20th year is $10,000,000. Glow expects these cash flows to increase at a rate of 1% thereafter. The company has a 15% WACC. Based on this information, the terminal value of the investment opportunity is:

$$\frac{\$10,000,000 \text{ final year cash flow}}{15\% \text{ WACC} - 1\% \text{ growth rate}} = \$71,429,000 \text{ Terminal value}$$

Inclusions in Cash Flow Analysis

There can be a number of variations on the possible cash flows associated with a business decision, making the present value calculation more difficult to derive. The following factors may also need to be considered:

- *Cash from sale of asset.* If an asset is to be purchased, also assume that some cash will be received at a later date from the eventual sale of that asset.
- *Maintenance costs.* If there will be incremental costs incurred to maintain a purchased asset, include the cash flows associated with these costs. Do not include any cash flows related to maintenance personnel who will still be paid, irrespective of the presence of the asset.
- *Working capital.* If there will be an incremental change in the amount invested in accounts receivable or inventory as the result of a purchase decision, include these cash flows in the analysis. If the asset is to be eventually sold off, this may mean that the related working capital investment will be terminated at the same time.
- *Tax payments.* Include any property taxes related to assets that are acquired. Also, include the amount of any incremental income taxes paid, if the acquired asset generates profits.
- *Depreciation effect.* Include the effect on income taxes paid of the depreciation expense associated with an acquired asset. This effect is caused by the tax deductibility of depreciation.

In short, discounted cash flow analysis is an effective way to aggregate and review the cash flows associated with a business decision that are spread over a number of time periods, though some analysis may be required to ensure that all of the relevant cash flows have been included.

Summary

Discounted cash flow is one of the key tools used to analyze cash outflows related to the purchase of fixed assets. In the Capital Expenditures chapter, we will combine the concepts of discounted cash flow with the corporate cost of capital to engage in the analysis of capital expenditure decisions. While discounted cash flow is not the only way to review requests to acquire fixed assets (and is not necessarily the best method), it is considered one of the primary capital expenditure analysis techniques. Consequently, be familiar with how discounted cash flows are constructed and the situations in which they can be used.

Chapter 11
Working Capital Management

Introduction

A company can invest a startling amount of its funds in working capital. This is an area in which businesses tend to be somewhat lax in monitoring investment levels, and especially the reasons why there are changes in working capital. The result is typically a high degree of variability in working capital levels, for which either additional funding will be needed or there will be an unplanned surge in investments. In this chapter, we discuss the impact of working capital on corporate finance, and then describe a number of enhancements to working capital that can cause major reductions in the cash needed to fund it.

> **Related Podcast Episodes:** Episodes 150, 151, 153, and 154 of the Accounting Best Practices Podcast discuss managing in financial adversity, while Episode 211 discusses working capital management. These episodes are available at: **accountingtools.com/podcasts** or **iTunes**

The Impact of Working Capital on Corporate Finance

A particular area of opportunity for the reduction of an organization's capital needs is *working capital*. Working capital is primarily comprised of accounts receivable, inventory, and accounts payable. Accounts receivable and inventory are large consumers of cash, while accounts payable is essentially cash borrowed from suppliers, and so is a provider of cash.

The policies and systems used to manage these three areas can have a major impact on the amount of funds needed to operate a business. Constant attention to working capital is of particular importance in situations where a company is trying to fund rapid growth, or has minimal access to cash from outside sources. In these cases, it may make sense to create a team that continually analyzes how to wring more cash out of working capital. In the following sections, we will explore the specific policies and systems that can minimize the investment in working capital.

Accounts Receivable Enhancements

If a business offers sales on credit, it is committing to a potentially massive investment in accounts receivable, for which it will be necessary to secure sufficient funding to pay for the company's granting of credit. For example, a company with $10 million of sales offers credit terms to its customers, whereby they commit to pay the company 30 days after the invoice date. All of the customers (understandably) accept the credit terms. Due to collection difficulties and the time it takes for checks to travel from customers to the company, the actual number of days during which accounts receivable are outstanding turns out to be 40 days. This represents receivables turnover of approximately nine times per year (calculated as 365 days ÷ 40 days). This means that the company routinely has about $1.1 million of accounts receivable outstanding (calculated as $10 million annual sales ÷ 9 receivable turns per year). Thus, the company is investing an average of $1.1 million in its credit granting program, which is a substantial amount of cash for a $10 million company. This brief calculation of committed cash is subject to three additional points:

- *Bad debts*. In a cash-in-advance or cash-on-payment environment, there are no bad debts. In a credit environment, some invoices will never be paid, so there will be an additional reduction in cash caused by these bad debts.
- *Seasonality*. The $1.1 million cash investment noted in the preceding example assumes that sales are consistent from period to period. In reality, many businesses have a seasonal element, which means that the amount of cash committed to accounts receivable could sometimes spike to a much higher level.
- *Actual out-of-pocket cash*. Just because a company has a certain amount of accounts receivable outstanding does not mean that it has actually invested the same amount of cash in those receivables. Realistically, a company has only invested in those receivables the cash required to build or supply the related products or services. The remainder of a receivable represents the profit on each sale. Thus, the cash tied up in a high-margin software sale could be negligible, whereas the cash associated with the sale of heavy equipment could be substantial.

The preceding factors mean that the actual amount of cash invested in accounts receivable could differ wildly between companies with the same sales volume. Thus, it is necessary to engage in detailed receivables modeling to estimate the amount of cash that will be required before there is a decision to offer credit terms or alter existing terms.

The "accounts receivable" area encompasses the granting of credit to customers, the issuance of invoices, and the subsequent collection of customer payments. We deal with each of these topics through the remainder of this section.

Credit Enhancements

The enhancement of accounts receivable can begin in the credit granting process, before a customer is even allowed to buy from the company on credit. The company needs to decide upon the proper amount of credit that it will grant customers. Strictly from the perspective of keeping funding needs to a minimum, it makes the most sense to adopt a relatively restrictive credit policy, so that sales on credit are only made to those customers most capable of paying the company in full and within credit terms.

Of course, the situation is considerably more complex than simply adopting a stringent credit policy. The financial analysis staff may have determined that the company will earn more profits if it loosens its credit policy to allow more sales to customers whose finances are more questionable. The result may indeed be higher profits, though at the cost of increased bad debts and an increase in accounts receivable as the days required to obtain payment expand. This is particularly likely when the gross profit associated with each product or service sold is quite high, since the company has little to lose if a customer does not pay. Conversely, if profit margins are slim, management is more likely to be prudent in expanding its use of credit, and will be more likely to maintain a restrictive credit policy. In short, the use of cash is only one factor considered in decisions to adjust a company's policy for granting credit.

In addition to careful control of the amount of credit offered, any of the following actions may contribute to a reduction in the investment in accounts receivable:

- *Outside financing*. Arrange with a third-party lender to extend a loan or lease to the customer. By doing so, the company obtains cash immediately from the lender, rather than investing its own cash in accounts receivable.
- *Distributor access*. If there are distributors of the company's products, refer the customer to one of the distributors. As was the case with outside financing, this means that the distributor takes on the accounts receivable burden.
- *Shorten payment interval*. Cash flow can be accelerated by requiring that customers pay sooner. This can be difficult to achieve with larger customers who are more inclined to pay late, no matter what the payment terms may be.

Billing Enhancements

Once credit issues have been decided upon, consider the efficiency of the customer billing process. Ideally, it should result in an accurate invoice being delivered to the accounts payable system of a customer as soon as possible after a sales transaction has been completed. By accelerating this process, customers pay faster, which reduces accounts receivable. Consider the current state of the following process issues:

- *Invoice preparation time*. All customer invoices should be prepared within one day of the delivery of goods or services to a customer. The accounting staff may try to delay invoice preparation in order to do so more efficiently in a batch, but this harms the speed of cash receipt, and so should not be tolerated. If a company bills its customers at the end of each month for services provided during the month, see if customers will find it acceptable to instead be billed twice a month; this can greatly accelerate the speed with which payments are received.
- *Invoice accuracy*. If an invoice is for a large amount, is difficult to compile, or contains volumes of explanatory text, have it reviewed for accuracy before releasing it. Otherwise, customers may delay payment if they find an error.

- *Invoice delivery*. The process of mailing an invoice, having it delivered by the postal service, and then delivered internally to the customer's accounts payable department can consume a number of days. Instead, consider using any form of electronic transmission, and follow up to verify receipt.
- *Payment delivery*. The best form of customer payment is an electronic payment, since no additional internal processing is required. Instead, it is delivered directly into the company's bank account. If this option is not available, set up a lockbox arrangement with the company's bank. Under a lockbox arrangement, customers are asked to send their check payments to the lockbox address, where the bank opens the mail and deposits the checks into the company's account. The use of a lockbox typically reduces the time required to process a payment by one or two days.

Collection Enhancements

The final task needed to reduce accounts receivable is an active collections function. There should be a system in place for economically collecting payment on overdue invoices. The exact sequence and timing of events will depend upon the industry, but the following is a reasonable sequence of events to consider:

1. *Administrative call*. Contact customers in advance of payment dates for the larger invoices, to verify that payment will be made on the expected date and in full. If not, making this early administrative call leaves enough time to rectify the situation before the payment due date arrives.
2. *Dunning message*. If payments are slightly overdue and the amounts are not large, issue a dunning letter or e-mail message, politely reminding customers of their obligations to pay.
3. *Telephone call*. After it becomes clear that an invoice will not be paid on time, the collections staff should call the customer, ascertain the reason for the payment delay, and either obtain a promise to pay as of a specific date or begin the process of resolving the underlying issue. Resolving the issue may involve a number of approaches, such as:

    - Return the purchased goods
    - Adopt a payment plan
    - Place a credit hold on the customer
    - Accept payment in kind
    - Accept a reduced payment
    - Replace the purchased goods

4. *Attorney letter*. If the customer is still not responsive, consider contracting with a local attorney to issue an attorney letter. This approach relies upon the involvement of an attorney and a mildly threatening letter to convince a customer that paying is less expensive than a lawsuit in the near future.
5. *Small claims complaint*. Fill out a small claims court form and send a copy to the customer. This does not mean that the form is filed with the court,

only that the paperwork has been filled out. The receipt of such an official-looking document might convince the customer that you are serious. Small claims courts allow only smaller claims, so this approach is only available for unpaid invoices totaling less than $10,000.

6. *Collection agency.* If all of the preceding approaches have not worked, consider shifting the claim to a collection agency, which may engage in more vigorous collection techniques. These agencies may charge up to one-third of the total amount of each invoice as their fee (if they achieve a collection), so use the preceding techniques first, and use a collection agency only as a last resort.

Of the collection techniques noted here, the first three are typical ones that are an expected part of business between long-term business partners, and the exchanges are expected to be polite and professional. However, once matters progress to attorney letters, small claims complaints, and collection agencies, the assumption is that the company will no longer be doing business with the customer, since these actions are considerably more aggressive.

Accounts Receivable Policies

The following bullet points contain suggested policies that can be of assistance in enhancing cash flows related to accounts receivable:

- *Do not allow payment terms greater than __ days.* Do not allow the sales staff to offer terms to customers that exceed a specific number of days without prior approval by a senior manager.
- *The maximum credit offered a customer is ___.* Use a formula that best fits your industry to arrive at a reasonable maximum amount of credit to offer customers, over which a senior manager must approve the terms.
- *Stop customer credit once days outstanding exceed __ days.* This policy is designed to keep additional credit from being extended to a customer who is not paying in a timely manner.

All three of these policies are designed to put boundaries around the amount of credit that a customer is allowed to have, thereby creating a limitation on the amount of bad debt that may be incurred, as well as the amount of accounts receivable investment that a business is willing to make.

Summary

Collection problems are typically caused by issues elsewhere in a company, such as the improper granting of credit, lost invoices, and invoicing errors. The collections staff is all too often lambasted for having trouble collecting overdue accounts receivable, when in fact the problem was caused by someone else. Thus, the recommendations noted in this section *prior to* the collections discussion should be considered of particular importance.

Inventory Enhancements

When a company maintains an inventory of the goods it plans to sell, the inventory is comprised of the raw materials needed to manufacture the goods, work-in-process for items currently going through the production process, and finished goods that are ready for sale. Each of these categories of inventory has different implications from a cash management perspective, which are:

- *Raw materials.* A company may buy more raw materials than it immediately needs, which means that extra cash is tied up in inventory for an indeterminate period of time. Since some raw materials have a limited shelf life, a possible outcome is that the initial cash expenditure may never be converted back into cash.
- *Work-in-process.* The production process is generally relatively short, but can be of considerable duration in cases where output is highly customized or complex. In these latter cases, there is a risk of customer default during production, leaving the seller with incomplete goods that may not be sellable.
- *Finished goods.* These goods are ready for sale, and so are most easily converted into cash. Some types of finished goods can become obsolete, so there is a risk that some products will be sold off at clearance prices, resulting in a reduced level of conversion back into cash.

All of the preceding issues should make it clear that converting inventory into cash can be difficult, both in terms of how much cash the company will realize and when it will receive the cash. In addition, the amount of cash involved can be spectacularly high. For example, a company manufactures refrigerators in a competitive market where it earns a gross margin of 25% on total sales of $10 million. This means that the company's cost of goods sold is $7.5 million. Its inventory turns over an average of four times per year, which means that one-quarter of its annual cost of goods sold is on the premises at any point in time. Thus, the company must invest approximately $1.9 million of cash to support its inventory requirements.

In addition to the amount of cash tied up in inventory, there are a number of holding costs associated with inventory, which can range from a few percent to 20% of the total inventory valuation. These holding costs can include:

- *Facility costs.* This is the cost of the warehouse, which includes depreciation on the building and interior racks, utilities, building insurance, and warehouse staff. There are also utility costs, such as electricity and heating fuel for the building.
- *Cost of goods.* This is the interest cost of any funds that a company borrows in order to purchase inventory.
- *Risk mitigation.* This is not only the cost of insuring inventory, but also of installing any risk-management items needed to protect the inventory, such as fire suppression systems, security monitoring, and burglar alarms.

- *Taxes*. The business district in which the inventory is stored may charge some form of property tax on the inventory.
- *Obsolescence*. A certain amount of inventory will become unusable or unsellable over time, resulting in its disposition at a reduced price or no price at all.

In short, the decision to hold inventory involves not only a substantial cash investment, but also an ongoing holding cost. In this section, we will touch upon an array of issues that can reduce the investment in inventory, which in turn may favorably impact the amount of holding costs incurred.

Product Design

The marketing department may want to blanket the market with a full range of product options, thereby increasing the odds that customers will find the exact production configuration that they want. However, this also means that the company must invest in far more finished goods inventory, so that all product configurations are in stock. For example, selling a black widget in five additional colors mandates that five times the amount of finished goods inventory be maintained. The impact on working capital can be overwhelmingly negative. Instead of designing so many products, it is more efficient from a working capital perspective to use one of the following alternatives:

- Restrict products to those most likely to sell in the highest volume. The company deliberately ignores niche products, and leaves them for other companies to sell.
- Only produce a particular combination of product options that are popular with customers. This approach is commonly used by automobile manufacturers, who prepackage certain sets of features into their vehicles.
- Store partially finished goods, and make final configurations only after customers place their orders. This interesting option results in far less inventory, but is a viable alternative only for those companies that can ship direct to customers from central storage locations where final configurations can be made.

Another product design issue is developing products that use the same set of raw materials. By doing so, a company can restrict its raw materials inventory investment to a smaller set of items. For example, a washing machine manufacturer could require its product designers to always use the same type of screw in all of its products, so that the company only has to stock that one type of screw. The associated working capital reduction can be significant. However, this option requires a long-term commitment from the product design staff that may take an entire product cycle to yield results.

Product Record Keeping

An opportunity for inventory reduction can be found in the record keeping for products. When a product design is complete, a record of its component parts is compiled into a *bill of materials*, which is then used to order parts for the product. If the bill is incorrect, an incorrect number of parts will be ordered, which may result in an excess number of component parts being kept in stock.

Product record keeping is a particular problem when the engineering department institutes an engineering change order (ECO), in which one or more components are substituted for existing parts. If not handled properly, an ECO can result in either or both of the following problems:

- *No recordation.* The bill of materials is not updated with the ECO, so that the company continues to buy components that it is no longer using.
- *Residual stock elimination.* The ECO is implemented before the company has finished using up its stocks of the components that are to be replaced. The result is a cluster of components that will never be used.

To keep product record keeping issues from impacting cash flow, institute a cross-checking approval process for all new bills of material, have the internal auditors periodically examine the bills, and also institute a detailed procedure for ECO launches.

Inventory Acquisition

The general purchasing concepts that a company uses to acquire inventory have a profound impact on the amount of inventory that is kept on hand, and therefore on the amount of cash invested in inventory. By understanding these purchasing concepts and making alternative recommendations, it may be possible to reduce the investment in inventory.

One purchasing concept is the relationship between the amount of safety stock kept on hand and the distance from which raw materials are replenished. *Safety stock* is the extra amount of inventory kept on hand to guard against shortages while a supplier is fulfilling a replacement order. For example, if a company historically uses $10,000 of a certain inventory item each week, and the supplier of that component requires one week to fulfill a replenishment order, then the company will keep $10,000 of inventory on hand while it is waiting for the replenishment order to be delivered. If a company has elected to source some inventory items with unusually distant suppliers, the company must maintain a larger safety stock to guard against shortages during the longer delivery period. A possible option is to point out the amount of cash that is being tied up in safety stock, and suggest the use of closer suppliers who can deliver on shorter notice. The net effect of this improvement requires a long time to realize, since it involves the replacement of suppliers.

Another purchasing concept is the view that businesses must guess at how many of their products will be purchased. This means that the materials management staff is "flying blind" when it creates the production schedule that drives purchases. The inevitable result will be excess quantities of some products and shortages of others. This uncertainty can be eliminated by working with larger customers to gain access to their own inventory usage information. It is usually not practical or even possible to obtain such detailed information from smaller customers, so some guesstimating will still be required for inventory planning. Nonetheless, information linkages with customers can drive a substantial reduction in inventory levels.

Inventory Ownership

There are two situations in which a company can shift the ownership of inventory to suppliers, sometimes to the extent that the company eliminates its investment in inventory. However, we have noted in the following bullet points the limited circumstances under which this technique can be applied:

- *Supplier ownership of on-site inventory.* It is possible to sole-source some inventory items with certain suppliers, who maintain inventory on the company's premises and restock it as necessary. The company only pays for these inventory items when it transfers them out of the warehouse. This practice is more common among the suppliers of fittings and fasteners. It can be expensive, since the designated suppliers have no competition, and also must expend extra effort to monitor inventory levels.
- *Drop shipping.* A company may outsource all of its production to a supplier, and has the supplier ship finished goods directly to customers. The supplier only bills the company when a sale occurs, so that cash from the sale is matched against the cost of the product shipped, resulting in a net cash in-flow to the company. This approach only works if a company is comfortable with having a third party manufacture what it is selling.

Manufacturing Process Flow

A manufacturing process can be designed to either "push" production jobs through it from beginning to end, or "pull" orders through the process as orders are received from customers. The first approach has a longer history. As typified by the material requirements planning system (MRP), it involves estimating likely unit quantities that will be needed for sale, and then releasing enough production orders into the manufacturing facility to generate the estimated number of units. The push system tends to focus on larger batch sizes, in the interests of lowering the per-unit cost of production. The trouble with the push system is that large production runs tend to require large amounts of in-process inventory, which increases the investment in working capital.

A better alternative is the pull system, since it is designed to produce in very small unit quantities, which reduces the amount of required inventory. Though the system initially appears to have a higher cost per unit produced, it avoids the cost of excess inventory and lowers scrap levels to such an extent that the overall cost of a pull system is lower than that of a push system.

Another cash-related benefit of a pull system is that it tends to involve the use of smaller production equipment, rather than the larger and more automated systems that are favored to manufacture the long production runs found in a push system. The result is a smaller investment in fixed assets, which improves a company's cash position.

Fulfillment

It can be extremely difficult to balance the opposing requirements of customer service and inventory management. The basic problem is that being able to fulfill 100% of all customer orders at once is nearly impossible, unless management is willing to commit to an overwhelming investment in inventory. In reality, customer orders will occasionally exceed the amount of inventory on hand, resulting in a backorder and therefore a reduction in the fulfillment percentage. A CEO who is determined to maintain a high order fulfillment rate will insist on maintaining very high inventory levels to ensure that *any* order can be fulfilled at once.

The insistence on a very high fulfillment rate has especially pernicious consequences for fashion products or anything with a short life span, since a company is more likely to be caught with excess quantities of inventory that it cannot liquidate. The result can be an ongoing series of low-price inventory liquidations.

The best solution to the fulfillment conundrum is an analysis of the tradeoff between each incremental percent of orders that are backordered and the corresponding change in inventory. This information can be used to give management a clear understanding of the cash investment associated with changes in the fulfillment percentage.

Either of the following suggestions may be reasonable alternatives to maintaining a high fulfillment rate:

- *Issue a $__ credit whenever goods are backordered.* A small credit paid back to customers may retain their loyalty even if a product is backordered. The cost of these credits will probably be far lower than the investment in inventory that would otherwise be required to maintain a higher fulfillment rate.
- *Sell a similar product.* Invest in a large enough customer support team to contact every customer who has experienced a backorder, and offer them a similar product that is in stock. Again, the cost of the support staff will probably be lower than the cost of maintaining more on-hand inventory.

Inventory Disposition

If there is a part of the inventory management function that tends to be less well managed (if not ignored), it is the disposition of inventory that is not selling well. These inventory items tend to languish in storage until they are so old that the company can only obtain a pittance for them.

A vastly better approach is to have an extremely active inventory disposition program. This group constantly monitors sales trends for all products, so that it can identify situations where on-hand stocks are probably not going to be sold off within a reasonable period of time. The disposition team should have developed alternative channels through which it can sell excess inventory at somewhat reduced prices, and also has contacts among third-party inventory liquidators who will buy goods at even lower prices. The result should be a program that proactively identifies and sells off inventory at the best possible prices.

A high-grade inventory disposition program is a boon from a funding perspective, since inventory turnover levels will be relatively high, ensuring that cash is extracted from the company's inventory investment as soon as possible.

Inventory Policies

The following bullet points contain suggested policies that can be of assistance in enhancing cash flows related to inventory:

- *Product designs shall incorporate an approved parts list.* Product designers are required to use a standard set of parts when creating new products, thereby reducing the number of components that must be kept in stock.
- *Bills of material shall be reviewed prior to release.* A review by a second person makes it less likely that incorrect components will be acquired for the construction of a product.
- *Suppliers shall be located no more than __ miles from the production facility.* While not always entirely achievable, this policy is designed to shorten the time required for suppliers to deliver raw materials to the company, which in turn reduces its safety stock requirements.
- *Drop shipped inventory is the preferred stocking method.* This policy shifts inventory ownership to the company's suppliers, who ship directly to the company's customers on its behalf.
- *The customer order first-time fulfillment goal is __%.* The fulfillment goal should be set at a level that reasonably balances the need for customer service with the lowest achievable investment in finished goods inventory.
- *Review inventory on hand exceeding __ days of usage.* This policy serves as a trigger point for a disposition analysis, which should lead to the elimination of excess inventory while a reasonable price can still be obtained for it.

Departmental Cooperation

Reducing the working capital investment in inventory is particularly difficult, for it requires the cooperation of many departments. The product design staff must agree to use a standard parts list, the marketing manager must be convinced to forego some product versions, auditors should review bills of material, the CEO must understand the costs associated with high fulfillment rates, and so forth. Given the impact of so many departments on inventory, the only practical way to exert any influence is through the CEO. This is likely to trigger an ongoing war between the departments, as they all present their arguments to the CEO regarding increases or decreases in the amount of inventory that the company should maintain.

Summary

If there is one area of working capital upon which to lavish attention, it is inventory. It can be extremely difficult to convert inventory into cash in the short term (if at all), so there should be a multitude of policies and controls designed to ensure that a company does everything possible to maintain a healthy rate of inventory turnover. Where possible, take a hard look at trying to outsource activities involving inventory storage to other parties, so there is no investment in inventory at all.

Accounts Payable Enhancements

From a corporate finance perspective, a good account payable is one that has not yet been paid, since accounts payable is a source of cash. Thus, the objective is to pay as late as possible, while remaining within the payment terms negotiated with each supplier. In this section, we focus on several factors that can optimize the amount of cash made available through accounts payable.

Terms Renegotiation

Whenever the purchasing department adds a supplier, it always negotiates a variety of terms, one of which is the number of days that the company has in which to pay the supplier's invoices. Emphasize to the purchasing manager that longer payment terms now have a higher priority. However, the purchasing negotiators will likely find that they must give way on other terms in exchange for longer payment terms, such as higher unit prices. It will be necessary to determine the cost-effectiveness of any change in terms to see if the overall package has not become excessively onerous in exchange for longer payment terms.

The impact of terms renegotiation is usually quite small over the short term. There are typically many suppliers to be contacted, and few qualified purchasing negotiators available to meet with them. Further, negotiations take time away from other activities that the purchasing staff might be engaged in, and which might also have an impact on cash flow. Also, discussions with some suppliers can be protracted, which extends the time required to meet with all suppliers. For these reasons, working capital improvement through terms renegotiation tends to be lower on the list of enhancements for many companies.

Early Payment Discounts

Some suppliers are willing to offer discounts in exchange for the early payment of invoices. Consider setting the minimum discount terms that the company will accept in exchange for early payment. Ideally, the minimum discount terms should be higher than the company's cost of capital. From a more practical perspective, it may be necessary to prohibit all early payment discounts, no matter what the terms may be, if the company does not have enough cash to make early payments. Assuming that there is enough cash, be aware of the calculation for determining the effective interest rate associated with early payment terms, which is:

(Discount % ÷ (1 – Discount %)) × (360 ÷ (Allowed payment days – Discount days))

Converted into the format of a procedure, this calculation is:

1. Calculate the difference between the payment date for those taking the early payment discount and the date when payment is normally due, and divide it into 360 days. For example, under "2/10 net 30" terms, you would divide 20 days into 360 to arrive at 18. Use this number to annualize the interest rate calculated in the next step.
2. Subtract the discount percentage from 100% and divide the result into the discount percentage. For example, under "2/10 net 30" terms, you would divide 2% by 98% to arrive at 0.0204. This is the interest rate being offered through the credit terms.
3. Multiply the result of both calculations together to obtain the annualized interest rate. To conclude the example, multiply 18 by 0.0204 to arrive at an effective annualized interest rate of 36.72%.

EXAMPLE

The CFO of Suture Corporation has received an early payment offer from a supplier, where Suture can take a 1% discount on any invoices paid, as long they are paid within 10 days of the invoice date. Otherwise, the company must pay the full amount after 30 days have passed from the invoice date. Using this information, the calculation of the effective interest rate of the offer is:

$$(1\% \text{ Discount} \div (1 - 1\% \text{ Discount}))$$
$$\times (360 \div (30 \text{ Allowed payment days} - 10 \text{ Discount days}))$$

$$= 18.2\%$$

As long as the cost of capital of Suture is lower than 18.2%, this is an acceptable offer that the CFO should authorize, if there is sufficient cash available to fund the early payment.

The table below shows some of the more common early payment discount terms, explains what they mean, and also notes the effective interest rate that suppliers are offering with each one.

Credit Terms	Explanation	Effective Interest Rate
1/10 net 30	Take a 1% discount if pay in 10 days, otherwise pay in 30 days	18.2%
2/10 net 30	Take a 2% discount if pay in 10 days, otherwise pay in 30 days	36.7%
1/10 net 60	Take a 1% discount if pay in 10 days, otherwise pay in 60 days	7.3%
2/10 net 60	Take a 2% discount if pay in 10 days, otherwise pay in 60 days	14.7%

Payment Processing Frequency

In some organizations, supplier payment processing is handled in batch mode, where all payments are made on one day of the week. Since payments are relatively infrequent, there is a tendency to pay those invoices that are not quite due for payment, resulting in a faster cash outflow than is mandated by supplier payment terms. If possible, consider scheduling payments more frequently, so that the company pays suppliers exactly when invoices are due, rather than too early.

Accounts Payable Policies

The following bullet points contain suggested policies that can be of assistance in extending cash flows related to accounts payable:

- *Do not pay accounts payable early.* Adopt a monitoring system that highlights any payment made earlier than the due date required by the supplier.
- *Require purchase orders for amounts exceeding $___.* This policy enforces an examination of larger expenditures before they are actually made.
- *Disallow purchases exceeding the department budget.* If a manager commits to a specific expenditure level for his department, do not allow expenditures above that level without approval by a senior manager. While this may seem excessively bureaucratic, it may at least push some purchases out into a later budget period.

These policies are designed to keep from disbursing cash too soon, as well as to avoid or delay some types of expenditures.

Researching Working Capital Enhancements

Besides the specific enhancement recommendations noted in the preceding sections, it is also possible to use several general tools for locating other potential improvements. These tools are:

- *Historical look back.* It is entirely possible that the amount of working capital used in prior years was less than it is today. If so, investigate which company policies have changed since then to increase the amount of working capital. For example, if inventory turnover has dropped from ten times per year to the current five times per year, you may be able to trace the cause to a policy decision to fulfill all customer orders within one day of receipt. This research can be invaluable for locating policies that should be reversed in order to achieve working capital reductions.
- *Subsidiary comparisons.* A particularly valuable enhancement method is to look for differences in business practices at the subsidiary level. It is entirely possible that one subsidiary is being run unusually well, and so has achieved low working capital levels. If so, consider copying its business practices over to the other subsidiaries. This approach works best when a system is in

place where managers throughout the company are constantly in communication.

> **Tip:** A bonus plan that rewards all employees for the overall performance of a business can spur employees of different subsidiaries to work together to implement improvements.

- *Benchmarking.* Consider looking outside of the company's industry to other areas where companies have achieved extraordinary reductions in working capital. Conduct site visits to understand how they achieved these reductions, and consider whether it is possible to import the associated best-in-class practices into the company's operations.

Working Capital Forecasting

It is entirely possible that working capital cannot be driven down, because of the strategic and tactical directions in which a company is going. For example, if there are plans to sell in a different country, common business practice in that country may mandate that longer payment terms are offered to customers. To extend this example, a company may find that it is expanding faster in a country where it already sells products, and in which payment terms are longer. Thus, it will be necessary to plan for obvious working capital changes, such as the development of new lines of business, as well as more subtle changes involving the expansion or contraction of existing businesses.

It can be extremely difficult to forecast changes in working capital, since companies do not always track working capital information by business unit, product line, or geographic region. Ideally, they should track working capital as a percentage of net sales at the most granular level possible, especially when there is a large investment in working capital. Only by doing so is it possible to understand where cash is being used within a business, how it may change over time, and where best to concentrate improvement activities.

Working Capital Strategy

The suggestions concerning working capital have largely involved the use of specific tactical improvements to existing systems to generate incremental reductions in the amount of working capital employed. It is also possible to view the working capital situation from a broader strategy-level perspective, which can generate much larger reductions in working capital. Here are several strategy-level alternatives to consider:

- *Eliminate sales on credit.* Rather than offering sales on credit, require payment in advance. This means taking payment upon order placement, rather than upon delivery of the goods. By doing so, a company completely eliminates its investment in receivables. This approach is considered normal for some consumer goods, but would be a much harder sell for more expensive items or where it is customary for customers to withhold payment until they have approved of the delivered product.

- *Outsource production.* Take the company out of the business of manufacturing its own goods. Instead, outsource all production to a contract manufacturer, and have the manufacturer ship goods directly to customers (known as drop shipping). Depending upon the arrangement, this can mean that the manufacturer takes on the working capital burden associated with raw materials and finished goods. However, doing so means that the company is exporting its product designs to a business that could become a competitor.
- *Minimize the number of suppliers.* If management is willing to sole source many of its raw materials, it may become such a large customer to the few remaining suppliers that they will be more willing to accept longer payment terms. This is only a valid option if the loss of the company's business would be a notable blow to a supplier.

The net effect of these strategic-level moves could even be a situation where a company has no working capital at all, or even negative working capital. The options noted here will only work under certain circumstances, but are worth consideration, given how large an impact they can have on the cash position of a company.

Summary

It is useful to engage in various analyses to show how policy and procedure changes can impact a company's use of funds. It is then necessary to continually communicate these results to the managers of other departments, and do whatever is necessary to convince them of the need to make proposed changes. In addition, continually monitor cash usage and create a feedback loop with the other managers, so that they know how their departments are impacting the availability of funds.

Another way to look at the working capital area is through an analysis of a company's cash conversion cycle, which is the time period from when cash is expended for the production of goods, until cash is received from customers in payment of those goods. We delve into the concept of the cash conversion cycle in the Corporate Finance Measurements chapter.

Chapter 12
Capital Expenditures

Introduction

Before a business expends funds on fixed assets, it should engage in a series of analysis steps to evaluate whether they should be purchased, usually including an analysis of the costs, related benefits, and impact on capacity levels of the prospective purchase. In this chapter, we describe several issues to consider when deciding whether to purchase a fixed asset.

> **Related Podcast Episodes:** Episodes 45, 144, 145, and 147 of the Accounting Best Practices Podcast discuss throughput capital expenditures, evaluating capital expenditure proposals, capital expenditures with minimal cash, and net present value analysis, respectively. The episodes are available at: **accountingtools.com/podcasts** or **iTunes**

Overview of Capital Expenditures

The normal capital expenditure analysis process is for the management team to request proposals to acquire fixed assets from all parts of the company. Managers respond by filling out a standard request form, outlining what they want to buy and how it will benefit the company. An analyst then assists in reviewing these proposals to determine which are worthy of an investment. Any proposals that are accepted are included in the annual budget, and will be purchased during the next budget year. Fixed assets purchased in this manner also require a certain number of approvals, with more approvals required by increasingly senior levels of management if the sums involved are substantial.

These proposals come from all over the company, and so are likely not related to each other in any way. Also, the number of proposals usually far exceeds the amount of funding available. Consequently, management needs a method for ranking the priority of projects, with the possible result that some proposals are not accepted at all. The traditional method for doing so is net present value (NPV) analysis, which focuses on picking proposals with the largest amount of discounted cash flows. A variation on the concept is the profitability index, which converts discounted cash flows into a ratio.

The trouble with NPV analysis is that it does not account for how an investment might impact the profit generated by the entire system of production; instead, it tends to favor the optimization of specific work centers, which may have no particular impact on overall profitability. Also, the results of NPV are based on the future projections of cash flows, which may be wildly inaccurate. Managers may even tweak their cash flow estimates upward in order to gain project approval, when they know that actual cash flows are likely to be lower.

A better method for judging capital expenditure proposals is constraint analysis, which focuses on how to maximize use of the bottleneck operation. The bottleneck operation is the most constricted operation in a company; if you want to improve the overall profitability of the company, then you must concentrate all attention on management of that bottleneck. This has a profound impact on capital expenditures, since a proposal should have some favorable impact on that operation in order to be approved.

There are two scenarios under which certain project proposals may avoid any kind of bottleneck or cash flow analysis. The first is a legal requirement to install an item. The prime example is environmental equipment, such as smokestack scrubbers, that are mandated by the government. In such cases, there may be some analysis to see if costs can be lowered, but the proposal *must* be accepted, so it will sidestep the normal analysis process.

The second scenario is when a company wants to mitigate a high-risk situation that could imperil the company. In this case, the emphasis is not on profitability at all, but rather on the avoidance of a situation. If so, the mandate likely comes from top management, so there is little additional need for analysis, other than a review to ensure that the lowest-cost alternative is selected.

A final scenario is when there is a sudden need for a fixed asset, perhaps due to the catastrophic failure of existing equipment or a strategic shift. These purchases can happen at any time, and so usually fall outside of the annual capital expenditure planning cycle. It is generally best to require more than the normal number of approvals for these items, so that management is made fully aware of the situation. Also, if there is time to do so, they are worthy of an unusually intense analysis, to see if they really must be purchased at once, or if they can be delayed until the next capital expenditure approval period arrives.

Once all items are properly approved and inserted into the annual budget, this does not end the review process. There is a final review just prior to actually making each purchase, with appropriate approval, to ensure that the company still needs each fixed asset.

Net Present Value Analysis

Any capital expenditure involves an initial cash outflow to pay for it, followed by a mix of cash inflows in the form of revenue, or a decline in existing cash flows that are caused by expense reductions. We can lay out this information in a spreadsheet to show all expected cash flows over the useful life of an investment, and then apply a discount rate that reduces the cash flows to what they would be worth at the present date. A discount rate is the interest rate used to discount a stream of future cash flows to their present value, typically using an organization's cost of capital. This cash flows calculation is known as *net present value*. These topics are expanded upon in the Cost of Capital chapter and the Discounted Cash Flows chapter.

EXAMPLE

Milagro Corporation is planning to acquire an asset that it expects will yield positive cash flows for the next five years. Its cost of capital is 10%, which it uses as the discount rate to construct the net present value of the project. The following table shows the calculation:

Year	Cash Flow	10% Discount Factor	Present Value
0	-$500,000	1.0000	-$500,000
1	+130,000	0.9091	+118,183
2	+130,000	0.8265	+107,445
3	+130,000	0.7513	+97,669
4	+130,000	0.6830	+88,790
5	+130,000	0.6209	+80,717
		Net Present Value	-$7,196

The net present value of the proposed project is negative at the 10% discount rate, so Milagro should not invest in the project.

In the "10% Discount Factor" column, the factor becomes smaller for periods further in the future, because the discounted value of cash flows are reduced as they progress further from the present day.

A net present value calculation that truly reflects the reality of cash flows will likely be more complex than the one shown in the preceding example. It is best to break down the analysis into a number of sub-categories, so that you can see exactly when cash flows are occurring and with what activities they are associated. Here are the more common contents of a net present value analysis:

- *Asset purchases.* All of the expenditures associated with the purchase, delivery, installation, and testing of the asset being purchased.
- *Asset-linked expenses.* Any ongoing expenses, such as warranty agreements, property taxes, and maintenance, that are associated with the asset.
- *Contribution margin.* Any incremental cash flows resulting from sales that can be attributed to the project.
- *Depreciation effect.* The asset will be depreciated, and this depreciation shelters a portion of any net income from income taxes, so note the income tax reduction caused by depreciation.
- *Expense reductions.* Any incremental expense reductions caused by the project, such as automation that eliminates direct labor hours.
- *Tax credits.* If an asset purchase triggers a tax credit (such as for a purchase of energy-reduction equipment), then note the amount of the credit.
- *Taxes.* Any income tax payments associated with net income expected to be derived from the asset.

- *Working capital changes.* Any net changes in inventory, accounts receivable, or accounts payable associated with the asset. Also, when the asset is eventually sold off, this may trigger a reversal of the initial working capital changes.

By itemizing the preceding factors in a net present value analysis, it is easier to review and revise individual line items.

Net present value is the traditional approach to evaluating capital expenditure proposals, since it is based on a single factor – cash flows – that can be used to judge any proposal arriving from anywhere in a company. However, the net present value method can be a poor evaluation method if you suspect that the cash flows used to derive an analysis are incorrect. If so, consider using scenario analysis and sensitivity analysis to make a closer examination of the situation.

Scenario analysis involves modeling of specific situations that can impact cash flows, such as the impact of an airliner crash on the willingness of the public to use air transport. Sensitivity analysis involves modeling changes in the key assumptions underlying an NPV analysis, such as market share or the costs of labor, utilities, and rent. These additional analyses are intended to note the extent to which cash flows may change. Here are several examples of the analyses that could be used for different types of capital expenditures:

- *Production equipment.* If equipment is being purchased to expand production capacity, use sensitivity analysis to examine the incremental increases in sales volume that are likely to be expected, with particular attention to the minimum amount of additional sales growth that must occur in order to generate enough cash flow to pay for the machinery.
- *Retail store.* Use sensitivity analysis to model seasonal sales levels to determine cash flows at different times of the year. Also use scenario analysis to model for the impact of a direct competitor opening a store within a short distance of the proposed location.
- *Distribution facility.* Use sensitivity analysis to model the impact of changes in labor costs on the operation of the proposed facility, as well as changes in the cost of fuel to move inventory into and out of the proposed location.
- *Transportation service.* Examples of transportation services are ferries, cruise lines, airlines, and tour buses. Use scenario analysis to model the impact on cash flows of major accidents within the industry, increases in fuel costs due to Middle East conflicts, and changes in public concerns about disease transmission in public spaces.

EXAMPLE

Explorer Cruise Lines is contemplating the construction of a cruise ship that will circumnavigate Africa on an ongoing basis. The intent is to dock at major ports frequently, and send passengers inland on multi-day safaris. The initial analysis of potential cash flows indicates that this venture could be extremely profitable. However, a scenario analysis addresses the public's perception of pirates off the east coast of Africa, and the presence of the Ebola virus along the west coast, as well as political unrest along the north coast. All of these scenarios point toward the potential for massive declines in the number of paying passengers. Consequently, Explorer elects to restrict the proposed travel route to the South African and Namibian coastal regions, which are perceived to be safer.

Breakeven Analysis

The breakeven point is the sales volume at which a project earns exactly no money. The concept can be used in the analysis of capital expenditures to determine the minimum sales level at which an investment will earn a profit of zero. This information can be used to develop the minimum baseline of activity that a proposed project must achieve. Management can then use its best judgment to decide whether this minimum activity level can be met.

To calculate the breakeven point, divide total fixed expenses by the contribution margin. Contribution margin is sales minus all variable expenses, divided by sales. The formula is:

$$\frac{\text{Total fixed expenses}}{\text{Contribution margin percentage}}$$

EXAMPLE

Sheep Chops is a meat processing company that is contemplating the construction of a new meat packing facility for sheep, to be located in Wyoming. The facility is expected to incur $6,000,000 of annual labor and other costs. Labor costs only vary slightly with volume, since approximately the same number of employees are needed to staff the production line. In essence, this means that the entire operational cost of the facility is fixed. The current market price for an unprocessed lamb is $0.80 per pound, and the wholesale price for processed lamb is $2.00. This means that the contribution margin of the facility will be 60%, which is calculated as follows:

($2.00 Processed price - $0.80 Unprocessed price) ÷ $2.00 Processed price = 60%

Based on the contribution margin, the breakeven sales level is $10,000,000, which is calculated as follows:

$$\frac{\$6,000,000 \text{ Total fixed expenses}}{60\% \text{ Contribution margin percentage}}$$

$$= \$10,000,000 \text{ Breakeven sales level}$$

The current "most likely" scenario indicates that the facility can generate $12,000,000 of sales at current price points, which equates to profitability of $1,200,000, which is calculated as follows:

($12,000,000 Sales × 60% Contribution margin) - $6,000,000 Fixed costs
= $1,200,000 Profit

A further analysis of the situation indicates that a large proportion of the world's sheep products are being diverted to China to meet an increased demand for lamb chops in that country. This increases the scarcity of lamb products in the United States, which will likely keep prices high. Management elects to enter into long-term supply contracts with several ranchers, thereby locking in an assured supply for the next ten years. The assumption of high prices and the action taken to assure supplies places the company in a position to reap excellent cash flows from the new facility for a number of years.

The Profitability Index

The profitability index measures the acceptability of a proposed capital investment. It does so by comparing the initial investment to the present value of the future cash flows associated with that project. The formula is:

$$\frac{\text{Present value of future cash flows}}{\text{Initial investment}}$$

If the outcome of the ratio is greater than 1.0, this means that the present value of future cash flows to be derived from a project is greater than the amount of the initial investment. At least from a financial perspective, a score greater than 1.0 indicates that an investment should be made. As the score increases above 1.0, so too does the attractiveness of the investment. The ratio could be used to develop a ranking of projects, to determine the order in which available funds will be allocated to them.

For example, a financial analyst is reviewing a proposed investment that requires a $100,000 initial investment. At the company's standard discount rate, the present value of the cash flows expected from the project is $140,000. This results in a strong profitability index of 1.4, which would normally be accepted.

There are a number of other considerations besides the profitability index to examine when deciding whether to invest in a project. Other considerations include:

- *The availability of funds.* A business may not have access to sufficient funds to take advantage of all potentially profitable projects.
- *The perceived riskiness of the project.* A risk averse management team may turn down a project with a high profitability index if the associated risk of loss is too great.
- *Mutual exclusivity.* The index cannot be used to rank projects that are mutually exclusive; that is, only one investment or the other would be chosen, which is a binary solution. In this situation, a project with a large total net present value might be rejected if its profitability index were lower than that of a competing but much smaller project.

The profitability index is a variation on the net present value concept. The only difference is that it results in a ratio, rather than a specific number of dollars of net present value.

The Payback Method

The simplest and least accurate capital expenditure evaluation technique is the payback method. This approach is still heavily used, because it provides a very fast "back of the envelope" calculation of how soon a company will earn back its investment. This means that it provides a rough measure of how long a company will have its investment at risk before earning back the original amount expended. Thus, it is a rough measure of risk. There are two ways to calculate the payback period, which are:

1. *Simplified.* Divide the total amount of an investment by the average resulting cash flow. This approach can yield an incorrect assessment, because a proposal with cash flows skewed far into the future can yield a payback period that differs substantially from when actual payback occurs.
2. *Manual calculation.* Manually deduct the forecasted positive cash flows from the initial investment amount from Year 1 forward, until the investment is paid back. This method is slower, but ensures a higher degree of accuracy.

EXAMPLE

Milagro Corporation's CFO has received a proposal from a manager, asking to spend $1,500,000 on equipment that will result in cash inflows in accordance with the following table:

Year	Cash Flow
1	+$150,000
2	+150,000
3	+200,000
4	+600,000
5	+900,000

The total cash flows over the five-year period are projected to be $2,000,000, which is an average of $400,000 per year. When divided into the $1,500,000 original investment, this results in a payback period of 3.75 years. However, the briefest perusal of the projected cash flows reveals that the flows are heavily weighted toward the far end of the time period, so the results of this calculation cannot be correct.

Instead, the CFO runs the calculation year by year, deducting the cash flows in each successive year from the remaining investment. The results of this calculation are:

Year	Cash Flow	Net Invested Cash
0		-$1,500,000
1	+$150,000	-1,350,000
2	+150,000	-1,200,000
3	+200,000	-1,000,000
4	+600,000	-400,000
5	+900,000	0

The table indicates that the real payback period is located somewhere between Year 4 and Year 5. There is $400,000 of investment yet to be paid back at the end of Year 4, and there is $900,000 of cash flow projected for Year 5. The CFO assumes the same monthly amount of cash flow in Year 5, which means that he can estimate final payback as being just short of 4.5 years.

The payback method is not overly accurate, does not provide any estimate of how profitable a project may be, and does not take account of the time value of money. Nonetheless, its extreme simplicity makes it a perennial favorite in many companies.

The accuracy of the payback method can be improved by incorporating the time value of money into the cash flows expected in each future year. However, doing so increases the complexity of this analysis method. To apply the time value of money to the calculation, follow these steps:

1. Create a table in which is listed the expected cash outflow related to the investment in Year 0.
2. In the following lines of the table, enter the cash inflows expected from the investment in each subsequent year.
3. Multiply the expected annual cash inflows in each year in the table by the applicable discount rate, using the same interest rate for all of the periods in the table. No discount rate is applied to the initial investment, since it occurs at once.
4. Create a column on the far right side of the table that lists the cumulative discounted cash flow for each year. The calculation in this final column is to add back the discounted cash flow in each period to the remaining negative balance from the preceding period. The balance is initially negative because it includes the cash outflow to fund the project.
5. When the cumulative discounted cash flow becomes positive, the time period that has passed up until that point represents the payback period.

EXAMPLE

We will continue with the preceding example. Milagro has a cost of capital of 7%, so the present value factor for 7% (see the Discounted Cash Flows chapter) is included in the payback table, with the following results:

Year	Cash Flow	7% Present Value Factor	Cash Flow Present Value	Net Invested Cash
0				-$1,500,000
1	+$150,000	0.9346	+$140,190	-1,359,810
2	+150,000	0.8734	+131,010	-1,228,800
3	+200,000	0.8163	+163,260	-1,065,540
4	+600,000	0.7629	+457,740	-607,800
5	+900,000	0.7130	+641,700	-33,900

The discounted payback calculation reveals that the payback period will be slightly longer than the five years of cash flows presented in the manager's original proposal.

Real Options

Another way to review a capital expenditure decision is to examine the value embedded in different strategic alternatives. This concept is known as a *real option*, which refers to the decision options available for a tangible asset. Most businesses ignore the real option concept, instead choosing to construct a net present value analysis for a single possible outcome. Instead, use the real options concept to examine a whole range of outcomes related to an investment. For example, a traditional investment analysis in an oil refinery might use a single price per barrel of oil for the entire investment period, whereas the actual price of oil will likely fluctuate far outside of the initial estimated price point over the course of the investment, and will also vary among the different products that the refinery can manufacture. An analysis based on real options would instead focus on the range of profits and losses that may be encountered over the course of the investment period as the prices of oil and petroleum products change over time. This analysis might lead the manager of an oil refinery to repeatedly switch production among different octane grades of gasoline, to take advantage of variations in market prices. These decision points will alter the cash flows of a project.

A comprehensive real options analysis begins with a review of the risks to which a project will be subjected, and then models for each of these risks or combinations of risks. To continue with the preceding example, an investor in an oil refinery project could expand the scope of the analysis beyond the price of oil, to also encompass the risks of possible new environmental regulations on the facility, the possible downtime caused by a supply shutdown, and the risk of damage caused by a hurricane.

A logical outcome of real options analysis is to be more careful in placing large bets on a single likelihood of probability. Instead, it can make more sense to place a series of small bets on different outcomes, and then alter the portfolio of investments over time as more information about the various risks becomes available. Once the key risks have been resolved, the best investment is easier to discern, so that a "bet the bank" investment can be made.

EXAMPLE

An agriculture company wants to develop a new crop strain for either wheat or barley, to be sold for export. The primary intended market is an area in which wheat is currently the preferred crop. The company estimates that it can generate a 20% return on investment by developing a new wheat variant at a cost of $30 million. Since wheat is already the primary type of crop being planted, the odds of success are high. However, if the company can successfully develop a barley variant at a total cost of $50 million, its projected profits are 50%. The key risk with the barley project is farmer acceptance. Given the high profits that could be derived from selling barley, the company makes a small initial $1 million investment in a pilot project. If the level of farmer acceptance appears reasonable, the company can then invest an additional $8 million for a further roll out of the concept, followed by additional expenditures for more extended rollouts.

This use of real options allows the company to invest a relatively small amount to test its assumptions regarding a possible alternative investment. If the test does not work, the company has only lost $1 million. If the test succeeds, the company can pursue an alternative that may ultimately yield far higher profits than the more assured investment in wheat.

The concept illustrated in the preceding example of placing a series of targeted bets can be expanded over an entire product life cycle. For example, if the pilot test for the barley variant works, the company could continue to develop options for the rollout of the product to farmers in other countries. The company may have identified certain parts of the world where cultural differences make it more or less likely that farmers will convert their fields to barley production. Accordingly, the company can invest in a target area in each of these geographic regions to measure acceptance levels, and then either proceed with a full-scale product rollout or withdraw from the market entirely. The following graphic illustrates how the process might work.

Real Options Rollout Plan for Barley Product

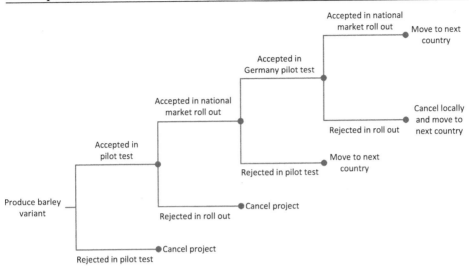

A concern with using real options is that competitors may be using the same concept at the same time, and may use the placing of small bets to arrive at the same conclusions as the company. The result may be that several competitors will enter the same market at approximately the same time, driving down the initially rich margins that management may have assumed were associated with a real option. Thus, the parameters of real options constantly change, and so must be re-evaluated at regular intervals.

Another concern relates to the last point that competitors may jump into the same market. This means that a business cannot evaluate the results of its options analyses in a leisurely manner. Instead, each option must be evaluated quickly and decisions made to make additional investments (or not) before the competition gets a jump on the situation.

Constraint Analysis

Under constraint analysis, the key concept is that an entire company acts as a single system, which generates a profit. Under this concept, capital expenditures revolve around the following logic:

1. Nearly all of the costs of the production system do not vary with individual sales; that is, nearly every cost is an operating expense; therefore,
2. You need to maximize the throughput (revenues minus totally variable costs) of the *entire* system in order to pay for the operating expense; and
3. The only way to increase throughput is to maximize the throughput passing through the bottleneck operation.

Consequently, give primary consideration to those capital expenditure proposals that favorably impact the throughput passing through the bottleneck operation.

From the perspective of constraint management, the only capital investments that should be made in a business are ones that will either increase throughput or reduce operating expenses. When this priority is assigned to capital requests, it is entirely likely that an organization will be able to avoid a number of asset purchases. The following asset requests can be avoided:

1. *Local optimization.* A request may be to increase the efficiency of a workstation that does nothing to increase throughput. If so, the investment is wasted, since the company invests funds and receives no return on its investment.

2. *Sprint capacity increase.* Sprint capacity is excess production capacity positioned upstream from the bottleneck operation. It is needed to ensure that inventory can be rushed to the bottleneck operation to keep it functioning at all times. A request may involve an increase in sprint capacity. If so, review the request to see if the size of the capacity increase is reasonable, based on the company's expectations for the amount of sprint capacity needed.

3. *Constraint capacity increase.* What if a proposed investment *is* designed to increase the capacity of the constraint? If so, compare the projected amount of incremental new capacity to the projected amount of capacity needed to fulfill throughput requirements. It is entirely possible that the investment will create too much capacity, which merely shifts the constraint to a different location in the company. The appropriate response is to scale back the amount of the investment to only build the required amount of additional capacity.

4. *Expense reduction.* If a capital request is not addressed by the preceding review steps, this means the only remaining justification is that the investment will reduce operating expenses. If so, subject the request to an especially detailed review, with a particular emphasis on the assumptions used to prove that expenses will indeed be reduced. Unless there is a high probability of an adequate expense reduction *and* a low probability of a cost overrun on the investment, reject the request.

The decision to increase the capacity of the constrained resource is a particularly important one. This resource is likely to be the constraint in the system precisely because it is quite expensive to increase the capacity level. Consequently, investments in this area require a considerable amount of investigation. A possible outcome is that these types of investments are delayed until such time as management has accumulated more information about the likelihood of future changes in capacity requirements.

Capital Expenditure Proposal Analysis

Reviewing a capital expenditure proposal does not necessarily mean passing judgment on it exactly as presented. A variety of modifications can be made to a proposal, which may result in a more precisely targeted investment. Here are some examples:

- *Asset capacity*. Does the asset have more capacity than is actually needed under the circumstances? Is there a history of usage spikes that call for extra capacity? Depending on the answers to these questions, consider using smaller assets with less capacity. If the asset is powered, this may also lead to reductions in utility costs, installation costs, and floor space requirements.

- *Asset commoditization*. Wherever possible, avoid custom-designed machinery in favor of standard models that are readily available. By doing so, it is easier to obtain repair parts, and there may even be an aftermarket for disposing of the asset when the company no longer needs it.

- *Asset features*. Managers have a habit of wanting to buy new assets with all of the latest features. Are all of these features really needed? If an asset is being replaced, then it is useful to compare the characteristics of the old and new assets, and examine any differences between the two to see if they are required. If the asset is the only model offered by the supplier, would the supplier be willing to strip away some features and offer it at a lower price?

- *Asset standardization*. If a company needs a particular asset in large quantities, then adopt a policy of always buying from the same manufacturer, and preferably only buying the same asset every time. By doing so, the maintenance staff becomes extremely familiar with the maintenance requirements of several identical machines, and only has to stock replacement parts for one model.

- *Extended useful life*. A manager may be applying for an asset replacement simply because the original asset has reached the end of its recommended useful life. But is it really necessary to replace the asset? Consider conducting a formal review of these assets to see if they can still be used for some additional period of time. There may be additional maintenance costs involved, but this will almost certainly be lower than the cost of replacing the asset.

- *Facility analysis*. If a capital proposal involves the acquisition of additional facility space, consider reviewing any existing space to see if it can be compressed, thereby eliminating the need for more space. For example, shift storage items to less expensive warehouse space, shift from offices to more space-efficient cubicles, and encourage employees to work from home or on a later shift. If none of these ideas work, then at least consider acquiring new facilities through a sublease, which tends to require shorter lease terms than a lease arranged with the primary landlord.

- *Monument elimination*. A company may have a large fixed asset around which the rest of the production area is configured; this is called a monument. If there is a monument, consider adopting a policy of using a larger number of lower-capacity assets. By doing so, you avoid the risk of having a single monument asset go out of service and stopping all production, in favor of having multiple units among which work can be shifted if one unit fails.

The Outsourcing Decision

It may be possible to avoid a capital purchase entirely by outsourcing the work to which it is related. By doing so, the company may be able to eliminate all assets related to the area (rather than acquiring more assets), while the burden of maintaining a sufficient asset base now shifts to the supplier. The supplier may even buy the company's assets related to the area being outsourced. This situation is a well-established alternative for high technology manufacturing, as well as for information technology services, but is likely not viable outside of these areas.

If there is an outsourcing opportunity, the cash flows resulting from doing so could be highly favorable for the first few years, as capital expenditures vanish. However, the supplier must also earn a profit and pay for its own infrastructure, so the cost over the long term will probably not vary dramatically from what a company would have experienced if it had kept a functional area in-house. There are three exceptions that can bring about a long-term cost reduction. They are:

- *Excess capacity.* A supplier may have such a large amount of excess capacity already that it does not need to invest further for some time, thereby potentially depressing the costs that it would otherwise pass through to its customers. However, this excess capacity pool will eventually dry up, so it tends to be a short-term anomaly.
- *High volume.* There are some outsourcing situations where the supplier is handling such a massive volume of activity from multiple customers that its costs on a per-unit basis decline below the costs that a company could ever achieve on its own. This situation can yield long-term savings to a company.
- *Low costs.* A supplier may locate its facility and work force in low-cost countries or regions within countries. This can yield significant cost reductions in the short term, but as many suppliers use the same technique, it is driving up costs in all parts of the world. Thus, this cost disparity is useful for a period of time, but is gradually declining as a long-term option.

There are risks involved in shifting functions to suppliers. First, a supplier may go out of business, leaving the company scrambling to shift work to a new supplier. Second, a supplier may gradually ramp up prices to the point where the company is substantially worse off than if it had kept the function in-house. Third, the company may have so completely purged the outsourced function from its own operations that it is now completely dependent on the supplier, and has no ability to take it back in-house. Fourth, the supplier's service level may decline to the point where it is impairing the ability of the company to operate. And finally, the company may have entered into a multi-year deal, and cannot escape from the contract if the business arrangement does not work out. These are significant issues, and must be weighed as part of the outsourcing decision.

The cautions noted here about outsourcing do not mean that it should be avoided as an option. On the contrary, a rapidly growing company that has minimal access to funds may cheerfully hand off multiple operations to suppliers in order to avoid the up-front costs associated with those operations. Outsourcing is less attractive to stable, well-established companies that have better access to capital.

Complex Systems Analysis

When analyzing a possible investment, it is useful to also analyze the system into which the investment will be inserted. If the system is unusually complex, it is likely to take longer for the new asset to function as expected within the system. The reason for the delay is that there may be unintended consequences that ripple through the system, requiring adjustments in multiple areas that must be addressed before any gains from the initial investment can be achieved.

It may initially appear that the multitude of factors to consider in a complex system can be accounted for by creating an equally complex analysis model. However, virtually all models, no matter how complex, are not entirely complete; there are always additional factors that have not been considered that can impact a model in unexpected ways. Further, some factors may interact in unexpected ways, resulting in outcomes that are well outside of what might be expected.

EXAMPLE

ABC Airlines is modeling whether to offer its customers a new route into Denver from Kansas City. ABC must consider a number of factors that can impact flight service, such as the impact of snowfall on the number of travelers to the area's ski resorts, whether a new high-speed train from Kansas City to Denver will impact the number of paying passengers, the extent to which upstart low-cost airlines may drive down prices, and how the price of aviation fuel will drive up ticket prices. ABC elects not to provide service, after which the International Olympic Committee grants Denver the next Winter Olympics, which triggers an upsurge in travel even in advance of the games. Thus, an outlier event arises that would not normally have been factored into the decision, but which has an impact on the decision.

A basic rule of investing in a complex environment is that it is impossible to understand the full impact of the investment. There may be any number of adjustments required that will call for additional investments of both time and money. Consequently, the more complex the environment, the more time and money should be allocated to an investment, even if there may not appear to be any immediate need for the additional investment.

Summary

This chapter addressed a variety of issues to consider when deciding whether to purchase a fixed asset. We put somewhat less emphasis on net present value analysis, which has been the primary analysis tool in industry for years, because it does not take into consideration the impact on throughput of a company's bottleneck operation. The best capital expenditure analysis is to give top priority to project proposals that have a strong favorable impact on throughput, and then use net present value to evaluate the impact of any remaining projects on cost reduction.

For a detailed explanation of bottlenecks and throughput, see the author's *Constraint Management* book, which is available on the accountingtools.com website.

Chapter 13
Investment Alternatives

Introduction

Any company will have occasional surges in cash flow, while wealthier ones may have substantial cash reserves. There should be a system in place for investing this cash, as defined by a number of restrictions that are primarily designed to protect the cash and make it readily accessible. In this chapter, we discuss the guidelines used for investing, cash availability scenarios, various investment strategies, and the investment instruments most commonly used.

Investment Guidelines

Though this chapter is entirely concerned with investments, we must emphasize that an organization keep cash reserves available for operational use; this is much more important than maximizing the return on investment. The following guidelines are designed to meet this cash availability goal:

- *Protect the cash.* Above all, do not lose the cash. No investment should be so risky that the company is unable to recover the cash that it initially placed in the investment. This is a particularly important consideration in situations where a company has a short-term operational need for cash, and is only parking it in an investment for a short time in order to gain some assured income.
- *Ready conversion to cash.* It should be easy to convert an investment into cash on little notice. It is critical to satisfy any short-term operational need for cash, even if it was not planned for in the cash forecast. This means that there should be an active secondary market for all investments, where someone else can readily be found to acquire an investment instrument held by the company.
- *Earn a return.* After the preceding two factors have been dealt with, it is then permissible to optimize the return on investment. This means that, if there are two possible investments that have identical risk profiles and liquidity, pick the one having the greater return on investment.

An additional investment consideration is the taxability of investment income. The interest earned on different types of federal, state, and municipal obligations may not be taxable. Taxability may be a consideration when making investments, but usually the preceding guidelines for protecting cash and cash convertibility override a possible boost in net interest income.

The interplay between these guidelines changes in relation to the duration of an investment. For example, a portfolio of investments that all have long-term maturities usually have returns associated with them that are locked in (assuming they are held to maturity), so there is a reduced risk related to the return that will be earned. Conversely, and depending upon the existence of a secondary market, it may be more difficult to liquidate these longer-term investments. For comparison purposes, a short-term investment is at considerable risk of a change in the rate of return, for the company is constantly buying new investments, each reflecting the most recent market rate of return; however, the shorter associated maturity makes it easier to liquidate these investments to meet short-term cash needs.

We must make it clear that it is critical to be exceedingly risk averse when investing company cash. All but the largest and wealthiest corporations will be harmed by an investment loss, so do not attempt to gain outsized returns on an investment when the accompanying risk level is too high.

> **Tip:** There should be a formal investment policy that confines the company to a narrow range of possible investments that are considered to be at low risk of default. A sample policy is listed later in this section.

There are several steps that can be taken to reduce the risk of losing invested funds, and which should be considered when engaging in investment activities. They are:

- *Diversification.* Only invest a limited amount of cash in the securities of a single entity, in case that entity defaults on its obligations. Similarly, only invest a limited amount in securities originating within one industry, in case economic circumstances lead to multiple defaults within the industry.
- *FDIC insurance.* The Federal Deposit Insurance Corporation (FDIC) protects depositors of insured banks against the loss of their deposits and accrued interest if an insured bank fails. This coverage includes deposits in checking accounts, savings accounts, money market deposit accounts, and certificates of deposit. The coverage does not include cash invested in stocks, bonds, mutual funds, life insurance proceeds, annuities, or municipal securities. The amount of this coverage is limited to $250,000 per depositor, per insured bank. Consequently, it may be worthwhile to monitor account balance levels and shift funds above the insurance cap to accounts in other banks. By doing so, a company can achieve an FDIC coverage level that is substantially higher than $250,000.
- *Sweep structure.* When a company elects to have cash automatically swept out of an account and into an interest-earning investment, it should insist on a *one-to-one sweep*, where its cash is used to acquire a specific investment instrument. If the bank handling the transaction were to enter bankruptcy, the company would have title to the acquired investment. A worse alternative is to engage in a *one-to-many sweep*, where the funds of multiple businesses are used to acquire an investment instrument. In this case, the bank handling the transaction has title to the investment instrument, which means

that the company would be reduced to filing a creditor claim that may eventually result in compensation for an amount less than its original investment.

All three of these risk reduction steps are to guard against admittedly unusual circumstances that a business may never experience. Nonetheless, if a counterparty were to fail, the potential loss could be quite large. Consequently, give strong consideration to these options when engaging in investment activities.

To ensure that investment guidelines are followed, they should be codified in a formal investment policy that is approved by the board of directors. The internal audit department can monitor compliance with this policy. A sample policy follows.

EXAMPLE

Suture Corporation's board of directors adopts the following investment policy.

General

In general, investments in securities with low liquidity levels shall be restricted to 15% of the company's total investment portfolio. There must be an active secondary market for all other investments.

Debt Investments

Debt investments are subject to the following restrictions:

- May only be made in high-quality intermediate or long-term corporate and Treasury bonds
- No more than 20% of the total debt investment can be made in a single industry
- Investments cannot comprise more than 5% of the debt issuances of the investee
- The average term to maturity cannot exceed __ years
- An investment must be terminated within one month if its Standard & Poor's credit rating drops below BBB
- Any bank acting as a counterparty shall have a capital account of at least $5 billion
- Short-term investments shall be pre-qualified by the investment advisory committee for the placement of funds

Equity Investments

Equity investments are subject to the following restrictions:

- May only be made in the common stock of companies trading on the New York Stock Exchange
- No more than 20% of the total equity investment can be made in a single industry
- Investments cannot comprise more than 5% of the capitalization of the investee

Control of Securities

All securities over which the company has physical control shall be consigned to an accredited third party.

Prohibitions

The company is prohibited from investing in any of the following types of investments without the prior approval of the board of directors:

- Commodities
- Foreign equity investments and commercial paper
- Leveraged transactions
- Real estate
- Securities with junk ratings
- Short sales or purchases on margin
- Venture capital

It is useful to periodically compare the company's investment policy to the actual structure and performance of its investment portfolio over the past few months, for the following reasons:

- *Compliance.* To ensure that employees have followed the guidelines set forth in the policy.
- *Performance.* To see if the company might have achieved better returns if the policy had been somewhat less restrictive.
- *Risk management.* To determine whether the company avoided or mitigated risks by adhering to the policy.
- *Liquidity.* To see if adherence to the policy allowed the company to routinely meet its liquidity requirements.

This analysis should be conducted by someone not directly associated with the treasury department, in order to avoid any bias in the results.

Cash Availability Scenarios

Before considering the type of investment strategy to follow, first determine the historical availability of cash that can be invested. A mix of the following situations will likely apply:

- *Daily operational needs.* For many organizations that operate at low profitability levels, nearly all cash on hand may be called upon to service the daily operational needs of the business. If so, the main emphasis is on highly liquid investments that will likely be called upon within the next few days.
- *Untouched cash.* If a business routinely has a baseline level of cash that is never used, these funds can be invested in longer-term and/or less liquid investments that have a higher rate of return. However, the duration of these investments should not exceed the end date of the corporate cash forecast, so that the organization is not caught in an investment when there is a need for funds.

- *Seasonal cash balances.* It is relatively common for a business to build up its cash balance following a seasonal spike in sales, and then use the accumulated funds during those parts of the year that experience lower activity levels. These changes in the seasonal accumulation and use of cash can be quite predictable. Investments should be tailored to make cash available as of the periods when cash outflows are anticipated.

- *Planned expenditures.* If there are upcoming capital purchases of considerable size, a business may accumulate cash in advance in order to pay for these purchases. This means there is a target date on which a specific amount of invested funds must be converted to cash. In this situation, the type of investment made must conform to the requirements of the planned expenditure.

- *Contingent expenditures.* A business may be anticipating a large cash outflow for which there is not a specific payout date, and needs to accumulate funds for that payment. An example of this situation is an anticipated payout from a lawsuit that the organization expects to lose. This situation calls for an investment of funds that is extremely liquid, so that it can be converted to cash on very short notice.

- *Corporate growth rate.* The rate at which an entity grows or shrinks will dictate the amount of cash available for investment, and the timing for when cash is needed. A rapidly-growing business will likely have an enormous need for cash that is fueled by rapid increases in working capital and fixed assets. In this situation, investment durations should be extremely short, so that cash can be put to use at once. Conversely, when a business is shrinking, there will be a gradual decline in working capital, which is converted back into cash. This can result in a large pool of cash for which there is no particular need; unless distributed to investors, this cash can be parked in longer-term investments.

- *Trapped cash.* Cash may be located in a country or other jurisdiction where cash flows are restricted, or where there are severe tax penalties associated with moving the cash elsewhere. If so, the cash will likely need to be invested locally. In this case, all of the preceding cash availability scenarios come into play. The proper investment will depend upon the level of planned or contingent expenditures, the corporate growth rate, and the variability of cash flows – but using local investments.

Investment Strategy

Within the preceding guidelines and cash availability scenarios, what strategy should be followed when investing cash? Several possibilities are noted in the following bullet points. When considering the options, please note that the more active ones require accurate cash forecasts, which may not be available.

- *Earnings credit.* The simplest investment option of all is to do nothing. Cash balances are left in the various bank accounts, where they accrue an earnings credit that is offset against the fees charged by the bank for use of the accounts. If cash balances are low, this can be an entirely acceptable strategy, since more active management of a small amount of cash will probably not glean a significantly larger return. However, the earnings credit can only be applied to fees charged in the current period; if the fees are less than the credit, the company loses the difference. This consideration puts a cap on the amount of funds that should be left in a bank account.

EXAMPLE

Suture Corporation has an African division that is in startup mode, and so has little excess cash. Currently, the division maintains an average of only $20,000 in its sole bank account. Its bank offers a 1.5% earnings credit on retained cash balances, which is $25 per month that can be offset against account fees. The best alternative is a money market fund that earns 2%, but which requires the manual transfer of funds several times per month.

Given the minor amount of the balance and the low return on other investment alternatives, management elects to accept an earnings credit, rather than taking any more aggressive investment actions.

- *Automated sweeps.* Sweep all excess cash into a central account, and shift the funds in that account to an overnight investment account. This strategy requires no staff time, but yields a low return on investment, since banks charge significant fees to manage this process.
- *Laddering.* The laddering strategy involves making investments of staggered duration, so that the company can take advantage of the higher interest rates typically associated with somewhat longer-term investments. For example, a business can reasonably forecast three months into the future, so it invests in a rolling set of investments that mature in three months. To begin this strategy, it invests a block of funds in an investment having a one-month maturity, another block in an investment with a two-month maturity, and yet another block in an investment with a three-month maturity. As each of the shorter investments matures, they are rolled into new investments having three-month maturities. The result is an ongoing series of investments where a portion of the cash is made available for operational use at one-month intervals, while taking advantage of the higher yields on three-month investments.
- *Match maturities.* An option requiring manual tracking is to match the maturities of investments to when the cash will be needed for operational purposes. This method calls for a highly accurate cash forecast, both in terms of the amounts and timing of cash flows. To be safe, maturities can be planned for several days prior to a forecasted cash need, though this reduces the return on investment.

- *Tiered investments.* If a business has more cash than it needs for ongoing operational requirements, conduct an analysis to determine how much cash is never or rarely required for operations, and use this cash in a more aggressive investment strategy. For example:

  o *Continual cash usage.* Cash usage levels routinely flow within a certain range, so there must be sufficient cash available to always meet these cash requirements. The investment strategy for the amount included in this investment tier should be concentrated in highly liquid investments that can be readily accessed, with less attention to achieving a high rate of return.

  o *Occasional cash usage.* In addition to cash usage for daily operating events, there are usually a small number of higher cash usage events that can be readily predicted, such as a periodic income tax or dividend payment. The strategy for this investment tier should focus on maturity dates just prior to the scheduled usage of cash, along with a somewhat greater emphasis on the return on investment. There should be a secondary market for these types of investments.

  o *No planned cash usage.* If cash usage levels have never exceeded a certain amount, all cash above this maximum usage level can be invested in longer-term instruments that have higher returns on investment, and perhaps with more limited secondary markets.

EXAMPLE

The CFO of Suture Corporation wants to adopt a tiered investment strategy. He finds that the company routinely requires a maximum of $200,000 of cash for various expenditures on a weekly basis. In addition, there are scheduled quarterly dividend payments of $50,000 per quarter, and quarterly income tax payments of $100,000, which fall on the same date. There have not been any instances in the past three years where cash requirements exceeded these amounts. Currently, Suture maintains cash reserves of $850,000 on a weekly basis. Based on the preceding information, the company could invest the cash in the following ways:

Investment Tier	Amount	Investment Type
Continual cash usage	$200,000	Money market
Occasional cash usage	150,000	Certificates of deposit, commercial paper
No planned cash usage	500,000	Bonds
Total	$850,000	

The tiered investment strategy requires close attention to the cash forecast, particularly in regard to the timing and amount of the occasional cash usage items. Otherwise, there is a risk of being caught with too much cash in an illiquid investment when there is an immediate need for the cash.

- *Ride the yield curve.* An investment manager can buy investments that have higher interest rates and longer maturity dates, and then sell these investments when the cash is needed for operational purposes. Thus, a company is deliberately buying investments that it knows it cannot hold until their maturity dates. If the yield curve is inverted (that is, interest rates are lower on longer-maturity investments), you would instead continually re-invest in very short-term instruments, no matter how far in the future the cash is actually needed again by the company.

EXAMPLE

The CFO of Suture Corporation has $300,000 available to invest for the next 90 days. He notes that the interest rate on 3-month T-Bills is 2.0%, while the rate on 6-month T-Bills is 2.25%. He elects to take advantage of this 0.25% difference in interest rates by investing the $300,000 in 6-month T-Bills, and then selling them on a secondary market in 90 days, when he needs the cash for operational purposes.

A variation on all of the preceding strategies is to outsource the investment task to an experienced third party money manager. This option works well if a company is too small or has too few cash reserves to actively manage its own cash. If outsourcing is chosen, be sure to set up guidelines with the money manager for exactly how cash is to be invested, primarily through the use of lower-risk investments that mitigate the possibility of losing cash. A variation on the outsourcing concept is to invest primarily in money market funds, which are professionally managed.

Types of Investments

Once an investment strategy has been decided upon, the next step is to shift funds into a preferred set of investments. In this section, we describe the most common types of investments, along with the characteristics of each one.

Repurchase Agreements

A repurchase agreement is a package of securities that an investor buys from a financial institution, under an agreement that the institution will buy it back at a specific price on a certain date, typically the next business day. The repurchase price incorporates the interest rate paid to the investor during the investor's holding period. It is most commonly used for the overnight investment of excess cash from a company's cash concentration account, which can be automatically handled by a company's primary bank.

The interest rate earned on this investment is equal to or less than the money market rate, since the financial institution takes a transaction fee that reduces the rate earned. Despite the low return, the automated nature of repurchase agreements makes them a popular investment choice for a business that does not want to spend the time manually entering into a short-term investment for residual funds.

Time Deposits

A time deposit is a bank deposit that pays a fixed interest rate, and requires an investment for a specific period of time, usually anywhere from one week to one year. This is essentially a loan from the company to a bank, with interest set at a level close to the interbank rate. Time deposits have the advantage of being set at fixed interest rates, so there is no risk of an interest rate decline. However, the interest rate is typically quite low.

Certificates of Deposit

A certificate of deposit (CD) is an interest-bearing certificate that is issued by a bank as a receipt for deposits invested with it. A CD can have a maturity of as little as a few weeks to several years. There is a secondary market for some CDs, so this type of investment can be liquidated relatively quickly. CDs are available in multiple currencies. In particular, two variations on the concept are:

- *Eurodollar CDs.* Denominated in U.S. dollars, and issued by entities outside the United States.
- *Yankee CDs.* Denominated in U.S. dollars, and issued by foreign entities with operations in the United States.

A CD is issued at its face value, with additional interest due to the investor in addition to the face amount. A shorter-term CD is usually issued at a fixed interest rate, with interest being paid at the end of each year or the maturity of the instrument.

A longer-term CD may instead use a floating interest rate that is based on a major benchmark interest rate, such as LIBOR. If so, the interest rate is usually re-set every three or six months.

Bankers' Acceptances

A banker's acceptance arises when a bank guarantees (or accepts) corporate debt, usually when it issues a loan to a corporate customer, and then sells the debt to investors. These acceptances are sold at a discount, and redeemed upon maturity at their face value. Because of the bank guarantee, a banker's acceptance is viewed as an obligation of the bank. If the bank has a good reputation, the acceptance can be re-sold in an open market, at a discount to its face value. A banker's acceptance is considered to be a very safe asset, and is used extensively in international trade. A banker's acceptance usually has a term of less than 180 days.

Commercial Paper

Commercial paper is a promissory note issued by a corporation, usually with a maturity of less than 180 days; thus, it is a short-term bond. The short maturity is designed to avoid the extra cost of registration with the Securities and Exchange Commission that would be required if the term were to exceed 270 days. Typical issuers of commercial paper include:

- Financial entities
- Industrial companies
- Insurance companies
- Public utilities

Entities issuing commercial paper have usually obtained a credit rating from one of the major credit rating agencies, such as Standard & Poor's, Moody's Investors Service, or Fitch Ratings. If the credit rating of an issuer were to decline, then the value of its commercial paper would decline as well (and vice versa), which can impact the value of investments if they are to be sold on a secondary market.

Commercial paper is usually sold at a discount from its face value, which means that the investor buys it at a discounted price, and is repaid on the maturity date at its face value. Most commercial paper is unsecured, which means that this type of investment carries a higher interest rate to reflect the increased level of risk associated with it – though the rate is still quite low. Commercial paper can be acquired directly from the issuing companies, but is also commonly available through banks that act as dealers.

Money Market Funds

A money market fund is a pool of short-term financial instruments operated by a fund manager, for which investors can purchase shares. A money market fund usually invests solely in federal government debt issuances, such as T-Bills and T-Notes. It is quite easy to invest in and move cash out of a money market fund, and so is ideal for extremely short-term investments. To attract investors, many of these funds offer late cutoff times for new investments, which allows a company to wait until later in the day to concentrate cash positions before making an investment in a fund.

There are some discernible differences in the risk associated with different money market funds, which is caused by some fund managers taking risks in order to outperform the market. Conversely, other fund managers do an excellent job of investment diversification in order to reduce risk. Some funds may also be able to defer redemptions under certain conditions. For these reasons, be sure to examine the stated objectives and rules of a fund before investing in it.

U.S. Government Debt Instruments

Despite the continuing increases in the debt of the United States government, its debt instruments are still considered among the lowest-risk in the world. The ones most commonly used by corporations for investment are Treasury Bills (T-Bills) and Treasury Notes (T-Notes). T-Bills have 3, 6, and 12-month maturities. T-Bills having maturities of 3 and 6 months are auctioned on a weekly basis, while T-Bills with 12-month maturities are auctioned once a month. T-Bills are sold at a discount, and redeemed upon maturity at their face value. There is a very active secondary market in T-Bills, so it is easy to sell them prior to their maturity dates.

The maturities of T-Notes range from 1 to 10 years. Two-year T-Notes are issued on a monthly basis, while T-Notes with other maturities are issued on a quarterly basis. T-Notes are available as both inflation-indexed and fixed-rate investments. Interest on T-Notes is paid semi-annually. T-Notes are traded on secondary markets at premiums or discounts to their face values, to reflect the current market interest rate (see the Effective Interest Rate section).

Treasury Bonds are also available. Bonds have similar characteristics to T-Notes, but have longer maturities. Maturities are generally in the range of 10 to 30 years.

Paradoxically, the trouble with U.S. government debt instruments is their safety – the United States government can obtain the lowest possible interest rates, so there is little return on funds invested in these instruments.

State and Local Government Debt

An interesting investment option is the debt obligations issued by state and local governments. These debt instruments are usually issued in conjunction with the revenue streams associated with large capital projects, such as airport fees and tolls from toll roads. Other instruments are based on general tax revenues. The maturities of these obligations are typically multi-year, so a company in need of cash must rely upon a vigorous aftermarket to liquidate them prior to their maturity dates. The returns on state and local debt obligations are higher than the yields on federal government issuances, and income from these investments is usually exempt from federal taxation.

Though it is rare for a state or local government to default on its debt, such cases are not unknown, so be mindful of the reliability of the cash flows supporting debt repayment.

Bonds

A bond is an obligation to pay a fixed amount to the bond holder, usually in the amount of $1,000 per bond, as of one or more dates specified in a bond agreement. The maturities of bonds can be extremely long, sometimes extending to 30 or even 40 years in the future.

There are many variations on the bond concept, but the two key types are based on differing methods for paying the bond holder. They are:

- *Coupon bond.* Each bond comes with a set of coupons, which are submitted to the issuer for payment of interest at regular intervals. The company does not track bond holder contact information for coupon bonds.

- *Registered bond.* The issuer maintains an updated list of the holders of its bonds, and sends interest payments to them at regular intervals.

The coupon bond is designed to be more easily transferrable between bond holders. This is of some importance, since there is an active secondary market in many bonds. The presence of a secondary market is critical for investors, especially when the maturity date is many years in the future, and the holder is uncertain of how long it wants to retain possession of the bond.

Several variations on bonds are noted below:

- *Secured/unsecured.* Some bond instruments provide specific collateral against which bondholders have a claim if the bonds are not paid. If there is a guideline to protect cash, then a business should only invest in secured bonds.
- *Convertible.* This is a bond that can be converted to stock using a pre-determined conversion ratio. This option is usually only available at set intervals, and conversion is at the discretion of the bondholder. The presence of conversion rights typically reduces the interest rate on a bond, since investors assign some value to the conversion privilege. If the main investment goal is obtaining a high return on investment, an organization should avoid convertible bonds, since they tend to have somewhat lower returns.
- *Callable.* This is a bond that the issuer can buy back prior to its maturity, usually because there has been a decline in interest rates since the issuance of the bond, and the issuer wants to refinance at a lower rate. The existence of a call provision tends to reduce the value of a bond, so investing organizations usually avoid this type of bond.

The Primary and Secondary Markets

A primary market refers to the original sale of a security to an investor. Whenever a security is sold thereafter among investors and market makers, it is referred to as the secondary market. The existence of a secondary market is critical to the investment operations of a business, since it allows for the liquidation of an investment prior to its maturity date. If there were no secondary market, investment activities would have to be limited to the most short-term investments, in order to ensure the availability of cash.

The secondary market is comprised of financial institutions and dealers. These entities can act as brokers, taking a commission on the transfer of an investment from a seller to a buyer. Alternatively, they can hold an inventory of investments on their own behalf, and sell them directly to buyers for a profit.

Secondary markets are particularly important when a company is aggressively investing in longer-term investments that generate higher interest rates. This activity, known as "riding the yield curve," is only possible if a business can promptly liquidate an investment well before its maturity date.

The Effective Interest Rate

If an entity buys or sells a financial instrument for an amount other than its face amount, this means that the interest rate it is actually earning or paying on the investment is different from the stated interest paid on the financial instrument. For example, if a company buys a bond for $95,000 that has a face amount of $100,000 and which pays interest of $5,000, then the actual interest it is earning on the investment is $5,000 ÷ $95,000, or 5.26%.

The *effective interest rate* exactly discounts estimated future cash payments or receipts over the expected life of a financial instrument. In essence, interest income or expense in a period is the carrying amount of a financial instrument multiplied by the effective interest rate.

EXAMPLE

Suture Corporation acquires a debt security having a stated principal amount of $100,000, which the issuer will repay in three years. The debt has a coupon interest rate of five percent, which it pays at the end of each year. Suture acquires the debt for $90,000, which is a discount of $10,000 from the principal amount of $100,000.

Based on a cash outflow of $90,000 to acquire the investment, three interest payments of $5,000 each, and a principal payment of $100,000 upon maturity, Suture calculates an effective interest rate of 8.95 percent. Using this interest rate, the CFO of Suture calculates the following amortization table:

Year	(A) Beginning Amortized Cost	(B) Interest and Principal Payments	(C) Interest Income [A x 8.95%]	(D) Debt Discount Amortization [C – B]	Ending Amortized Cost [A + D]
1	$90,000	$5,000	$8,055	$3,055	$93,055
2	93,055	5,000	8,328	3,328	96,383
3	96,383	105,000	8,617	3,617	100,000

The Discounted Investment Formula

Some investments, such as T-Bills and T-Notes, are sold at a discount and redeemed at their face value. The calculation used to determine the correct discount to pay for one of these instruments is:

$$\text{Face value} \times \text{Discount rate} \times \frac{\text{Day count}}{\text{Annual basis}} = \text{Amount of discount}$$

For example, a company wants to buy a 90-day $10,000,000 T-Bill at a discount of 2.5%. The calculation is:

$$\underset{\text{Face value}}{\$10,000,000} \times \underset{\text{Discount rate}}{0.025} \times \underset{\text{360 Days}}{\frac{90\ \text{Days}}{}} = \underset{\text{Discount}}{\$62,500}$$

When the discount is subtracted from the face value of the T-Bill, the amount to be paid is:

$10,000,000 Face value - $62,500 Discount = $9,937,500 Purchase price

Summary

While there are many investment alternatives available, it is entirely likely that an efficient organization will elect to concentrate its attention on just a few alternatives, and probably on those that are transactionally most efficient to engage in on a regular basis. For example, a business with modest cash balances may enter into an automated overnight repurchase arrangement with its primary bank, and essentially forget about any additional investment activities. An alternative where there is more investable cash on hand is to make all investments through an investment portal that conveniently links participants with a specific cluster of available investment instruments. Thus, convenience may prove to be the key reason for continually investing excess cash in the same types of investments.

If there is an interest in looking beyond the most convenient investments and exploring other options, the next most critical element of the investment decision will likely be the presence of an active secondary market. If there is such a market, it is much easier to liquidate an investment before its maturity date. The result can be a broader range of choices when cash is available for investment even over a relatively short period of time.

Chapter 14
Dividends and Other Payouts

Introduction

A question for the board of directors is whether to pay out dividends, and if so, the appropriate amount to pay. This decision tends to be based on an understanding of what investors want and the alternative uses to which cash can be put, rather than a specific formula. In this chapter, we address the payment of dividends from the perspectives of both the investor and the company, and how these viewpoints drive the payment of dividends. In addition, we address related courses of action, which are the stock buyback option and the stock dividend.

Dividend Mechanics

A dividend is a payment made by a corporation to each of the holders of its stock as of a specific date. Dividends are authorized by a company's board of directors, which may authorize dividends once a month, quarter, or year, or possibly semi-annually. Dividends are most commonly issued on a quarterly basis. Key dates in the process of issuing dividends are as follows:

- *Declaration date.* The date on which the board of directors declares that a dividend payment will be made.
- *Record date.* Payments are made to those investors recorded as holding the company's stock as of a specific date after the declaration date.
- *Payment date.* The date on which dividend payments will be issued to shareholders of record.

EXAMPLE

During its January 10 board meeting, the board of directors of Cranky Corporation passes a resolution to pay a dividend of $0.25 per share on February 28 to all shareholders of record on February 16. The declaration date is January 10, the record date is February 16, and the payment date is February 28.

An additional date to be aware of is the *ex-dividend date.* This is the first date following the declaration of a dividend on which the holder of stock is not entitled to receive the next dividend payment. This is normally two days before the record date. Thus, if an investor buys shares between the ex-dividend date and the payment date, he will not receive a dividend; the dividend will instead be paid to a prior shareholder. Since the cash flows of a shareholder will be reduced as of the ex-dividend date, the market price of the stock will fall on this date to reflect the impact of the dividend that the current holder will no longer receive. The amount of the price decline should be the amount of the dividend, less the tax effect to the shareholder.

EXAMPLE

The market price of Cranky Corporation's common stock is $10 just prior to the ex-dividend date. The average tax bracket for investors is 15%, and a $0.25 dividend is being paid. The price of the company's stock as of the ex-dividend date should reflect a decline of $0.21, which is calculated as follows:

$$\$0.25 \text{ Dividend} \times (1 - 15\% \text{ Tax bracket})$$

$$= \$0.25 \times 0.85$$

$$= \$0.21 \text{ Price decline}$$

Types of Dividends

A dividend is generally considered to be a cash payment. However, there are several types of dividends, some of which do not involve the payment of cash to shareholders. These dividend types are:

- *Cash dividend.* The cash dividend is by far the most common of the dividend types used.
- *Stock dividend.* A stock dividend is the issuance by a company of its common stock to its common shareholders without any consideration. This is described later in the Stock Dividend section.
- *Property dividend.* A company may issue a non-monetary dividend to investors, rather than making a cash or stock payment. This distribution is recorded at the fair market value of the assets distributed. Since the fair market value is likely to vary somewhat from the book value of the assets, the issuing company will likely record the variance as a gain or loss. This accounting rule can sometimes lead a business to deliberately issue property dividends in order to alter its taxable and/or reported income.
- *Scrip dividend.* A company may not have sufficient funds to issue dividends in the near future, so instead it issues a scrip dividend, which is essentially a promissory note (which may or may not include interest) to pay shareholders at a later date. This dividend creates a note payable.
- *Liquidating dividend.* When the board of directors wishes to return the capital originally contributed by shareholders as a dividend, the payout is called a liquidating dividend, and may be a precursor to shutting down the business.

The Investor Viewpoint

The financial performance and dividend payout policy of a company will attract a certain type of investor. If the company has a history of consistently issuing a certain amount of dividends, then it will attract investors who want this steady stream of income. Conversely, if a business chooses to instead plow its earnings back into operations, it will attract a different set of investors that wants to profit from presumed increases in the company's share price. In the latter case, an increase in share price may be taxed at the capital gains rate, which results in more after-tax income to the investor.

In the former case, investors who want a dividend will evaluate a company based on its *dividend payout ratio*. This ratio is the percentage of a company's earnings paid out to its shareholders in the form of dividends. There are two ways to calculate the dividend payout ratio; each one results in the same outcome. One version is to divide total dividends paid by net income. The calculation is:

$$\frac{\text{Total dividends paid}}{\text{Net income}}$$

The alternative version essentially calculates the same information, but at the individual share level. The formula is to divide total dividend payments over the course of a year on a per-share basis by earnings per share for the same period. The calculation is:

$$\frac{\text{Annual dividend paid per share}}{\text{Earnings per share}}$$

EXAMPLE

The Conemaugh Cell Phone Company paid out $1,000,000 in dividends to its common shareholders in the last year. In the same time period, the company earned $2,500,000 in net income. The dividend payout ratio is:

$$\frac{\$1,000,000 \text{ Dividends paid}}{\$2,500,000 \text{ Net income}}$$

$$= 40\% \text{ Dividend payout ratio}$$

Investors interested in the long-term viability of a series of dividend payments will likely track the dividend payout ratio on a trend line, to see if a business is generating enough income to support its dividend payments over a number of years. If not, they may sell off their shares, thereby driving down the stock price. If an investor sees that the payout ratio is nearly 100% or greater than that amount, then the current dividend level is probably not sustainable. Conversely, if the ratio is quite low, investors will consider the risk of a dividend cutback to also be low, and so will be more inclined to buy the stock, thereby driving up its price.

Investors may also look at the reverse of the dividend payout ratio to see how much of earnings are being retained within a business. If the retention amount is declining, this indicates that the company does not see a sufficient return on investment to be worthy of plowing additional cash back into the business. From this perspective, a declining retention rate will drive away those growth-oriented investors who rely on an increasing share price.

In short, investors rely on ratio analysis on a trend line to determine whether a business is issuing an appropriate amount of dividends, and may alter their stock holdings based on the outcome of this analysis.

The Company Viewpoint

A company typically issues dividends under three circumstances, which are:

- Certain shareholders have sufficiently large stock holdings to force the company to pay out dividends; or
- There are not sufficient profitable internal uses for the cash being spun off by operations, so the excess amount is returned to investors in the form of a dividend; or
- Management believes it can bolster the company's stock price by issuing dividends.

In the first case, dividends being forcibly extracted from a company tend to be one-time events, and so require little financial analysis.

The second case is by far the most common reason for issuing dividends. Typically, a business needs to employ all of its cash internally during its initial growth stage, and so is not capable of issuing a dividend. Once the business matures, it may begin to spin off more cash than it needs to maintain its market position, which can be returned to investors in the form of a dividend.

The third case is a misguided one, for (as noted in the last section), investors are already holding company stock based on expectations regarding how the company is employing its cash. If the company suddenly pays a dividend, the stock price may initially decline, because the dividend is a signal to the existing group of growth-oriented investors that management no longer feels there are enough growth opportunities for the company. The stock price should eventually recover as income-oriented investors take the place of growth investors, so there may be no net change in the price of the stock over time.

The change in the type of investor is neither good nor bad, but it does mean that there will be an increased amount of turnover among shareholders for a period of time. During this transition period, it is possible that the share price will be somewhat more volatile than usual.

If the board of directors wants to find a use for excess cash, but does not want to turn away its growth-oriented investors, then some alternative uses for the cash are making acquisitions, paying off liabilities in advance of their scheduled payment dates, or buying back shares (see the next section).

If the board of directors elects to go forward with an initial dividend payment, it is important to signal to the marketplace that the company intends to continue to issue dividends at regular intervals. Otherwise, a one-time distribution to shareholders via a dividend will merely send growth-oriented investors to the exits without creating an incentive for income-oriented investors to take their place, thereby creating downward pressure on the stock price.

> **Tip:** When initially announcing a dividend, point out the timing and expected size of future dividends, so that the investment community can properly value the shares on which dividends are being paid.

When embarking on a strategy of issuing ongoing dividends, it is of some importance to begin with a small dividend that the company can easily support from its current resources and expected cash flows. By doing so, the board of directors can comfortably establish a gradual increase in the size of the dividend that the investment community can rely upon, which should result in a slow increase in the price of the company's stock. Conversely, the worst type of dividend is one so large that the company has a difficult time scraping together the cash needed to pay it, which can endanger its ability to operate on an ongoing basis.

It is also useful for the board of directors to consider the negative implications of not having sufficient cash to continue paying a dividend. If this were to happen, the income-oriented investors who are holding the stock precisely because of those dividends will sell their shares; this will trigger a supply and demand imbalance that will lower the price of the stock. Eventually, value-oriented investors will buy the stock when it has dropped by a sufficient amount, in hopes of a recovery in the stock price. Nonetheless, a dividend cancellation almost always triggers a steep stock price decline.

In short, the decision to issue dividends should be considered in light of the message being sent to the investment community, as well as the long-term ability of a business to continue paying dividends.

The Stock Buyback Option

Companies sometimes engage in stock buybacks, where the board of directors authorizes that a certain amount of cash be set aside for a repurchase program. The stock buyback can be considered an alternative to issuing dividends. There are three reasons why a company may engage in a buyback:

- *Increase earnings per share.* To reduce the number of shares outstanding, which should increase the amount of earnings per share, and therefore provide pressure to increase the share price.
- *Set price floor.* Because management believes that the share price is currently too low, and does not adequately reflect the true market value of the business. Thus, if a buyback plan is announced that the company will

buy back shares whenever the share price falls below a certain price point, there will be a tendency for the stock price to stay above that trigger point.

- *Reduce shares.* To mop up excess shares that have been created through the issuance of stock options and warrants.

An additional situation is a targeted repurchase, where a business buys shares back from a specific shareholder. This approach may be used in order to avert a possible takeover, or to turn away an investor who is threatening to present proposals at the next shareholders meeting to alter the management structure or general direction of the organization.

EXAMPLE

The Hegemony Toy Company has 5,000,000 shares of its common stock outstanding. These shares currently trade at $20. In the fiscal year just ended, Hegemony reported net profits of $2,000,000, which results in reported earnings per share of $0.40 (calculated as $2,000,000 profits ÷ 5,000,000 shares).

Hegemony's board of directors approves a $10,000,000 stock buyback. At the current $20 market price, this means the company can acquire 500,000 shares. By doing so, there will now be 4,500,000 shares outstanding. The altered share total changes the earnings per share figure to $0.444.

There are some problems with a stock buyback. One is that there will be fewer shares in circulation after the buyback has been completed, which reduces the liquidity of the stock. If a company already suffers from an excessively small number of shares outstanding, this is a valid objection to a buyback.

Another problem is that companies have a strong tendency to acquire shares when they are flush with cash, which is usually at a point in their life cycles when they have a very high stock price. Thus, they are converting a relatively small number of shares to treasury stock in exchange for a large amount of cash, which does little to boost the earnings per share for the remaining shares outstanding. This is the reverse of what would be considered prudent behavior for an investor, who attempts to buy low and sell high. If a company were as prudent as an investor, it would only buy back shares when its stock price was very low.

When a company has excess cash, it should consider a stock buyback to be one of the last uses for that cash. Instead, the sequence of possible uses should roughly follow this series of decision options:

1. *Invest in company operations.* This is assumed to be the best profit generator.
2. *Acquire related companies.* This approach is riskier than internal growth, but still focuses the company on its primary markets.

3. *Pay down debt.* This reduces the risk of not paying back loans. The approach can be extended to paying off leases and even reducing the amount of accounts payable.
4. *Build a reserve.* There is nothing wrong with building a large cash reserve to guard against a downturn in the company's fortunes.
5. *Buy back stock.* If all of the preceding steps have been taken, only then is a buyback warranted, and only if the stock is trading at a reasonably low price.

Deciding Between a Dividend and a Buyback

There may be a situation where the board of directors has already made a determination to make a payout to investors, and is deciding between a dividend and a stock buyback. What are the differentiating factors between these choices? Here are several considerations:

- *Level of commitment.* A stock buyback is the logical choice if the board does not want to commit to a long-term series of dividend payments to investors. This decision can be based on the stability of a company's underlying cash flows. If there is a rock-solid amount of cash flow produced each year, it could be reasonable to allocate a portion of that cash flow to dividends. However, if cash flows have a history of spiking and plunging from one period to the next, there is not enough reliability to form the basis for a long-term series of dividend payments, so a one-time buyback would be a better choice.
- *Cash flow consistency.* A continuation of the last comment is that a company could issue dividends to draw down that portion of its cash flows that consistently recur, year after year. If there are additional one-time surges in cash flow, these additional funds could be transferred to shareholders through a one-time stock buyback, thereby not establishing a higher level of dividend payments that might be construed as a long-term payout commitment.
- *Impact on options.* As noted earlier in the Dividend Mechanics section, the price of a company's stock will decline following the issuance of a dividend. This price decline does not happen when there is a stock buyback. Consequently, the holders of a company's stock options are more likely to suffer when dividends are paid, since the potential profit they can earn from exercising an option is reduced. If members of management have a large number of options, their personal interest in the situation could result in pressure on the board of directors to favor the use of buybacks.

EXAMPLE

The president of Cantilever Construction has been granted 1,000,000 stock options, with an exercise price of $5. The market price of the company's stock is currently $8, and the board of directors is contemplating a large $2 dividend. If the dividend is declared, the ex-dividend price of the stock will likely drop by the amount of the dividend, to $6. This has a direct impact on the president, since his potential profit from exercising his options (excluding the impact of taxes) will drop from $3,000,000 to $1,000,000. The difference is calculated as follows:

($8 Market price - $5 Exercise price) × 1,000,000 Options = $3,000,000 Profit

($6 Market price - $5 Exercise price) × 1,000,000 Options = $1,000,000 Profit

Given the prospective change in personal income, the president lobbies the board of directors to buy back shares, rather than issuing a dividend.

The Stock Dividend

A stock dividend is the issuance by a company of its common stock to its common shareholders without any consideration. For example, when a company declares a 15% stock dividend, this means that every shareholder receives an additional 15 shares for every 100 shares he already owns.

A company usually issues a stock dividend when it does not have the cash available to issue a normal cash dividend, but still wants to give the appearance of having issued a payment to investors.

In reality, the total market value of a company does not change just because a company has issued more shares, so the same market value is simply spread over more shares, which likely reduces the value of individual shares to compensate for the increased number of shares. For example, if a company has a total market value of $10 million and it has one million shares outstanding, then each share should sell on the open market for $10. If the company then issues a 15% stock dividend, there are now 1,150,000 shares outstanding, but the market value of the entire firm has not changed. Thus, the market value per share after the stock dividend is now $10,000,000 ÷ 1,150,000 shares, or $8.70.

If a company's shares are selling for such a large amount on a per-share basis that it appears to be keeping investors from buying the stock, a large stock dividend might sufficiently dilute the market value per share that more investors would be interested in buying the stock. This might result in a small net increase in the market value per share, and so would be useful for investors. However, a high stock price is rarely an impediment to an investor who wants to buy stock.

A problem with a stock dividend is that it may use up the remaining amount of authorized shares. For example, the board of directors may have initially authorized 15 million shares, and 10 million shares are outstanding. If the company issues a 50% stock dividend, this increases the number of shares outstanding to 15 million shares. The board will now have to authorize more shares before the company can issue any additional stock.

In short, any advantages of using a stock dividend are minor, and so its use is not recommended in most cases.

Summary

The board of directors should think long and hard about the decision to begin issuing dividends. Dividends work best when followed consistently over a long period of time, but doing so requires consistent cash flows. Any inability to meet a dividend obligation will trigger a rapid stock price decline. Thus, always consider a decision to issue dividends as a long-term strategic issue, not just a short-term payout. It is useful to model for the board of directors a series of worst-case scenarios that reveal the company's ability to pay dividends even in the face of serious revenue declines; doing so may keep the board from committing to excessively large dividend payments.

Chapter 15
Mergers and Acquisitions

Introduction

Corporate finance is essentially about obtaining and deploying funds. One of the most massive deployments of funds that any organization can engage in is the purchase of another business. This purchase can be a difficult one, for a large part of the money spent may be lost – either due to a bad valuation or because the acquirer did not closely adhere to a strategy for how the acquired business was to be used. In this chapter, we delve into these issues by first examining the different types of acquisition strategies, and then moving on to the different methods used to assign a value to and pay for an acquisition.

> **Related Podcast Episode:** Episode 75 of the Accounting Best Practices Podcast discusses acquisition valuation. The episode is available at: **accounting-tools.com/podcasts** or **iTunes**

Acquisition Strategy

Many acquirers do not have a specific acquisition strategy. Instead, they examine any acquisition that comes to their attention. Over time, serial acquirers will likely find that one particular approach to acquisitions works best for them, and so they will use it as the primary basis for engaging in additional acquisitions. While other strategies may occasionally be employed, these acquirers are most likely to follow the strategy that has worked for them in the past. In this section, we review a number of different reasons for engaging in acquisitions – some of which yield better results than others.

The Sales Growth Strategy

One of the most likely reasons why a business acquires is to achieve greater growth than it could manufacture through internal, or *organic*, growth. It is very difficult for a business to grow at more than a modest pace through organic growth, because it must overcome a variety of obstacles, such as bottlenecks, hiring the right people, entering new markets, opening up new distribution channels, and so forth. Conversely, it can massively accelerate its rate of growth with an acquisition. Consider the following calculation of growth rates:

- A company has $1,000,000 of sales, and is growing at a reasonable 10% per year. Assuming a consistent rate of growth for five years, the business will have grown to $1,611,000 in sales at the end of that period.

- The same company buys a competitor whose sales are $500,000, so that its initial combined sales are $1,500,000. Assuming the same rate of growth per year, the business will have grown to $2,416,000 after five years.

The difference in ending sales between the two scenarios is $805,000. If we also subtract out the $500,000 in sales that were purchased through the acquisition, there is still $305,000 of new incremental sales. This incremental difference is the result of growing the acquired business at 10% per year for the five-year period. Thus, the acquirer has jump-started its growth by increasing the baseline level of sales to which its normal growth rate is applied. Of course, this line of thinking assumes that the same growth rate applies to both the acquiring and acquired businesses.

Another version of the growth strategy is when the expansion rate of a business is slowing down or has stalled, possibly because it is located in a market niche that has a slow rate of growth. The company could acquire a business located in a faster-growing niche, thereby giving the company as a whole a faster rate of growth. It may be possible to engage in a series of such acquisitions, continually skipping from niche to niche within an industry to position the business in the fastest-growing areas.

The Geographic Growth Strategy

A business may have gradually built up an excellent business within a certain geographic area, and wants to roll out its concept into a new region. This can be a real problem if the company's product line requires local support in the form of regional warehouses, field service operations, and/or local sales representatives. Such product lines can take a long time to roll out, since the business must create this infrastructure as it expands.

The geographical growth strategy can be used to accelerate growth in this situation. This involves finding another business that has the geographic support characteristics that the company needs, such as a regional distributor, and rolling out the product line through the acquired business. Under this approach, an acquirer would likely need to find an acquisition in each area in which it plans to conduct a geographic expansion. It can be difficult to find suitable target companies in less-populated regions, so a business may have to build its own distribution systems in those areas, while growing through acquisitions elsewhere.

The Product Supplementation Strategy

An acquirer may want to supplement its product line with the similar products of another company. This is particularly useful when there is a hole in the acquirer's product line that it can immediately fill by making an acquisition. This approach is most useful in the following situations:

- *Customer progression.* Customers may progress from an introductory model to a more complex model over time. If the company does not have more complex models to sell, it will eventually lose customers to its competitors.

- *Competitor marketing.* Competitors may be marketing their wares by publishing comparison charts in which they point out the absence of certain products or product features from the product line of the company.

However, the acquirer should also examine its acquisitions under this strategy for several characteristics, to see if the products will be a good fit. They are:

- *Branding coverage.* Can the acquirer easily shift the acquired products under the umbrella of its corporate or product-line brand without too much trouble? The acquired products cannot be so different that they are not seen by customers as being a good fit within the company's product line.
- *Field servicing.* Is the company's own field service or in-house warranty repair staff capable of repairing these products? This is a particular problem for more complex products. It can also be a problem when an entirely different set of parts must be stocked for the acquired products.
- *Manufacturability.* Can the acquired products be produced within the company's production facilities, or do they require such different manufacturing processes that they must remain within their current production facilities?
- *Product life cycle.* Are the products to be acquired near the end of their life cycles, and does the acquiree have replacement products ready for release? If not, the new products may not last long in the marketplace.
- *Product strength.* The products must be considered among the most competitive in the industry. There is no point in acquiring products that are considered substandard.
- *Profitability.* Do the products have price points and cost structures that allow them to generate a reasonable profit?

The number of considerations just presented should make it clear that the product supplementation strategy requires considerable due diligence to see if the products of a target company can actually be integrated into the product line of the acquirer. Realistically, this will be difficult to achieve, and may only make this strategy possible in a minority of situations.

The Full Service Strategy

An acquirer may have a relatively limited line of products or services, and wants to reposition itself to be a full-service provider. This calls for the pursuit of other businesses that can fill in the holes in the acquirer's full-service strategy. This approach usually involves the combination of products with supporting services, which may then be extended into multiple geographic regions.

The Vertical Integration Strategy

A company may want to have complete control over every aspect of its supply chain, all the way through to sales to the final customer. This control may involve buying the key suppliers of those components that the company needs for its products, as well as the distributors of those products and the retail locations in which they are sold.

A company does not normally engage in a comprehensive vertical integration strategy, but instead focuses on those suppliers who control key raw materials and production capacity, as well as those sales channels that generate the most profit.

A problem with the vertical integration strategy is that the upstream suppliers owned by the corporate parent have an assured customer, so they tend to be less watchful in controlling their costs, which can eventually impact the cost structure of the entire group of businesses. This problem can be overcome by allowing downstream companies within the group to buy their materials from outside suppliers; this forces each company within the business group to remain competitive. Alternatively, the transfer price at which goods are sold within the company should be based on the market price. A transfer price is the price at which one part of an entity sells a product or service to another part of the same entity.

The Adjacent Industry Strategy

An acquirer may see an opportunity to use one of its competitive strengths to buy into an adjacent industry. This approach may work if the competitive strength gives the company a major advantage in the adjacent industry. Examples of adjacent industry strategies are:

- A company devises an extremely low-cost method for heating a home, and wants to move the technology into the adjacent commercial heating market.
- A company creates a popular web site store for sports equipment, and wants to expand the items distributed into the home furnishings market.
- A company uses enormous production volume to become the low-cost leader in the automobile industry, and wants to expand into the golf cart industry, where most of its cost efficiencies can be applied to build very low-cost golf carts.

However, it is usually dangerous to rely upon a few strengths, no matter how large they may be, to move into a new market space. For example, a company may feel that it can bring impressive new technology into an adjacent industry, only to find that competition in that industry is based more on control over distribution channels than technology. Consequently, it is important to make acquisitions in adjacent industries where acquirees have the competitive advantages that the acquirer lacks.

The Diversification Strategy

A company may elect to diversify away from its core business in order to offset the risks inherent in its own industry. These risks usually translate into highly variable cash flows which can make it difficult to remain in business when a bout of negative cash flows happen to coincide with a period of tight credit where loans are difficult to obtain.

For example, a business environment may fluctuate strongly with changes in the overall economy, so a company buys into a business having more stable sales. Or, a business specializes in winter activities, and so buys a business whose sales are primarily in the summer months. Further examples of the diversification strategy are:

- *Season based.* A store that specializes in ski and snowboard equipment acquires another business that specializes in baseball and football equipment, and merges them into the same store, thereby ensuring a consistent sales level throughout the year.
- *Economy based.* A company that builds homes finds that its industry is a leading indicator of swings in the general economy, so it acquires a dam-building company, which is involved in decade-long projects that are less subject to swings in the economy.
- *Credit based.* A mortgage lender finds that its ability to generate lending revenue fluctuates with the level of interest rates, so it acquires a chain of payday loan shops, where customers are less sensitive to interest rates.

The trouble with the diversification strategy is that there are usually few synergies to be gained, since the businesses are so different from each other. On the contrary, it usually requires *more* expenses for an additional layer of corporate oversight to manage the disparate businesses. Thus, the main benefit of the diversification strategy is more consistent cash flows, rather than more profits.

To reduce the risk of diversification, an acquirer can buy businesses in adjacent market spaces, or in different niches within the same market, rather than acquiring too far afield. By doing so, it may be able to profit from some revenue enhancement or cost reduction synergies, while still mitigating some of the risk of its original operations.

The Market Window Strategy

A company may see a window of opportunity opening up in the market for a particular product or service. It may evaluate its own ability to launch a product within the time period during which the window will be open, and conclude that it is not capable of doing so. If so, its best option is to acquire another company that is already positioned to take advantage of the window with the correct products, distribution channels, facilities, and so forth. Such an acquisition will allow the acquirer to gain market share in an area where it otherwise would have had no chance of competing at all. Here are several examples of business features that might be attractive to a buyer under a market window strategy:

- A key patent needed to compete in a new market area
- A government certification needed to bid for work in an area that just received an infusion of government funding
- A distribution network already in place to distribute goods into a country that just loosened its import restrictions

The downside of the market window strategy is that correctly-positioned target companies know they are valuable commodities, and so may be entertaining offers from multiple bidders. Thus, a business that wants to use acquisitions to improve its market window positioning will likely pay high prices to do so.

The Bolt-on Strategy

One of the more successful acquisition strategies is to only acquire similar businesses in the same market, where the acquirer has a deep knowledge of how businesses are operated. This is called a bolt-on acquisition, since the acquired business is typically added directly onto the acquirer's existing business lines.

The bolt-on strategy pursues enhanced value by two avenues, which are increased aggregate revenues and reduced aggregate expenses. These two objectives have substantially different success levels, as noted below:

- *Revenue enhancement synergies.* Revenue enhancement can be achieved by multiple means, such as cross-selling the products of the two businesses, placing acquired products under the brand name of the other business, and selling acquired products through additional distribution channels. The trouble with this type of synergy is that it depends upon the generation of entirely new sales, which in turn depends upon the cooperation of customers. Thus, it is difficult to quantify the synergies that might be gained from revenues, which makes it dangerous to base an acquisition valuation on this type of synergy. In practice, many acquirers find that combined revenue levels *decline* following an acquisition, due to customer uncertainty and the depredations of competitors who view this as an opportunity to steal customers.

- *Cost reduction synergies.* Cost reduction synergies arise from the identification and elimination of overlapping functional areas within a business, as well as from overall cost reductions due to economies of scale. Cost reductions can come from such areas as overlapping administrative positions, duplicate warehouse systems, duplicate computer systems, excess production capacity, and volume purchase discounts. A particularly fine cost reduction synergy is when the acquirer has excellent operational knowledge, and is able to impose it on the operations of acquired companies (usually in the manufacturing area). It is relatively easy to quantify and implement cost reduction synergies, especially since they are entirely under the control of the acquirer. Many serial acquirers only rely upon cost reduction synergies when reviewing target companies and formulating offer prices for them.

The Low-Cost Strategy

In many industries, there is one company that has rapidly built market share through the unwavering pursuit of the low-cost strategy. This approach involves offering a baseline or mid-range product that sells in large volumes, and for which the company can use best production practices to drive down the cost of manufacturing.

It then uses its low-cost position to keep prices low, thereby preventing other competitors from challenging its primary position in the market.

This type of business needs to first attain the appropriate sales volume to achieve the lowest-cost position, which may call for several acquisitions. Under this strategy, the acquirer is looking for businesses that already have significant market share, and products that can be easily adapted to its low-cost production strategy. In addition, a business pursuing the low-cost strategy is more likely to acquire another business that enters its market space and which is following the same strategy.

In short, this strategy can be used both to initially expand into the role of the dominant player in an industry, and as a competitive weapon for taking over any business that threatens its position.

The Industry Roll-up Strategy

The industry roll-up strategy involves buying up a number of smaller businesses with small market shares to achieve a consolidated business with significant market share. While attractive in theory, this is not that easy a strategy to pursue. In order to create any value, the acquirer needs to consolidate the administration, product lines, and branding of the various acquirees, which can be quite a chore. There is a further risk in that a roll-up involves multiple acquisitions within a relatively short period of time, which makes the integration goals even harder to achieve. Further, an acquirer that is good at the legal aspects of buying many other businesses may not have an equivalent level of expertise in integrating them, which leads to more of a conglomeration of companies than a seamless, well-oiled business machine.

An interesting variation on this strategy is to aggregate several quite small businesses, so that the combined group is now larger than the minimum acquisition threshold of a major industry acquirer. Larger acquirers understand that it is not cost-effective to buy very small businesses, since they must spend nearly the same amount of time and money on due diligence that they would on a larger target company. The trouble with this strategy is that the acquirer engaged in the initial roll-up will spend a considerable amount of time on its own due diligence, as well as on the consolidation and rebranding of the acquirees, before it can make any money by flipping the company to a larger acquirer.

Valuation of a Target Company

There are many ways to value a business, which can yield widely varying results, depending upon the basis of each valuation method. Some methods assume a valuation based on the assumption that a business will be sold off at bankruptcy prices, while other methods focus on the inherent value of intellectual property and the strength of a company's brands, which can yield much higher valuations. There are many other valuation methods lying between these two extremes.

We need all of these methods, because no single valuation method applies to all businesses. For example, a rapidly-growing business with excellent market share may produce little cash flow, and so cannot be valued based on its discounted cash flows. Alternatively, a company may have poured all of its funds into the development of intellectual property, but has no market share at all. Only through the application of multiple valuation methods can we discern what the value of a business may be.

In this section, we cover how to arrive at a valuation. You will see not only the calculation methodology, but also the assumptions underlying each one, and the situations to which they might be applied. They are presented beginning with those likely to yield the lowest valuations, and progress through other methods that usually result in higher valuations.

Related Podcast Episode: Episode 75 of the Accounting Best Practices Podcast discusses acquisition valuation. The episode is available at: **accounting-tools.com/podcasts** or **iTunes**

Liquidation Value

Liquidation value is the amount of funds that would be collected if all assets and liabilities of the target company were to be sold off or settled. Generally, liquidation value varies depending upon the time allowed to sell assets. If there is a very short-term "fire sale," then the assumed amount realized from the sale would be lower than if a business were permitted to liquidate over a longer period of time.

The liquidation value concept is based on the assumption that a business will terminate, for one that continues in business has additional earning power from its intellectual property, products, branding, and so forth. Thus, liquidation value sets the lowest possible valuation for a business. The concept is useful for the acquirer to address even in cases where it intends to pay a great deal more for a target company. The reason is that the difference between the liquidation value and the amount actually paid is the amount for which the acquirer is at risk, in case there are problems with the target company that require it to be liquidated.

Real Estate Value

If a company has substantial real estate holdings, they may form the primary basis for the valuation of the business. This approach only works if nearly all of the assets of a business are various forms of real estate. Since most businesses lease real estate, rather than owning it, this method can only be used in a small number of situations.

If the acquirer has no experience in dealing with real estate, and plans to sell off the real estate, then it may apply a discount to the real estate values that it derives. However, since the real estate valuation is being used as the primary source of information for the valuation, and the acquirer expects to sell the real estate, this brings up the issue of why the acquirer is making an offer at all.

From the perspective of a seller that wants to be sold, it may make more sense to gradually sell off the real estate in such a manner as to maximize prices, and use the funds to either buy back shares or issue a large cash dividend to shareholders. This approach shifts all of the cash directly to the shareholders, without worrying about any discount that might be applied by a prospective acquirer. Company management can then pursue the sale of the remainder of the business to realize any residual cash, which also goes to the shareholders.

Relief-from-Royalty Method

What about situations where a company has significant intangible assets, such as patents and software? Is it possible to create a valuation for them? A possible approach is the relief-from-royalty method, which involves estimating the royalty that the company would have paid for the rights to use an intangible asset if it had to license it from a third party. This estimation is based on a sampling of licensing deals for similar assets. These deals are not normally made public, so it can be difficult to derive the necessary comparative information.

Under this method, any savings from not licensing an asset are considered on an after-tax basis. The reason is that, if the company had indeed licensed the rights from a third party, there would have been a licensing expense that reduced taxable income.

The relief-from-royalty method is hardly one that can be used to value an entire enterprise, since it only addresses intangible assets. Nonetheless, it is one of the few methods available for putting a price tag on intangible assets, and so can be of use in situations where intangibles comprise a large part of the assets of a target company.

Enterprise Value

What would be the value of a target company if an acquirer were to buy all of its shares on the open market, pay off any existing debt, and keep any cash remaining on the target's balance sheet? This is called the enterprise value of a business, and the calculation is:

+	Market value of all shares outstanding
+	Total debt outstanding
-	Cash
=	Enterprise value

Enterprise value is only a theoretical form of valuation, because it does not factor in the effect on the market price of a target company's stock once the takeover bid is announced. In addition, the current market price may not be indicative of the real value of the business if the stock is thinly traded, since a few trades can substantially alter the market price. Further, the removal of cash from the target company does not indicate the need for that cash in order to continue operating the target business. Nonetheless, enterprise value is of some use in determining the "raw" valuation prior to estimating other factors that typically boost the valuation of a business.

EXAMPLE

High Noon Armaments is preparing the valuation of a target company, and the CFO wants to know the amount of its enterprise value. The target has one million shares, and today's market price is $12.50 per share. According to its most recent quarterly Form 10-Q filing, the target has $2.4 million of outstanding debt, and $200,000 of cash on hand. Based on this information, its enterprise value is:

+ Market value (1,000,000 shares × $12.50/share)	$12,500,000
+ Debt	2,400,000
- Cash	-200,000
= Enterprise value	$14,700,000

Multiples Analysis

It is quite easy to compile information based on the financial information and stock prices of publicly-held companies, and then convert this information into valuation multiples that are based on company performance. These multiples can then be used to derive an approximate valuation for a specific company. The typical approach is as follows:

1. Create a list of the top ten publicly-held companies most comparable to the company for which a valuation is being compiled.
2. Find the current market valuation for each business, which is easily obtained through Yahoo Finance or Google Finance.
3. Obtain the revenue information for the past 12 months for each business, either from SEC filings or the Internet sites just noted. Compare revenues to the total company market valuation to arrive at a sales-to-market-value multiple.
4. Obtain the EBITDA information for the past 12 months for each business, either from SEC filings or the Internet sites just noted. EBITDA is earnings before interest, taxes, depreciation, and amortization. It is a rough measure of the cash flows of a business. Compare EBITDA to the total company market valuation to arrive at an EBITDA-to-market-value multiple.
5. Multiply the target company's revenue and EBITDA amounts for the past 12 months by the median multiples for the target group to derive valuations.

The following example illustrates the concept.

EXAMPLE

High Noon Armaments routinely acquires other businesses within the firearms industry, and so conducts an annual review of the revenue and EBITDA multiples associated with the smaller publicly-held companies in the same industry. Accordingly, the acquisitions staff prepares the following multiples analysis.

Multiples Analysis
Firearms Industry
As of January 10, 20xx
(000s)

Name	Market Capitalization	One Year Revenues	One Year EBITDA	Revenue Multiple	EBITDA Multiple
Arbuckle Weapons	$145,000	$174,000	$19,300	1.2x	7.5x
Billy the Kid Designs	90,000	117,000	11,500	1.3x	7.8x
Heston Shotguns	128,000	160,000	24,200	0.8x	5.3x
Patton Siege Guns	210,000	210,000	30,000	1.0x	7.0x
Plasma Weapons	52,000	24,000	3,900	2.2x	13.2x
Quigley Artillery	360,000	240,000	42,400	1.5x	8.5x
Rifled Custom Guns	76,000	19,000	3,200	4.0x	24.0x
Totals	$1,061,000	$944,000	$134,500	1.1x	7.9x

Thus, the review shows a weighted-average revenue multiple of 1.1x and a weighted-average EBITDA multiple of 7.9x.

One month later, High Noon is engaged in a valuation analysis of a prospective acquisition, which has annual sales of $6.8 million and EBITDA of $400,000. Based on the multiples analysis, High Noon arrives at the following possible valuations for the company:

	Revenue	EBITDA
Target company results	$6,800,000	$400,000
× Industry average multiple	1.1x	7.9x
= Valuation based on multipliers	$7,480,000	$3,160,000

The results suggest quite a broad range of possible valuations, from $3,160,000 to $7,480,000. It is possible that the target company has unusually low EBITDA in comparison to the industry, which is causing its EBITDA-based multiplier to be so low. This means that High Noon might want to push for a lower valuation if it proceeds with the acquisition.

It is most common to multiply the valuation multiples by the revenue and EBITDA information for the target company for its last 12 months. This is known as *trailing revenue* or *trailing EBITDA*. This is the most valid information available, for it represents the actual results of the business in the immediate past. However, if a target company expects exceptional results in the near future, then it prefers to use *forward revenue* or *forward EBITDA*. These measurements multiply expected results for the next 12 months by the valuation multipliers. While the use of forward measurements can create a good estimate of what a business will be worth in the near future, it generally incorporates such optimistic estimates that it tends to result in excessively high valuations.

A multiplier analysis that is based on revenues is useful in cases where a business is in high-growth mode, where there are typically fewer profits. This is because such businesses have elevated expenditure levels to hire staff, acquire more facilities, and other issues related to faster growth. However, creating a valuation based solely on revenues is dangerous, since a target company may be generating those revenues by selling at such rock-bottom prices that it will be impossible for the acquirer to turn a profit. Also, high revenues do not mean that a business is being well run. In short, a revenue-based multiplier should be supplemented by other valuation techniques.

The EBITDA multiple is a much better basis for a valuation than the revenue multiple, since it reflects the ability of a business to generate a profit. However, you should examine the EBITDA for the past few years as well, to see if the management of the target company is cutting back on expenditures in the current year in order to make the business appear more profitable.

There are several problems with multiples analysis to be aware of. They are:

- *Company size.* The information used for multiples analysis comes from publicly-held companies, and those companies are generally larger ones. Thus, the multiples that they command may not be applicable to smaller, privately-held organizations.
- *Market capitalization.* A very large publicly-held company may have higher multiples than smaller companies, if only because it has a more liquid market for its shares and more institutional investors authorized to own its shares. Thus, comparing a larger firm's multiples to a small private company can be misleading.
- *Outliers.* It is quite common for a few companies in the comparison analysis to have unusually high or low multiples. It is also common for an acquirer to fixate on those businesses with the lowest multiples, while target companies do the reverse. Instead, throw out the high and low outliers and focus on the median multiples, which give the best general idea of valuation.
- *Price swings.* The stock price of a company may vary significantly over just a few days, so the specific date on which a multiples table is compiled can have a resounding impact on multiples. This difficulty can be mitigated by using the average stock price for the past month.
- *Thin trading.* A public company whose shares trade over-the-counter rather than on a stock exchange will likely be thinly traded, which means that even a few trades may significantly alter share prices, resulting in unusual multiples.

- *Transitory revenue.* Both the revenue and EBITDA multiples can be skewed if the target company has recorded transitory sales. These are typically larger, one-time sales that are not expected to recur. Examine the underlying details of a business and strip away these sales before applying any revenue or EBITDA multiples.
- *Underlying quality.* A major problem with using multiples to derive valuations is that you are assuming the business being valued is about the same as every other company included in the multiples analysis. If the business has much better fundamentals than other companies, such as a more recent product line, then it may be worth much more than the multipliers would indicate. Conversely, a poorly-run business with low-quality assets may not justify the valuation that a multiplier analysis would indicate for it.

The last point, regarding the underlying quality of a target company, underscores the main problem with multiples analysis. In short, this may seem to be an ideally quantitative type of analysis that yields a strong justification for a particular valuation, but in reality it only suggests what an average business may be worth, based on a cluster of other average businesses. A company with unusual business fundamentals could be worth substantially more or less than multiples analysis would indicate.

Discounted Cash Flows

One of the most detailed and justifiable ways to value a business is through the use of discounted cash flows (DCF). See the Discounted Cash Flows chapter for more information about DCF concepts. Under this approach, the acquirer constructs the expected cash flows of the target company, based on extrapolations of its historical cash flow and expectations for synergies that can be achieved by combining the two businesses. A discount rate is then applied to these cash flows to arrive at a current valuation for the business. The steps in the process are:

1. Create an estimate of the cash flows to be derived from the target company in each of the next five years, including any expected synergies.
2. After the five-year period, estimate a second set of cash flows that are assumed to continue in perpetuity at a certain rate of growth (or decline) per year. This is typically based on the cash flows in year five. We use this approach after year five, because it is impossible to estimate cash flows with much precision so far in the future.
3. Calculate the net present value of all future cash flows, using a discount rate. The result is the present value of the target company.

There can be a considerable amount of manipulation involved in adjusting the items to be included in a discounted cash flow analysis. The seller invariably wants to exclude selected expenses from the calculation, on the grounds that they were one-time events that the acquirer will not experience in the future. The seller will also identify a large number of expense exclusions that are based on presumed synergies.

The result, according to the seller, is likely to be startlingly high cash flow that the target would be unlikely to ever achieve in practice. It is the task of the acquirer to sort through these alleged expense reductions and verify which ones may actually be achieved.

The following example illustrates the compilation of cash flows for a target company, as well as their reduction to net present value using a discount rate.

EXAMPLE

The CFO of High Noon Armaments is constructing a discounted cash flow forecast for Sinclair Side Arms. The CFO begins with the cash flow for the preceding 12-month period, which was $5,800,000. The Sinclair management team claims that the following items should be added back to the cash flow figure:

- One-time charge of $200,000 related to lawsuit judgment
- One-time bonus payment of $120,000 made to the management team
- Elimination of $60,000 for CEO travel and entertainment expenses that would go away once the CEO is terminated
- Reduction of $400,000 in salary and payroll taxes related to the CEO, who will be terminated
- Reduction of $92,000 for a leased warehouse that the management team had not quite gotten around to terminating on its own

The CFO does not exclude the $200,000 lawsuit judgment, on the grounds that Sinclair has incurred a series of similar judgments from similar lawsuits in the past, and there is a significant possibility that it will continue to do so in the future. The CFO also does not exclude the $120,000 bonus payment, since further investigation reveals that this was a performance-based bonus, and there is an expectation in the industry for this type of bonus to be paid; further, the amount is not unreasonable. The CFO accepts the combined $460,000 expense reduction related to the CEO, since that expenditure will not be required in the future. Finally, the CFO elects not to exclude the $92,000 warehouse lease, on the grounds that there is no evidence yet that the company can operate without the additional warehouse space.

In addition, the CFO's due diligence team comes up with the following suggestions, which are added back to the cash flow report for valuation purposes:

- $200,000 for duplicated corporate staff who can be terminated
- $80,000 from volume purchasing discounts
- $320,000 from the consolidation of leases
- $38,000 from the elimination of duplicated software maintenance charges

The due diligence team also notes that Sinclair's fixed assets are very old, and will require $2,000,000 of expenditures in years two, three, and four to bring them up to standard.

Finally, the due diligence team prudently recommends that High Noon assume that Sinclair's cash flow will likely drop 5% in the year following the merger, as uncertainty causes some customers to switch to competitors. Cash flow growth thereafter should be 5% per year.

The CFO combines this information into the following table, in which he estimates the most likely cash flow scenario for the next five years. High Noon has a cost of capital of 9%, which is used to derive the discount rates noted in the table.

	Year 1	Year 2	Year 3	Year 4	Year 5
Beginning* cash flow	$5,800,000	$6,608,000	$6,938,000	$7,285,000	$7,649,000
Base level % change	-290,000	+330,000	+347,000	+364,000	+382,000
CEO expense reduction	+460,000				
Fixed asset replacements		-2,000,000	-2,000,000	-2,000,000	
Duplicate staff	+200,000				
Volume discounts	+80,000				
Lease consolidation	+320,000				
Software maintenance	+38,000				
Net cash flow	$6,608,000	$4,938,000	$5,285,000	$5,649,000	$8,031,000
Discount rate	0.9174	0.8417	0.7722	0.7084	0.6499
Present value of cash flows	$6,062,000	$4,156,000	$4,081,000	$4,002,000	$5,219,000
Present value grand total	$23,520,000				

* Considered to be the cash flow for the year, based on prior year results, not including fixed asset replacements

The CFO did not include any valuation for Sinclair after five years, citing the uncertainty of cash flow projections that far in the future.

In summary, the DCF model incorporates considerable detail about the cash flows of a target company and the synergies to be expected from it, though there is an increasing amount of uncertainty as cash flows go further into the future. The resulting model gives what is likely to be the most realistic view of the valuation of a business. However, it also incorporates many estimates regarding future events, so the model must be constructed carefully to yield results that can be attained in practice.

Replication Value

An acquirer can place a value on a target company based upon its estimate of the expenditures it would have to incur to build that business "from scratch." Doing so would involve building customer awareness of the brand through a lengthy series of advertising and other brand building campaigns, as well as building a competitive product through several iterative product cycles. It may also be necessary to obtain regulatory approvals, depending on the products involved. There is also the prospect of engaging in a price war in order to unseat the target company from its current market share position. Here is a summary of the more likely expenditures to include in the derivation of replication value:

- Product development
- Production design and investment in new production equipment
- Working capital to support new product line
- Startup scrap and spoilage costs
- Branding expenditures
- Expenditures to set up and support a new distribution channel
- Cost of additional sales force or retraining of existing sales force

Further, if the acquirer could have bought a target company at once to avoid the preceding replication expenses, also include in the replication value the present value of foregone profits that the company could have earned during the process of replicating the business of the target company. In short, it is usually a very expensive process to replicate a business.

EXAMPLE

A target company is resisting a $5 million buyout offer by High Noon Armaments, so High Noon examines the cost of replicating the product line that it wants to acquire. It estimates the following information:

	Cost Estimate	Time Estimate
Product development	$420,000	10 months
Production line redesign	100,000	2 months
Startup scrap costs	20,000	--
Branding expenditures	180,000	6 months
New distribution setup	110,000	4 months
	$830,000	22 months

The analysis shows that the replication value is less than $1 million. Also, High Noon estimates that the present value of the profits that it would forego in the next 22 months by *not* purchasing the company is $570,000. This leaves an incremental acquisition cost of $3.6 million associated with buying the company right now. Also, the replication process will require nearly two years.

High Noon needs to decide if it is worth offering more than the $3.6 million incremental cost of buying the company in order to be in the market with an active product line right now, rather than in two years.

The replication cost requires an additional analysis, which is how long the replication will take. If the acquirer wants to jump into a market in the near future, replication of a target company is a near impossibility, since doing so may require multiple years of effort. Thus, the analysis of replication cost and time may lead an acquirer to assign quite a high price to a target company. In many instances, this results in what may appear to be an inordinately high valuation for a target company that is not generating much cash flow.

The analysis of replication value is an interesting one, for it involves the collection of estimates from within the company about replication costs, rather than the more typical analysis of a target company. This does not mean that the resulting information is more accurate – on the contrary, the acquirer does not own the products and businesses under consideration, and so may arrive at quite inaccurate estimates of replication costs. For this reason, always consider replication cost to be a supplemental analysis method, and use a more detailed analysis, such as discounted cash flows, as the primary valuation technique.

Comparison Analysis

A common form of valuation analysis is to comb through listings of acquisition transactions that have been completed over the past year or two, extract those for companies located in the same industry, and use them to estimate what a target company should be worth. The comparison is usually based on either a multiple of revenues or cash flows. This is a very easy approach, since the information is available in a number of merger and acquisition databases. Any company that wants to be sold will engage the services of an investment banker who will use sales multiples to derive the value of the business. However, there are a number of problems with the sales multiple valuation method, including the following:

- *Link to profits.* A target company may generate sales by setting its prices extremely low. Doing so means that profits and cash flow will be low, if they exist at all. Thus, someone paying a multiple based on sales may find that it has acquired an essentially worthless business that will never generate a profit.
- *Comparison group.* The seller will attempt to match itself to whichever industry niche has generated the highest sales multiples. The acquirer must verify that the target company actually engages in the same line of business as those in the comparison group, and not a different group in another industry niche for which sales multiples are lower.
- *Fundamentals.* Another company may have obtained a high sales multiple, but for a very specific reason that was attractive to the acquirer, such as a key patent or distribution channel. If the target company does not have a similar feature that is worthwhile to the acquirer, there is no reason to apply the comparison sales multiple to the proposed transaction.
- *Outliers.* A target company may collect a group of unusually high sales multiples from other transactions and attempt to apply them to the proposed sale transaction. The acquirer should be wary of these selective comparable transactions, which may in fact be outliers in comparison to the normal sales multiples typically obtained in the industry.

In short, the sales multiple is more of a tool for the target company, not for the acquirer. It can distort the valuation of a business, since the comparison solely to sales does not account for any other factors, such as profitability or cash flow, with which an acquirer should be deeply concerned.

The Strategic Purchase

The ultimate valuation strategy from the perspective of the target company is the strategic purchase. This is when the acquirer is willing to throw out all valuation models and instead consider the strategic benefits of owning the target company. For example, an acquirer can be encouraged to believe that it needs to fill a critical hole in its product line, or to quickly enter a product niche that is considered key to its future survival, or to acquire a key piece of intellectual property. In this situation, the price paid may be far beyond the amount that any rational examination of the issues would otherwise suggest.

The downside of a strategic purchase is that the buyer is more likely to dismantle the target company and fully integrate the business into its own operations, on the grounds that the strategic value gained must be maximized by rolling it into the acquirer's organization to the greatest extent possible. Thus, this type of valuation certainly maximizes the return to shareholders, but sometimes at the cost of the complete elimination of the underlying business as a cohesive unit.

The Control Premium

When investors purchase stock in a business, they gain the right to dividends, any appreciation in the market price of the stock, and any final share in the proceeds if the business is sold. If an investor buys at least a 51% controlling interest in a business, then it also obtains the right to redirect the business in any way it chooses. Consequently, obtaining a controlling interest is worth an additional price, which is known as the control premium. This premium can be an insignificant issue if the target is on the verge of bankruptcy, since the presumably short-term nature of the business makes the control premium essentially irrelevant. However, if the target is a robust business that can be enhanced by the acquirer, then the control premium can be a significant factor. Historical evidence shows that control premiums for healthy businesses can range from 30% to 75% of the market price of a company's stock.

The Valuation Floor and Ceiling

We have presented a number of ways to create a valuation for a target company. The trouble is that if you were to use all of them, there would be an incredibly broad range of possible valuations from which to choose. There may be orders of magnitude between the valuation indicated by a liquidation analysis and the price an acquirer is willing to pay for a strategic purchase. How do you find your way amongst these numbers?

The key issue is that, eventually, most acquisitions must present positive cash flow to the acquirer, even if it takes some optimistic forecasts to arrive at positive cash flow projections. Consequently, the discounted cash flow model should be the key valuation methodology that every acquirer uses.

While you should always use a discounted cash flow analysis, this does not mean that it should be used to the exclusion of all other methodologies. In the following bullet points, we have clustered those valuation methods that tend to yield low, medium, and high valuations. You should select one valuation method from each of these clusters in order to establish a range of valuations. Doing so provides some leeway in regard to what the final price will be. Thus, you will be more comfortable using the valuation based on discounted cash flows, but will push for a price closer to liquidation value, and may accept a price closer to the amount indicated by a strategic purchase analysis. The valuations are:

Low valuation tendency

- *Liquidation value.* Tends to yield the lowest possible valuation. This is useful for establishing the amount the acquirer can sell the business for if an acquisition does not go as planned, rather than for establishing the price the acquirer will insist on paying.
- *Real estate value.* Tends to be close to liquidation value, and only applies to target companies with significant real estate holdings.
- *Relief-from-royalty method.* Is only used to measure the royalties avoided by owning an intangible asset.

Medium valuation tendency

- *Enterprise value.* States the current amount at which you could buy a business. It only applies to those businesses for which there is a ready market for its stock, and does not include a control premium. Thus, it tends to be one of the lower valuations.
- *Multiples analysis.* Is based on the valuations of other publicly-held businesses in the same industry, and so is similar to the enterprise measurement approach; and like that measurement, it does not include a control premium. Thus, it also tends to be one of the lower valuations.
- *Discounted cash flows.* Based on estimated future cash flows. If these cash flows are carefully reviewed and tested against historical results, this can yield excellent results. The results tend to be in the middle of the cluster of valuations.
- *Replication value.* Indicates the "go it alone" cost required to duplicate a business that an acquirer wants to buy. This can yield one of the higher valuations. Since it is largely based on estimates, it is not sufficient as the sole source of valuation information.
- *Comparison analysis.* Estimates the valuation based on the prices paid when similar businesses were sold in the recent past. This analysis includes the control premium, and so tends to yield a higher valuation.

High valuation tendency

- *Strategic purchase.* Based on other considerations than cash flow, and can yield a startlingly high price.

In summary, you might consider spending a modest amount of time establishing liquidation value, certainly calculate a detailed discounted cash flow, possibly also compile a comparison analysis, and then establish the high-end valuation by engaging in a strategic purchase review.

Payment Structures

In the preceding section, we talked about creating a valuation for a business. The valuation must now be translated into a form of payment to the owners of the target company. The structure of this deal has ramifications for both the buyer and seller in terms of risk, tax liabilities, liquidity, and other issues. In this section, we will address the various reasons both for and against the use of stock, debt, or cash in the structure of the deal. When reviewing these options, please note that a typical deal is not black-and-white, using only one form of payment. Instead, a deal that meets the needs of both the acquirer and the seller may need to incorporate elements of several types of payments.

The Stock-for-Stock Exchange

In a stock-for-stock exchange, the shareholders of the selling entity swap their shares for the shares of the acquirer. A stock-for-stock exchange is useful for the seller when its shareholders do not want to recognize taxable gains in the near term. Instead, they pay income taxes only when they sell the shares paid to them by the acquirer. They will pay taxes only on the difference between their cost basis in the stock of the acquiree and the price at which they sell the stock of the acquirer. However, this also means that shareholders will not have liquid investment positions in the short term.

In a stock-for-stock exchange, the seller shares with the acquirer the risk that the benefits of the acquisition are not realized. Thus, if the acquirer derives a purchase price based on the realization of synergy gains and those gains are not achieved, it is quite possible that the market will then force down the price of its shares. If the seller's shareholders now own some of those shares, the value of the payment to them will decline.

The seller should only accept shares as part of the payment structure under the following circumstances:

- *Registration rights.* Unless the shares were already registered with the Securities and Exchange Commission (SEC) through a shelf registration (which is the registration of a new issuance of securities with the SEC in advance of their distribution), the shareholders will have to either wait for them to be registered or wait for a mandatory holding period to expire under Rule 144, after which they can sell the shares. The SEC's Rule 144 allows the holder of stock to sell shares on the open market after an initial holding period has been completed, but only in small quantities over a relatively long period of time. Acquirers tend to resist pressure to register shares, since the process is both time-consuming and expensive. The inclusion of registration rights is *the* issue in a stock-for-stock exchange, since the stock recipient otherwise has no way to sell the shares.

- *Registration timing.* The acquirer must guarantee that shares will be registered within a certain period of time. Otherwise, the seller is holding shares that may decline in value over time. The deal structure may include a penalty clause, such as issuing more shares to the seller if the registration is not completed within a certain number of months following the purchase.

In addition, the seller must examine the market for the acquirer's shares to see if there is sufficient trading volume for the seller's shareholders to sell off their shares within a reasonably short time period, and without driving down the price of the stock. This is a serious issue if the acquirer is a smaller public company, and especially if its stock is not traded on a major stock exchange.

Another issue for the seller to consider is the trading history of the stock. If the acquirer has been publicly-held for a long time, its stock trades on an exchange, and it has a well-run investor relations department, then its stock probably trades consistently within a relatively narrow price range. This is the ideal situation in which to accept a stock-for-stock exchange, since the shares received are more likely to retain their value.

If a privately-held acquirer proposes a stock-for-stock exchange with no prospect of registration rights, then the ability of the seller's shareholders to eventually convert the stock to cash is exceedingly tenuous. In these cases, the seller should seriously question the proposed deal, if not reject it outright. If the seller decides to proceed with the deal, it should at least impose a sharp discount on the value of the acquirer's stock in comparison to what it would have accepted in cash.

The issuance of stock could present a control problem for the managers of the acquirer. When a significant proportion of company shares are issued to pay for an acquiree, the newly-minted shareholders may be in a position to vote for their own members of the board of directors, or to pressure the board to take actions that it would not usually consider, such as issuing dividends. The situation could be particularly serious if the company's bylaws require that a supermajority approve certain measures, such as the sale of the company, and the new shareholders have enough shares to swing this vote. Consequently, the existence of a potential shareholder control situation could mean that payment in stock is not an option.

The Exchange Ratio

A stock-for-stock exchange is accomplished through the derivation of an *exchange ratio*. The exchange ratio is the number of shares of the acquirer that it is offering to exchange for each share of the seller. This calculation is based on the market price of the shares of the acquirer and the price offered for the seller.

EXAMPLE

The shares of High Noon Armaments are currently trading at $14 per share. It is contemplating the acquisition of Bolton Body Armor for $4,000,000. Bolton has 500,000 shares of common stock outstanding, so each share is valued at $8 per share.

Based on this information, High Noon offers an exchange ratio of 0.57143 shares of High Noon stock for each share of Bolton stock. The exchange ratio calculation is:

$8 Bolton share price ÷ $14 High Noon share price = 0.57143 exchange ratio

Thus, the Bolton shareholders receive a total of 285,715 shares of High Noon stock. At the current trading price of $14 per share, the High Noon shares issued to the Bolton shareholders are worth $4,000,000.

The derivation of the exchange ratio can be quite a contentious one when the shares of the acquirer are not publicly traded. If so, there is no market to independently value the shares, resulting in a value that is largely based on opinion.

Issues Impacting the Stock Payment Decision

An acquirer is more inclined to offer stock-for-stock deals when it believes its stock price is unusually high. During these times, it can offer fewer shares to pay for an acquisition. Conversely, if it feels that the market is assigning it an unusually low share price, it will be less inclined to pay with stock, for it must issue more shares. The seller is placed in the reverse situation if it believes the acquirer's stock to be selling at too high a level, since there is a higher risk that the share price will subsequently decline, and along with it the effective price paid to the seller.

EXAMPLE

The market is currently assigning a high $20 share price to the stock of High Noon Armaments, well above its usual $12 trading price. Within the past year, its stock has traded as low as $10 per share. High Noon is contemplating the purchase of a competitor for $8,000,000. If it were to pay with stock, it would only issue 400,000 shares at the current stock price. The number of shares would usually be 666,667 shares at the normal trading price, or 800,000 at the lowest trading price.

If the acquirer believes that it has obtained a good (i.e., low) price for an acquisition, it will be less inclined to pay with its own stock. If it were to do so, the price of the stock should increase, and the shareholders of the seller would share in that increase. In such a situation, the acquirer should be more interested in buying for cash; doing so means that all share price increases will accrue to the benefit of existing shareholders.

EXAMPLE

High Noon Armaments makes a low-ball offer for Black Powder Weaponry, which is currently having cash flow problems. The price is $6,000,000, and High Noon believes that the actual value of Black Powder is closer to $10,000,000. High Noon currently has 2,000,000 shares of common stock outstanding, at a market price of $12 per share, which gives the company a total market valuation of $24,000,000. High Noon could pay with 500,000 shares of its stock (calculated as $6,000,000 price ÷ $12 per share). However, High Noon must consider the impact on its current shareholders if the market later increases the price of its stock to reflect the full value of the Black Powder deal. The impact is noted in the following table:

Deal Structure	Stock Price Calculation
Pay in cash	($24,000,000 Current valuation + $10,000,000 Incremental valuation - $6,000,000 Cash) ÷ 2,000,000 Shares = $14.00/Share
Pay in stock	($24,000,000 Current valuation + $10,000,000 Incremental valuation) ÷ (2,000,000 Existing shares + 500,000 New shares) = $13.60/Share

Thus, paying with stock for the Black Powder acquisition reduces the eventual price per share that the original High Noon shareholders would realize by $0.40.

If the seller drives an extremely hard bargain, where there is little room for the acquirer to earn a profit from the transaction, the acquirer should be more inclined to offer stock as part of the deal structure. By doing so, the seller's shareholders take on some of the risk that the value of the shares with which they are paid will decline in value.

Stock Payment Based on Fixed Share Count or Fixed Price

There are two ways in which a stock-for-stock deal can be structured. They are:

- *Fixed share count.* Under this method, the exact number of shares to be paid is incorporated into the purchase agreement. This introduces some risk to the seller, in that the market value of the acquirer's shares could change in the days leading up to the purchase date. However, it also gives the seller a fixed percentage of ownership in the acquirer, irrespective of changes in the stock price.
- *Fixed price.* Under this method, the total price to be paid is incorporated into the purchase agreement. The actual payment is based on the market price of the acquirer's stock on the effective date of the agreement. This method reduces the risk to the seller that the value of the underlying shares will decline in the days leading up to the acquisition.

The problem with stock price variability and its impact on the purchase price is sometimes resolved through the use of a collar agreement. A collar agreement is a clause within a stock-for-stock purchase transaction, where the number of shares paid to the shareholders of the seller will be adjusted if the market price of the acquirer's shares trade above or below certain predetermined levels, which are usually 10-20% above and below the midpoint stock price. The agreement may also allow either party to terminate the acquisition arrangement if stock prices fluctuate beyond specific price points.

There are several variations on the collar concept. In a *fixed-price collar*, the price is fixed within the collar boundaries. For example, the price might be set at $10.00 per share, within a share price range of $9.00 to $11.00. In this case, the width of the collar is $2.00. If the price of the acquirer's stock moves outside of the collar, then the price is based on an exchange ratio. In this situation, the seller benefits from gaining more shares if the acquirer's stock price falls below the lower collar, while the acquirer benefits from issuing fewer shares if its share price increases above the higher collar. Thus, the price is fixed within the collar and variable outside of the collar. The fixed-price collar works well when the seller wants to be sure of obtaining a specific valuation amount.

In a *fixed-exchange collar*, the exchange ratio is locked between the collar boundaries. This means that the acquirer is setting a fixed number of shares that will be paid within the boundaries of the collar. Outside of the upper and lower boundaries of the collar, the price is fixed. In this situation, the acquirer keeps from having to issue more of its own shares if its share price plummets below the lower collar, while the seller benefits from an increase in the share price of the acquirer above the upper collar. Thus, the price is variable within the collar and fixed outside of the collar. The fixed-exchange collar works well when:

- The acquirer wants to preserve for itself any upside potential in its stock price
- The seller wants to establish a floor on the value of the consideration it receives

The collar agreement is particularly important in two situations:

- *Volatility.* Stock prices in some industries are unusually volatile, making it difficult to pin down a price to use for the exchange ratio.
- *Time to close.* If regulatory approval is required, it will lengthen the time required to close the purchase transaction. This means there is some risk that the acquirer's share price will gradually drift away from the amount at which the exchange ratio was first calculated. For these longer closing transactions, it is customary to adopt fairly wide collars.

In short, the collar agreement is useful for preserving the value of the compensation that the seller receives, at least for the time period covered by the collar agreement.

The Debt Payment

The acquirer may include debt in the structure of its deal to buy the acquiree. This can be beneficial to the seller's shareholders, since they do not pay income taxes until they receive the debt payments.

The seller should not accept this form of payment unless it is very certain of the financial condition of the acquirer. Otherwise, if the acquirer were to enter bankruptcy, the seller's shareholders would simply be categorized among other creditors to be paid out of any remaining assets. The seller can mitigate this risk to some extent by placing the holders of the debt in the most senior position of all debt holders. However, most companies already have assigned senior debt positions to other lenders, so the shareholders are instead placed in a junior debt position. The seller could place a lien on the assets of the acquiree, but the seller will have no control over those assets once the purchase agreement is finalized; this means that the acquirer could sell off the assets and use the proceeds, or simply let the equipment run down over time without proper maintenance, leaving little for the seller's shareholders to recover.

Even if the seller is certain of the financial condition of the acquirer, accepting debt means that the shareholders will have no access to cash until the debt payments begin. This can be a problem if the shareholders previously received dividends or other distributions from the target company, and are no longer receiving that cash flow. Also, now that they are debt holders, rather than shareholders, they have no ability to vote for a new board of directors, and so have no control over the business that owes them money.

Payment in debt also means that the acquirer is in a position to profit from 100% of any stock appreciation caused by the acquisition, while the seller is locked into a fixed payment plan.

The acquirer is more likely to offer debt, if only because it can then conserve its cash. The use of debt may be the only alternative when it is difficult for the acquirer to obtain credit from lenders. It is an especially useful tool when the acquirer can force the seller to accept a junior debt position behind its other lenders, thereby effectively placing the seller's shareholders in a position not much better than that of its general creditors.

In short, despite the favorable tax impact of debt payments, this is the worst alternative for the seller. On the flip side of the deal, it is usually the best alternative for the seller. Thus, the two sides are quite likely to dicker over the presence of debt in a deal, the terms associated with the debt, and its convertibility into the acquirer's stock.

The Cash Payment

The form of payment generally preferred by shareholders is cash. It is particularly appreciated by shareholders who are unable to sell their stock by other means, which is the case for most privately-held companies. In addition, they no longer have to worry about the future performance of their company impacting the amount that they will be paid. The degree to which cash is preferred is indicated by the extent to which sellers are generally willing to accept a smaller amount of cash rather than a larger payment in stock or debt. However, a cash payment also means that the selling shareholders must pay income taxes on any gains immediately.

From the perspective of the acquirer, a cash payment presents both pluses and minuses. One advantage is that, in a competitive bidding situation, the bid of the buyer willing to pay cash is more likely to be accepted by the seller. Also, not paying in stock means that any future upside performance generated by the acquisition accrues solely to the existing shareholders of the acquirer – the shareholders of the acquiree are taking cash instead, so they are blocked from the gains.

The main disadvantage of paying with cash is the availability of cash to the acquirer. If the purchase will use up the bulk of its cash on hand, and the borrowing environment is difficult, the acquirer could place itself in a tenuous financial position. However, using cash places greater financial discipline on an acquirer, who may therefore be more prudent in setting an offer price than a company that is willing to pay with vast amounts of stock.

A possible point of contention is the tax effect of a cash payment. The seller's shareholders must immediately pay income taxes on any gain resulting from a cash transaction, so they may want additional compensation to pay for the taxes. The acquirer typically resists this pressure, on the grounds that cash is a scarce commodity, and that the taxation status of the individual shareholders of the seller is not under the control of the acquirer.

Practical Considerations

Much of the preceding discussion has addressed a number of theoretical considerations of the benefits of various types of deal structures. In reality, the type of payment will be driven by that entity having the most power in an arrangement. Here are several scenarios to consider:

- *Bankruptcy*. The acquirer may be required by the bankruptcy court to pay in cash, and would be more likely to do so in any event, since it is likely buying at a low price and wants the residual value to accrue to its shareholders.
- *Controlling acquirer shareholder*. If there is a controlling shareholder of the acquirer, that individual or business may want to avoid having its share holdings watered down by the issuance of stock to a seller.
- *Controlling seller shareholder*. Whoever owns the controlling interest in the seller can dictate the terms of the deal structure, as long as there are multiple bidders.
- *Hostile bid*. If an acquirer is making an unwelcome bid, it will likely need to offer cash in order to win over the shareholders of the target company.
- *Management ownership of seller*. If the managers of the seller own a large part of its shares, they are more likely to demand a stock-for-stock deal, on the grounds that they will then become large shareholders of the acquirer, and so may be able to influence their continuing employment by the acquirer.

- *Multiple bidders.* In a multi-bidder environment, the bid with the largest proportion of cash usually wins.
- *Sole bidder.* If the seller is motivated to sell and there is only one bidder, then the bidder can adopt a take-it-or-leave-it attitude and impose a range of possible deal structures.

Thus, the key determinant of the deal structure can swing between the acquirer and the seller, depending on the circumstances.

Summary

Of the valuation methods described in this chapter, the most quantitatively precise one is the discounted cash flows method. However, even that method is derived from a number of estimates of future results, as well as estimates of expenses that can be eliminated due to synergies. In short, even the DCF method can yield results that turn out to vary widely from subsequent actual results.

Valuation depends to a great extent upon the timing of the situation. If the target company finds itself in a difficult financial situation and there are few potential bidders, then an acquirer may be able to snap it up for an amount at the far lower end of what would normally be considered reasonable. Conversely, a business that is carefully built to provide a strategic advantage in a new market, and for which multiple bidders see a strong strategic advantage, may sell at a price well beyond the price created by most rational valuation calculations.

When negotiating a deal structure, the two parties must take into account their respective financial positions, expectations for future gains, and tax requirements. The following table shows the respective issues of both parties.

Deal Structure Considerations

Deal Structure	Acquirer	Acquiree
Stock	• Shares future stock gains • Preserves cash • May dilute earnings per share	• No immediate liquidity • Defers income taxes
Debt	• Takes all future stock gains • Preserves cash • Accepts liens on some assets • Does not dilute earnings per share	• No share of future stock gains • At risk of non-payment • Defers income taxes
Cash	• Takes all future stock gains • More likely to win in bidding war • At risk of not having sufficient cash • Requires more discipline • Does not dilute earnings per share	• Gains liquidity • No share of future stock gains • Immediate tax liability

However, if there is only one possible buyer, and that buyer is having trouble obtaining financing for the deal, then all of the various permutations just noted do not factor into the deal structure. Instead, the acquirer simply assembles the only available funding package and presents it to the seller for approval; there is no negotiation of structure, for the seller cannot negotiate. Instead, the seller is faced with a binary solution – to either accept or reject the deal as offered.

Chapter 16
Foreign Exchange Risk Management

Introduction

A business may engage in transactions with customers and suppliers located in other countries. If so, the company will likely need to either pay out or accept foreign exchange as part of these transactions. When there is a delay in the payment or receipt dates of these transactions, the organization is subject to some risk of loss if the exchange rate were to shift during the delay period. In this chapter, we describe the different types of foreign exchange risk, as well as the tools for mitigating this risk.

Foreign Exchange Risk Overview

When a business enters into transactions that involve foreign currencies, there is a risk that changes in the exchange rate can cause significant losses for the business. In this section, we describe the types of foreign exchange risks to which an organization can be subjected.

A company may incur *transaction exposure*, which is derived from changes in foreign exchange rates between the dates when a transaction is booked and when it is settled. For example, a company in the United States may sell goods to a company in the United Kingdom, to be paid in pounds having a value at the booking date of $100,000. Later, when the customer pays the company, the exchange rate has changed, resulting in a payment in pounds that translates to a $95,000 sale. Thus, the foreign exchange rate change related to a transaction has created a $5,000 loss for the seller. The following table shows the impact of transaction exposure on different scenarios.

Risk When Transactions Denominated in Foreign Currency

	Import Goods	Export Goods
Home currency weakens	Loss	Gain
Home currency strengthens	Gain	Loss

When a company has foreign subsidiaries, it denominates the recorded amount of their assets and liabilities in the currency of the country in which the subsidiaries generate and expend cash. This *functional currency* is typically the local currency of the country in which a subsidiary operates. When the company reports its consolidated results, it converts these valuations to the home currency of the parent company, which may suffer a loss if exchange rates have declined from the last time when the financial statements were consolidated. This type of risk is known as *translation exposure*.

EXAMPLE

Hammer Industries has a subsidiary located in England, which has its net assets denominated in pounds. The home currency of Hammer is U.S. dollars. At year-end, when the parent company consolidates the financial statements of its subsidiaries, the U.S. dollar has depreciated in comparison to the pound, resulting in a decline in the value of the subsidiary's net assets.

The following table shows the impact of translation exposure on different scenarios.

Risk When Net Assets Denominated in Foreign Currency

	Assets	Liabilities
Home currency weakens	Gain	Loss
Home currency strengthens	Loss	Gain

There are also several types of economic risk related to the specific country within which a company chooses to do business. These risks include:

- *Political risk* is based on the actions of a foreign government that can impact a company, such as the expropriation of assets. Political risk can also encompass the violence that may accompany a change in government. There can be a significant risk of expropriation when a company has a large asset base within a country.
- *Convertibility risk* is the inability to convert a local currency into a foreign currency, because of a shortage of hard currencies. This tends to be a short-term problem.
- *Transfer risk* is the inability to transfer funds across a national border, due to local-country regulatory restrictions on the movement of hard currencies out of the country. Thus, a company may find that a local subsidiary is extremely profitable, but the parent company cannot extract the profits from the country.

Country-specific risks call for strategic-level decisions in the executive suite, not in the accounting or treasury departments. The senior management team must decide if it is willing to accept the risks of expropriation or of not being able to extract cash from a country. If not, the risk is eliminated by refusing to do business within the country.

Please note that the *type* of risk has an impact on the time period over which a company is at risk. For example, transactional risk spans a relatively short period, from the signing date of the contract that initiates a sale, until the final payment date. The total interval may be only one or two months. However, translation risk and the various types of economic risks can extend over many years. There tends to be an inordinate focus in many companies on the short-term transactional risk, when more emphasis should be placed on hedging against these other risks that can result in substantial losses over the long term.

Foreign Exchange Risk Management

As noted in the last section, a company is at risk of incurring a loss due to fluctuations in any exchange rates that it must buy or sell as part of its business transactions. What can be done? Valid steps can range from no action at all to the active use of several types of hedges. In this section, we address the multitude of options available to mitigate foreign exchange-related risks. When perusing these options, keep in mind that the most sophisticated response is not necessarily the best response. In many cases, the circumstances may make it quite acceptable to take on some degree of risk, rather than engaging in a hedging strategy that is not only expensive, but also difficult to understand.

Take No Action

There are many situations where a company rarely engages in transactions that involve foreign exchange, and so does not want to spend time investigating how to reduce risk. There are other situations where the amounts of foreign exchange involved are so small that the risk level is immaterial. In either case, a company will be tempted to take no action, which may be a reasonable course of action. The question to consider is, at what level of foreign exchange activity should a business begin to consider risk management alternatives?

The question cannot be answered without having an understanding of a company's *risk capacity*. Risk capacity is the maximum amount of a loss that a business can sustain before a financial crisis is triggered. The following are examples of maximum losses:

- A loss that would require the tapping of all remaining borrowing capacity
- A loss that would breach one or more debt covenants
- A loss that would reduce capital levels below those mandated by regulatory authorities

The preceding examples provide hard quantitative numbers for a firm's total risk capacity, all of which threaten the company's existence. This does not mean that management should routinely expose a business to threat levels that could destroy it. Instead, it is necessary to arrive at a much less quantitative number, which is the maximum risk tolerance that management is willing to operate under on an ongoing basis before it will take steps to reduce risk. The risk tolerance figure is likely to be far lower than total risk capacity – perhaps just 5% or 10% of a firm's risk capacity. The exact amount of risk tolerance will depend upon the willingness of managers to accept risk. A more entrepreneurially inclined group may be willing to bet the company on risky situations, while professional managers will probably begin managing risk at lower tolerance levels.

Avoid Risk

A company can avoid some types of risk by altering its strategy to completely sidestep the risk. Complete avoidance of a specific product, geographic region, or business line is an entirely reasonable alternative under the following circumstances:

- The potential loss from a risk condition is very high
- The probability of loss from a risk condition is very high
- It is difficult to develop a hedge against a risk
- The offsetting potential for profit does not offset the risk that will be incurred

For example, a company located in the United States buys the bulk of its supplies in China, and is required under its purchasing contracts to pay suppliers in yuan. If the company does not want to undertake the risk of exchange rate fluctuations in the yuan, it can consider altering its supply chain, so that it purchases within its home country, rather than in China. This alignment of sales and purchases within the same country to avoid foreign currency transactions is known as an *operational hedge*.

As another example, a company wants to sell products into a market where the government has just imposed severe restrictions on the cross-border transfer of funds out of the country. The government also has a history of nationalizing industries that had been privately-owned. Under these circumstances, it makes little sense for the company to sell into the new market if it cannot extract its profits, and if its assets in the country are subject to expropriation.

Shift Risk

When a company is either required to pay or receive payment in a foreign currency, it is taking on the risk associated with changes in the foreign currency exchange rate. This risk can be completely eliminated by requiring customers to pay in the company's home currency, or suppliers to accept payment in the company's home currency. This is a valid option when the company is a large one that can force this system of payment onto its suppliers, or when it sells a unique product that forces customers to accept the company's terms.

> **Tip:** Never give customers a choice of currency in which to pay the company, since they will likely pay with their home currency, leaving the company to bear the risk of exchange rate changes.

Another possibility is to charge business partners for any changes in the exchange rate between the date of order placement and the shipment date. This is an extremely difficult business practice to enforce, for the following reasons:

- *Continual rebillings.* There will always be some degree of variation in exchange rates between the order date and shipment date, so it is probable that a company would have to issue an invoice related to exchange rate adjustments for every order, or at least include a line item for the change in every invoice.
- *Two-way rebillings.* If a company is going to insist on billing for its exchange rate losses, it is only fair that it pay back its business partners when exchange rates shift in its favor.
- *Purchase order limitations.* Customers routinely place orders using a purchase order than only authorizes a certain spending level. If the company later issues an incremental billing that exceeds the total amount authorized for a purchase, the customer will probably not pay the company.

To mitigate these issues, billing a business partner for a change in exchange rates should only be enacted if the change is sufficiently large to breach a contractually-agreed minimum level. The minimum level should be set so that this additional billing is a rare event.

Example: An outsourcing company enters into long-term services contracts with its customers, and so is at considerable foreign exchange risk. It offers customers a fixed price contract within a 5% currency trading band, outside of which customers share the risk with the company. If the company gains from a currency shift outside of the trading band, it discounts the contract price.

The conditions under which currency risk can be shifted elsewhere are not common ones. Most companies will find that if they insist on only dealing in their home currencies, such behavior will either annoy suppliers or drive away customers. Thus, we will continue with other risk management actions that will be more palatable to a company's business partners.

Time Compression

Large variations in exchange rates are more likely to occur over longer periods of time than over shorter periods of time. Thus, it may be possible to reduce the risk of exchange rate fluctuations by reducing the contractually-mandated payment period. For example, 30 day payment terms could be compressed to 10 or 15 days. However, delays in shipping, customs inspections, and resistance from business partners can make it difficult to achieve a compressed payment schedule. Also, a customer being asked to accept a shorter payment schedule may attempt to push back with lower prices or other benefits, which increases the cost of this option.

The time compression concept can take the form of a company policy that does not allow standard credit terms to foreign customers that exceed a certain number of days. By doing so, a company can at least minimize the number of days during which exchange rates can fluctuate.

Payment Leading and Lagging

If there is a pronounced trend in exchange rates over the short term, the accounts payable manager can be encouraged to alter the timing normally associated with payables payments to take advantage of expected changes in exchange rates. For example, if a foreign currency is becoming more expensive, it may make sense to pay those payables denominated in it as soon as possible, rather than waiting until the normal payment date to pay in a more expensive currency. Similarly, if a foreign currency is declining in value, there may be an opportunity to delay payments by a few days to take advantage of the ongoing decline in the exchange rate. The latter case may be too much trouble, since suppliers do not appreciate late payments.

Build Reserves

If company management believes that there is just as great a risk of a gain as a loss on a currency fluctuation, it may be willing to accept the downside risk in hopes of attaining an upside profit. If so, it is possible to build cash and debt reserves greater than what would normally be needed, against the possibility of an outsized loss. This may entail investing a large amount of cash in very liquid investments, or retaining extra cash that might otherwise be paid out in dividends or used for capital expenditures. Other options are to obtain an unusually large line of credit that can be called upon in the event of a loss, or selling more stock than would typically be needed for operational purposes.

Building reserves will protect a business from foreign exchange risk, but the cost of acquiring and maintaining those reserves is substantial. Cash that is kept on hand could have earned an investment, while a commitment fee must be paid for a line of credit, even if the line is never used. Similarly, investors who buy a company's stock expect to earn a return. Thus, there is a noticeable cost associated with building reserves. A less expensive option is hedging, which we will address in the next section.

Maintain Local Reserves

If the company is routinely engaging in the purchase and sale of goods and services within another country, the answer may be to maintain a cash reserve within that country, which is denominated in the local currency. Doing so eliminates the cost of repeatedly buying and selling currencies and paying the related conversion commissions. The downside of maintaining local reserves is that a company is still subject to translation risk, where it must periodically translate its local cash reserves into its home currency for financial reporting purposes – which carries with it the risk of recording a translation loss.

Hedging

When all operational and strategic alternatives have been exhausted, it is time to consider buying hedging instruments that offset the risk posed by specific foreign exchange positions. Hedging is accomplished by purchasing an offsetting currency exposure. For example, if a company has a liability to deliver 1 million euros in six months, it can hedge this risk by entering into a contract to purchase 1 million euros on the same date, so that it can buy and sell in the same currency on the same date. The ideal outcome of a hedge is when the distribution of probable outcomes is reduced, so that the size of any potential loss is reduced. The following exhibit shows the effect of hedging on the range of possible outcomes.

Impact of Hedging on Risk Outcome

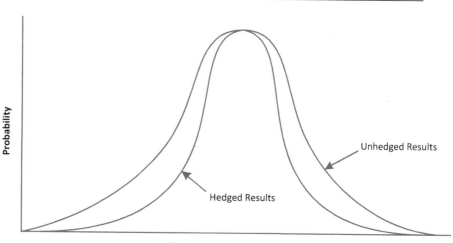

When a company has a multi-year contract with a customer, it may be necessary to create a long-term hedge to offset the related risk of currency fluctuations. If the customer subsequently terminates the contract early, the company may have to incur a significant cost to unwind the related hedge before its planned termination date. If this scenario appears possible, or if a business has experienced such events in the past, it may make sense to include in the contract a clause stating that the customer bears the cost of unwinding the hedge if there is an early contract termination.

> **Tip:** When entering into a long-term contract for which a hedge is anticipated, be sure to estimate the cost of the hedge in advance, and include it in the formulation of the price quoted to the customer.

Various types of hedges are described in the next section.

Summary

Clearly, there are many risk management alternatives available to a company that must deal with foreign exchange situations. We recommend avoiding active hedging strategies as long as possible, in favor of more passive methods that are easier to understand, implement, and monitor. If the risk situation is too extreme to be completely addressed by passive means, then an active hedging strategy is probably the answer. In the next section, we address several types of active hedging activities.

Types of Foreign Exchange Hedges

This section describes a number of methods for hedging foreign currency transactions. The first type of hedge, which is a loan denominated in a foreign currency, is designed to offset translation risk. The remaining hedges target the transaction risk related to the currency fluctuations associated with either specific or aggregated business transactions.

Loan Denominated in a Foreign Currency

When a company is at risk of recording a loss from the translation of assets and liabilities into its home currency, it can hedge the risk by obtaining a loan denominated in the functional currency in which the assets and liabilities are recorded. The effect of this hedge is to neutralize any loss on translation of the subsidiary's net assets with a gain on translation of the loan, or vice versa.

EXAMPLE

Hammer Industries has a subsidiary located in London, and which does business entirely within England. Accordingly, the subsidiary's net assets are denominated in pounds. The net assets of the subsidiary are currently recorded at £10 million. To hedge the translation risk associated with these assets, Hammer acquires a £10 million loan from a bank in London.

One month later, a change in the dollar/pound exchange rate results in a translation loss of $15,000 on the translation of the subsidiary's net assets into U.S. dollars. This amount is exactly offset by the translation gain of $15,000 on the liability associated with the £10 million loan.

> **Tip:** An ideal way to create an offsetting loan is to fund the purchase or expansion of a foreign subsidiary largely through the proceeds of a long-term loan obtained within the same country, so that the subsidiary's assets are approximately cancelled out by the amount of the loan.

There are two problems with this type of hedge. First, it can be difficult to obtain a loan in the country in which the net assets are located. Second, the company will incur an interest expense on a loan that it would otherwise not need, though the borrowed funds could be invested to offset the interest expense.

The Forward Contract

A forward contract is an agreement under which a business agrees to buy a certain amount of foreign currency on a specific future date, and at a predetermined exchange rate. Forward exchange rates can be obtained for twelve months into the future; quotes for major currency pairs can be obtained for as much as five to ten years in the future.

The exchange rate is comprised of the following elements:

- The spot price of the currency
- The bank's transaction fee
- An adjustment (up or down) for the interest rate differential between the two currencies. In essence, the currency of the country having a lower interest rate will trade at a premium, while the currency of the country having a higher interest rate will trade at a discount. For example, if the domestic interest rate is lower than the rate in the other country, the bank acting as the counterparty adds points to the spot rate, which increases the cost of the foreign currency in the forward contract.

The calculation of the number of discount or premium points to subtract from or add to a forward contract is based on the following formula:

$$\text{Exchange rate} \quad \times \quad \text{Interest rate differential} \quad \times \quad \frac{\text{Days in contract}}{360} \quad = \quad \text{Premium or discount}$$

Thus, if the spot price of pounds per dollar were 1.5459 and there were a premium of 15 points for a forward contract with a 360-day maturity, the forward rate (not including a transaction fee) would be 1.5474.

By entering into a forward contract, a company can ensure that a definite future liability can be settled at a specific exchange rate. Forward contracts are typically customized, and arranged between a company and its bank. The bank will require a partial payment to initiate a forward contract, as well as final payment shortly before the settlement date.

EXAMPLE

Hammer Industries has acquired equipment from a company in the United Kingdom, which Hammer must pay for in 60 days in the amount of £150,000. To hedge against the risk of an unfavorable change in exchange rates during the intervening 60 days, Hammer enters into a forward contract with its bank to buy £150,000 in 60 days, at the current exchange rate.

60 days later, the exchange rate has indeed taken a turn for the worse, but Hammer's CFO is indifferent, since he obtains the £150,000 needed for the purchase transaction based on the exchange rate in existence when the contract with the supplier was originally signed.

A forward contract is designed to have a specific settlement date, but the business transaction to which it relates may not be so timely. For example, a business has a contract to sell £10,000 in 60 days, but may not be able to do so if it has not yet received funds from a customer. A *forward window contract* is designed to work around this variability in the timing of receipts from customers by incorporating a range of settlement dates. You can then wait for a cash receipt and trigger settlement of the forward contract immediately thereafter.

The primary difficulties with forward contracts relate to their being customized transactions that are designed specifically for two parties. Because of this level of customization, it is difficult for either party to offload the contract to a third party. Also, the level of customization makes it difficult to compare offerings from different banks, so there is a tendency for banks to build unusually large fees into these contracts. Finally, a company may find that the underlying transaction for which a forward contract was created has been cancelled, leaving the contract still to be settled. If so, one can enter into a second forward contract, whose net effect is to offset the first forward contract. Though the bank will charge fees for both contracts, this arrangement will settle the company's obligations.

The Futures Contract

A futures contract is similar in concept to a forward contract, in that a business can enter into a contract to buy or sell currency at a specific price on a future date. The difference is that futures contracts are traded on an exchange, so these contracts are for standard amounts and durations. An initial deposit into a margin account is required to initiate a futures contract. The contract is then repriced each day, and if cumulative losses drain the margin account, a company is required to add more funds to the margin account. If the company does not respond to a margin call, the exchange closes out the contract.

Given that futures contracts are standardized, they may not exactly match the timing and amounts of an underlying transaction that is being hedged, which can lead to over- or under-hedging. However, since these contracts are traded on an exchange, it is easier to trade them than forward contracts, which allows you to easily unwind a hedge position earlier than its normal settlement date.

In a forward contract, the bank includes a transaction fee in the contract. In a futures contract, a broker charges a commission to execute the deal.

The Currency Option

An option gives its owner the right, but not the obligation, to buy or sell an asset at a certain price (known as the *strike price*), either on or before a specific date. In exchange for this right, the buyer pays an up-front premium to the seller. The income earned by the seller is restricted to the premium payment received, while the buyer has a theoretically unlimited profit potential, depending upon the future direction of the relevant exchange rate.

Currency options are available for the purchase or sale of currencies within a certain future date range, with the following variations available for the option contract:

- *American option.* The option can be exercised on any date within the option period, so that delivery is two business days after the exercise date.

213

- *European option.* The option can only be exercised on the expiry date, which means that delivery will be two business days after the expiry date.
- *Burmudan option.* The option can only be exercised on certain predetermined dates.

The holder of an option will exercise it when the strike price is more favorable than the current market rate, which is called being *in-the-money*. If the strike price is less favorable than the current market rate, this is called being *out-of-the-money*, in which case the option holder will not exercise the option. If the option holder is inattentive, it is possible that an in-the-money option will not be exercised prior to its expiry date. Notice of option exercise must be given to the counterparty by the notification date stated in the option contract.

A currency option provides two key benefits:

- *Loss prevention.* An option can be exercised to hedge the risk of loss, while still leaving open the possibility of benefiting from a favorable change in exchange rates.
- *Date variability.* An option can be exercised within a predetermined date range, which is useful when there is uncertainty about the exact timing of the underlying exposure.

There are a number of factors that enter into the price of a currency option, which can make it difficult to ascertain whether a quoted option price is reasonable. These factors are:

- The difference between the designated strike price and the current spot price. The buyer of an option can choose a strike price that suits his specific circumstances. A strike price that is well away from the current spot price will cost less, since the likelihood of exercising the option is low. However, setting such a strike price means that the buyer is willing to absorb the loss associated with a significant change in the exchange rate before seeking cover behind an option.
- The current interest rates for the two currencies during the option period.
- The duration of the option.
- Volatility of the market. This is the expected amount by which the currency is expected to fluctuate during the option period, with higher volatility making it more likely that an option will be exercised. Volatility is a guesstimate, since there is no quantifiable way to predict it.
- The willingness of counterparties to issue options.

Banks generally allow an option exercise period of no more than three months. Multiple partial currency deliveries within a currency option can be arranged.

Exchange traded options for standard quantities are available. This type of option eliminates the risk of counterparty failure, since the clearing house operating the exchange guarantees the performance of all options traded on the exchange.

EXAMPLE

Hammer Industries has an obligation to buy £250,000 in three months. Currently, the forward rate for the British pound is 1.5000 U.S. dollars, so that it should require $375,000 to buy the £250,000 in 90 days. If the pound depreciates, Hammer will be able to buy pounds for less than the $375,000 that it currently anticipates spending, but if the pound appreciates, Hammer will have to spend more to acquire the £250,000.

Hammer's CFO elects to buy an option, so that he can hedge against the appreciation of the pound, while leaving open the prospect of profits to be gained from any depreciation in the pound. The cost of an option with a strike price of 1.6000 U.S. dollars per pound is $3,000.

Three months later, the pound has appreciated against the dollar, with the price having changed to 1.75 U.S. dollars per pound. The CFO exercises the option, and spends $400,000 for the requisite number of pounds (calculated as £250,000 × 1.6000). If he had not purchased the option, the purchase would instead have cost $437,500 (calculated as £250,000 × 1.7500). Thus, Hammer saved $34,500 by using a currency option (calculated as the savings of $37,500, less the $3,000 cost of the option).

Currency options are particularly valuable during periods of high currency price volatility. Unfortunately from the perspective of the buyer, high volatility equates to higher option prices, since there is a higher probability that the counterparty will have to make a payment to the option buyer.

The Cylinder Option

Two options can be combined to create a *cylinder option*. One option is priced above the current spot price of the target currency, while the other option is priced below the spot price. The gain from exercising one option is used to partially offset the cost of the other option, thereby reducing the overall cost of the hedge. In effect, the upside potential offered by one option is being sold for a premium payment in order to finance the protection afforded by the opposing option.

The cylinder option is configured so that a company can acquire the right to buy currency at a specified price (a call option) and sell an option to a counterparty to buy currency from the company at a specified price (a put option), usually as of the expiry date. The premium the company pays for the purchased call is partially offset by the premium payable to the company for the put option that it sold.

If the market exchange rate remains between the boundaries established by the two currency options, the company never uses its options and instead buys or sells currency on the open market to fulfill its currency needs. If the market price breaches the strike price of the call option, the company exercises the call option and buys currency at the designated strike price. Conversely, if the market price breaches the strike price of the put option, the counterparty exercises its option to sell the currency to the company.

A variation on the cylinder option is to construct call and put options that are very close together, so that the premium cost of the call is very close to the premium income generated by the put, resulting in a near-zero net hedging cost to the company. The two options have to be very close together for the zero cost option to work, which means that the effective currency price range being hedged is quite small.

Swaps

If a company has or expects to have an obligation to make a payment in a foreign currency, it can arrange to swap currency holdings with a third party that already has the required currency. The two entities engage in a swap transaction by agreeing upon an initial swap date, the date when the cash positions will be reversed back to their original positions, and an interest rate that reflects the comparative differences in interest rates between the two countries in which the entities are located.

Another use for a currency swap is when a forward exchange contract has been delayed. In this situation, you would normally sell to a counterparty the currency that it has just obtained through the receipt of an account receivable. If, however, the receivable has not yet been paid, the company can enter into a swap agreement to obtain the required currency and meet its immediate obligation under the forward exchange contract. Later, when the receivable is eventually paid, the company can reverse the swap, returning funds to the counterparty.

A swap arrangement may be for just a one-day period, or extend out for several years into the future. Swap transactions generally do not occur in amounts of less than $5 million, so this technique is not available to smaller businesses.

A potentially serious problem with swaps is the prospect of a default by the counterparty. If there is a default, the company once again assumes its foreign currency liability, and must now scramble to find an alternative hedge.

Netting

There are circumstances where a company has subsidiaries in multiple countries that actively trade with each other. If so, they should have accounts receivable and payable with each other, which could give rise to a flurry of foreign exchange transactions in multiple currencies that could trigger any number of hedging activities. It may be possible to reduce the amount of hedging activity through *payment netting*, where the corporate parent offsets all accounts receivable and payable against each other to determine the net amount of foreign exchange transactions that actually require hedges. A centralized netting function may be used, which means that each subsidiary either receives a single payment from the netting center, or makes a single payment to the netting center. Netting results in the following benefits:

- Foreign exchange exposure is no longer tracked at the subsidiary level
- The total amount of foreign exchange purchased and sold declines, which reduces the amount of foreign exchange commissions paid out
- The total amount of cash in transit (and therefore not available for investment) between subsidiaries declines

> **Tip:** It is easier to create an intracompany netting system when there is already a centralized accounts payable function for the entire business, which is called a *payment factory*.

The same concept can be applied to payables and receivables with outside entities, though a considerable amount of information sharing is needed to make the concept work. In some industries where there is a high level of trade between companies, industry-wide netting programs have been established that routinely offset a large proportion of the payables and receivables within the industry. The net result is that all offsetting obligations are reduced to a single payment per currency per value date between counterparties.

A related concept is *close-out netting*, where counterparties having forward contracts with each other can agree to net the obligations, rather than engaging in a large number of individual contract settlements. Before engaging in close-out netting, discuss the concept with corporate counsel. A case has been made in some jurisdictions that close-out netting runs counter to the interests of other creditors in the event of a bankruptcy by one of the counterparties.

The only downside of netting is that the accounting departments of the participating companies must sort out how their various transactions are settled. This requires a procedure for splitting a group of netted transactions into individual payments and receipts in the cash receipts and accounts payable modules of their accounting systems.

Summary

We have described a number of tools for dealing with foreign exchange risk, some of which require advanced knowledge of the underlying financial instruments. Since there is a risk of incorrectly setting up and unwinding these risk mitigation strategies, it always makes sense to give priority to the *least* complicated risk mitigation strategies. Once the organization is comfortable with these alternatives, it can move on to the various swaps, options, forward contracts, and futures contracts that can be tailored to the specific needs of the business and provide more comprehensive risk mitigation.

Chapter 17
Interest Rate Risk Management

Introduction

A business may borrow or invest funds. If so, the organization is at risk of loss from changes in the underlying interest rate. There could be an unexpected increase in the rate on borrowed funds, or a decline in the rate on invested funds. In this chapter, we describe the types of interest rate risk, as well as the tools for mitigating this risk.

Interest Risk Overview

Interest rate risk involves the risk of increases in interest rates on debt, as well as reductions in interest rates for investment instruments, with the attendant negative impact on profitability. This risk can take the following forms:

- *Absolute rate changes.* The market rate of interest will move up or down over time, resulting in immediate variances from the interest rates paid or earned by a company. This rate change is easily monitored.
- *Reinvestment risk.* Investments must be periodically re-invested and debt re-issued. If interest rates happen to be unfavorable during one of these rollover periods, a company will be forced to accept whatever interest rate is available.
- *Yield curve risk.* The yield curve shows the relationship between short-term and long-term interest rates, and typically slopes upward to indicate that long-term debt carries a higher interest rate to reflect the risk to the lender associated with such debt. If the yield curve steepens, flattens, or declines, these relationships change the debt duration that a company should use in its borrowing and investing strategies.

Interest risk is a particular concern for those businesses using large amounts of debt to fund their operations, since even a small increase in the interest rate could have a profound impact on profits, when multiplied by the volume of debt employed. Further, a sudden boost in interest expense could worsen a company's interest coverage ratio, which is a common covenant in loan agreements, and which could trigger a loan termination if the minimum ratio covenant is not met.

Interest Rate Risk Management

The primary objective of interest risk management is to keep fluctuations in interest rates from impacting company earnings. Management can respond to this objective in many ways, ranging from a conscious decision to take no action, passing through a number of relatively passive alternatives, and culminating in several active techniques for risk mitigation. We provide an overview of each option in this section.

Take No Action

There may be situations where a company has minimal investments that earn interest, or issues only minor amounts of debt. If so, it is certainly acceptable to not implement an aggressive risk management campaign related to interest rates. However, this state of affairs does not typically last for long, after which there will be some degree of risk related to interest rates. In anticipation of such an event, it is useful to model the amount of interest rate change that must occur before there will be a serious impact on company finances. Once that trigger point is known, you can begin to prepare any of the risk mitigation alternatives noted later in this section.

Avoid Risk

The risk associated with interest rates arises between external entities and a business; it does not arise between the subsidiaries of the same business. Thus, a company can act as its own bank to some extent, by providing intercompany lending arrangements at interest rates that are not subject to fluctuations. This is particularly useful in a multi-national corporation, where cash reserves in different currencies may be scattered throughout the business, and can be lent back and forth to cover immediate cash needs.

Another way to avoid risk is to operate the business in such a conservative manner that the company has no debt, thereby eliminating the risk associated with interest rates on debt. The same result can be achieved by using invested funds to pay off any outstanding debt. The main downside of the low-debt method is that a company may be constraining its growth by not taking advantage of a low-cost source of funds (i.e., debt).

Asset and Liability Matching

A key trigger for interest rate risk is when short-term debt is used to fund an asset that is expected to be held for a long period of time. In this situation, the short-term debt must be rolled over multiple times during the life span of the asset or until the debt is paid off, introducing the risk that each successive debt rollover will result in an increased interest rate. To avoid this risk, arrange for financing that approximately matches the useful life of the underlying asset. Thus, spending $1 million for a machine that is expected to have a useful life of 10 years should be funded with a loan that also has a 10-year life.

Hedging

Interest rate hedging is the practice of acquiring financial instruments whose effects offset those of the underlying scenario causing interest rate fluctuations, so that the net effect is minimized rate fluctuations. Hedges fall into two categories:

- *Forward rate agreements and futures.* These financial instruments are designed to lock in an interest rate, so that changes in the actual interest rate above or below the baseline interest rate do not impact a business. These instruments do not provide any flexibility for taking advantage of favorable changes in interest rates.
- *Options.* These financial instruments only lock in an interest rate if the holder wants to do so, thereby presenting the possibility of benefiting from a favorable change in an interest rate.

The various types of interest rate hedges are discussed next.

Types of Interest Rate Hedges

This section describes a number of methods for hedging the variability in interest rates. These options are mostly designed for high-value transactions, and so are not available to smaller companies.

The Forward Rate Agreement

A forward rate agreement (FRA) is an agreement between two parties to lock in a specific interest rate for a designated period of time, which usually spans just a few months. Under an FRA, the parties are protecting against opposing exposures: the FRA buyer wants to protect against an increase in the interest rate, while the FRA seller wants to protect against a decrease in the interest rate. Any payout under an FRA is based on a change in the reference interest rate from the interest rate stated in the contract (the FRA rate). An FRA is not related to a specific loan or investment – it simply provides interest rate protection.

The FRA rate is based on the yield curve, where interest rates usually increase for instruments having longer maturities. This means that the FRA rate typically increases for periods further in the future.

Several date-specific terms are referred to in a forward rate agreement, and are crucial to understanding how the FRA concept works. These terms are:

1. *Contract date.* The date on which the FRA begins.
2. *Expiry date.* The date on which any variance between the market rate and the reference rate is calculated.
3. *Settlement date.* The date on which the interest variance is paid by one counterparty to the other.
4. *Maturity date.* The final date of the date range that underlies the FRA contract.

In essence, these four dates anchor the two time periods covered by an FRA. The first period, which begins with the contract date and ends with the expiry date, spans the term of the contract. The second period begins with the settlement date and ends with the maturity date, and spans the period that underlies the contract. This date range is shown graphically in the following example.

Relevant FRA Dates

July 1
(contract date)

September 30
(expiry date)

October 1
(settlement date)

December 31
(maturity date)

The FRA rate is based on a future period, such as the period starting in one month and ending in four months, which is said to have a "1 × 4" FRA term, and has an effective term of three months. Similarly, a contract starting in three months and ending in six months is said to have a "3 × 6" FRA term, and also has an effective term of three months.

At the *beginning* of the designated FRA period, the interest rate stated in the contract is compared to the reference rate. The reference rate is usually a well-known interest rate index, such as the London Interbank Offered Rate (LIBOR). If the reference rate is higher, the seller makes a payment to the FRA buyer, based on the incremental difference in interest rates and the notional amount of the contract. The payment calculation is shown in the following example. If the reference rate is lower than the interest rate stated in the contract, the buyer makes a payment to the FRA seller. The payment made between the counterparties must be discounted to its present value, since the payment is associated with the FRA underlying period that has not yet happened. Thus, the discount assumes that the money would actually be due on the maturity date, but is payable on the settlement date (which may be months before the maturity date). The calculation for discounting the payment between counterparties is:

$$\frac{\text{Settlement amount}}{1 + (\text{Days in FRA underlying period}/360 \text{ Days} \times \text{Reference rate})} = \frac{\text{Discounted}}{\text{Payment}}$$

The reason why the contract payment is calculated at the *beginning* of the designated FRA period is that the risk being hedged by the contract was from the initial contract date until the date on which the FRA buyer expects to borrow money and lock in an interest rate. For example, a company may enter into an FRA in January, because it is uncertain of what the market interest rate will be in April, when it intends to borrow funds; the period at risk is therefore from January through April. The following example illustrates the concept.

EXAMPLE

Hammer Industries has a legal commitment to borrow $50 million in two months, and for a period of three months. Hammer's CFO is concerned that there may be an increase in the interest rate during the two-month period prior to borrowing the $50 million. The CFO elects to hedge the risk of an increase in the interest rate by purchasing a three-month FRA, starting in two months. A broker quotes a rate of 5.50%. Hammer enters into an FRA at the 5.50% interest rate, with 3rd National Bank as the counterparty. The notional amount of the contract is for $50 million.

Two months later, the reference rate is 6.00%, so 3rd National pays Hammer the difference between the contract rate and reference rate, which is 0.50%. At the same time, Hammer borrows $50 million at the market rate (which happens to match the reference rate) of 6.00%. Because of the FRA, Hammer's effective borrowing rate is 5.50%.

The amount paid by 3rd National to Hammer is calculated as:

(Reference rate – FRA rate) × (FRA days/360 days) × Notional amount = Profit or loss

or

(6.00% - 5.50%) × (90 days/360 days) × $50 million = $62,500

Since the payment is made at the beginning of the borrowing period, rather than at its end, the $62,500 payment is discounted and its present value paid. The discounting calculation for the settlement amount is:

$$\frac{\$62,500}{1 + (90/360 \text{ Days} \times 6.00\%)} = \$61,576.35$$

What if the reference rate had fallen by 0.50%, instead of increasing? Then Hammer would have paid 3rd National the discounted amount of $62,500, rather than the reverse. Hammer would also end up borrowing the $50 million at the new market rate of 5.00%. When the payment to 3rd National is combined with the reduced 5.00% interest rate, Hammer will still be paying a 5.50% interest rate, which is what it wanted all along.

From the buyer's perspective, the result of an FRA is that it pays the expected interest rate – no higher, and no lower.

The Futures Contract

An interest rate futures contract is conceptually similar to a forward contract, except that it is traded on an exchange, which means that it is for a standard amount and duration. The standard size of a futures contract is $1 million, so multiple contracts may need to be purchased to create a hedge for a specific loan or investment amount. The pricing for futures contracts starts at a baseline figure of 100, and declines based on the implied interest rate in a contract. For example, if a futures contract has an implied interest rate of 5.00%, the price of that contract will be 95.00. The calculation of the profit or loss on a futures contract is derived as follows:

Notional contract amount × Contract duration/360 Days × (Ending price – Beginning price)

Most trading in interest rate futures is in Eurodollars (U.S. dollars held outside of the United States), and are traded on the Chicago Mercantile Exchange.

Hedging is not perfect, since the notional amount of a contract may vary from the actual amount of funding that a company wants to hedge, resulting in a modest amount of either over- or under-hedging. For example, hedging a $15.4 million position will require the purchase of either 15 or 16 $1 million contracts. There may also be differences between the time period required for a hedge and the actual hedge period as stated in a futures contract. For example, if there is a seven month exposure to be hedged, one could acquire two consecutive three-month contracts, and elect to have the seventh month be unhedged.

Tip: If the buyer wants to protect against interest rate variability for a longer period, such as for the next year, it is possible to buy a series of futures contracts covering consecutive periods, so that coverage is achieved for the entire time period.

EXAMPLE

The CFO of Hammer Industries wants to hedge an investment of $10 million. To do so, he sells 10 three-month futures contracts with contract terms of three months. The current three-month LIBOR is 3.50% and the 3 × 6 forward rate is 3.75%. These contracts are currently listed on the Chicago Mercantile Exchange at 96.25, which is calculated as 100 minus the 3.75% forward rate.

When the futures contracts expire, the forward rate has declined to 3.65%, so that the contracts are now listed at 96.35 (calculated as 100 minus the 3.65 percent forward rate). By engaging in this hedge, Hammer has earned a profit of $2,500, which is calculated as follows:

$10,000,000 × (90/360) × (0.9635 Ending price − 0.9625 Beginning price) = $2,500

When the buyer purchases a futures contract, a minimum amount must initially be posted in a margin account to ensure performance under the contract terms. It may be necessary to fund the margin account with additional cash (a *margin call*) if the market value of the contract declines over time (margin accounts are revised daily, based on the market closing price). If the buyer cannot provide additional funding in the event of a contract decline, the futures exchange closes out the contract prior to its normal termination date. Conversely, if the market value of the contract increases, the net gain is credited to the buyer's margin account. On the last day of the contract, the exchange marks the contract to market and settles the accounts of the buyer and seller. Thus, transfers between buyers and sellers over the life of a contract are essentially a zero-sum game, where one party directly benefits at the expense of the other.

It is also possible to enter into a bond futures contract, which can be used to hedge interest rate risk. For example, a business that has borrowed funds can hedge against rising interest rates by selling a bond futures contract. Then, if interest rates do in fact rise, the resulting gain on the contract will offset the higher interest rate that the borrower is paying. Conversely, if interest rates subsequently fall, the borrower will experience a loss on the contract, which will offset the lower interest rate now being paid. Thus, the net effect of the contract is that the borrower locks in the beginning interest rate through the period of the contract.

> **Tip:** A bond futures contract is not a perfect hedge, for it is also impacted by changes in the credit rating of the bond issuer.

When a purchased futures contract expires, it is customary to settle it by selling a futures contract that has the same delivery date. Conversely, if the original contract was sold to a counterparty, then the seller can settle the contract by buying a futures contract that has the same delivery date.

The following table notes the key differences between forward rate agreements and futures contracts. Similarities between the two instruments are excluded from the table.

Differences between a Futures Contract and FRA

Feature	Futures Contract	Forward Rate Agreement
Trading platform	Exchange-based	Between two parties
Counterparty	The exchange	Single counterparty
Collateral	Margin account	None
Agreement	Standardized	Modified
Settlement	Daily mark to market	On expiry date

The preceding table reveals two key differences between a futures contract and an FRA. First, there can be significant counterparty risk in an FRA, since the contract period can be lengthy, and financial conditions can change markedly over that time. Second, a futures contract is settled every day, which can create pressure to fund a margin call if there are significant losses on the contract.

The Interest Rate Swap

An interest rate swap is a customized contract between two parties to swap two schedules of cash flows that could extend for anywhere from one to 25 years, and which represent interest payments. Only the interest rate obligations are swapped, not the underlying loans or investments from which the obligations are derived. The counterparties are usually a company and a bank. There are many types of rate swaps; we will confine this discussion to a swap arrangement where one schedule of cash flows is based on a floating interest rate, and the other is based on a fixed interest rate. For example, a five-year schedule of cash flows based on a fixed interest rate may be swapped for a five-year schedule of cash flows based on a floating interest rate that is tied to the LIBOR rate.

> **Tip:** To prevent confusion, replicate the same swap terms across all swap agreements. Replicated terms should include the reference rate, the interest calculation method, and the coupon frequency. Other terms, such as the notional amount and swap term, will probably vary by agreement.

The most common reason to engage in an interest rate swap is to exchange a variable-rate payment for a fixed-rate payment, or vice versa. Thus, a company that has only been able to obtain a floating-rate loan can effectively convert the loan to a fixed-rate loan through an interest rate swap. This approach is especially attractive when a borrower is only able to obtain a fixed-rate loan by paying a premium, but can combine a variable-rate loan and an interest rate swap to achieve a fixed-rate loan at a lower price.

A company may want to take the reverse approach and swap its fixed interest payments for floating payments. This situation arises when there is a belief that interest rates will decline during the swap period, and wants to take advantage of the lower rates.

A swap contract is settled through a multi-step process, which is:

1. Calculate the payment obligation of each party, typically once every six months through the life of the swap arrangement.
2. Determine the variance between the two amounts.
3. The party whose position is improved by the swap arrangement pays the variance to the party whose position is degraded by the swap arrangement.

Thus, a company continues to pay interest to its banker under the original lending agreement, while the company either accepts a payment from the rate swap counterparty, or issues a payment to the counterparty, with the result being that the net amount of interest paid by the company is the amount planned by the business when it entered into the swap agreement.

EXAMPLE

Hammer Industries has a $15 million variable-rate loan outstanding that matures in two years. The current interest rate on the loan is 6.5%. Hammer enters into an interest rate swap agreement with Big Regional Bank for a fixed-rate 7.0% loan with a $15 million notional amount. The first scheduled payment swap date is in six months. On that date, the variable rate on Hammer's loan has increased to 7.25%. Thus, the total interest payments on the swap date are $543,750 for Hammer and $525,000 for Big Regional. Since the two parties have agreed to swap payments, Big Regional pays Hammer the difference between the two payments, which is $18,750.

Hammer issues an interest payment of $543,750 to its bank. When netted with the cash inflow of $18,750 from Big Regional, this means that the net interest rate being paid by Hammer is 7.0%.

Several larger banks have active trading groups that routinely deal with interest rate swaps. Most swaps involve sums in the millions of dollars, but some banks are willing to engage in swap arrangements involving amounts of less than $1 million. There is a counterparty risk with interest rate swaps, since one party could fail to make a contractually-mandated payment to the other party. This risk is of particular concern when a swap arrangement covers multiple years, since the financial condition of a counterparty could change dramatically during that time.

If there is general agreement in the marketplace that interest rates are headed in a certain direction, it will be more expensive to obtain a swap that protects against interest rate changes in the anticipated direction.

Interest Rate Options

An option gives its owner the right, but not the obligation, to trigger a contract. The contract can be either a call option or a put option. A *call option* related to interest rates protects the option owner from rising interest rates, while a *put option* protects the option owner from declining interest rates. The party selling an option does so in exchange for a one-time premium payment. The party buying an option is doing so to mitigate its risk related to a change in interest rates.

An interest rate option can be relatively inexpensive if there has been or is expected to be little volatility in interest rates, since the option seller does not expect interest rates to move enough for the option to be exercised. Conversely, if there has been or is expected to be interest rate volatility, the option seller must assume that the option will be exercised, and so sets a higher price. Thus, periods of high interest rate volatility may make it cost-prohibitive to buy options.

> **Tip:** An interest rate hedge using an option may not be entirely successful if the reference rate used for the option is not the same one used for the underlying loan. For example, the reference rate for an option may be LIBOR, while the rate used for the underlying loan may be a bank's prime rate. The result is a hedging mismatch that can create an unplanned gain or loss.

An interest rate option sets a *strike price*, which is a specific interest rate at which the option buyer can borrow or lend money. The contract also states the amount of funds that the option buyer can borrow or lend (the *notional amount*). Rate increases and declines are measured using a *reference rate*, which is typically a well-known interest rate index, such as LIBOR. There is also an option expiration date, or *expiry date*, after which the option is cancelled. The buyer can specify the exact terms needed to hedge an interest rate position with a customized option.

If an option buyer wants to be protected from increases in interest rates, a *cap* (or ceiling) is created. A cap is a consecutive series of options, all having the same strike price. The buyer of a cap is paid whenever the reference rate exceeds the cap strike price on an option expiry date. For example, if a company wants to hedge its interest risk for one year with a strike price of 6.50%, beginning on January 1, it can buy the following options:

Desired Coverage Period	Option Number	Expiry Date	Option Term	Strike Price
January - March	--	Not applicable*	Not available*	N/A*
April - June	1	April 1	4 to 6 months	6.50%
July – September	2	July 1	7 to 9 months	6.50%
October - December	3	October 1	10 to 12 months	6.50%

* There is no option available for the first three-month period, since the expiry date is at the beginning of the contract period, so the expiry date will be reached immediately.

With a cap arrangement, the buyer is only subject to interest rate changes up to the cap, and is protected from rate changes above the cap if the reference rate exceeds the cap strike price on predetermined dates. If the reference interest rate is below the cap at the option expiration, the option buyer lets the option expire. However, if the reference rate is above the cap, the buyer exercises the option, which means that the option seller must reimburse the buyer for the difference between the reference rate and the cap rate, multiplied by the notional amount of the contract.

A cap may be included in a loan agreement, such that the borrower is guaranteed not to pay more than a designated maximum interest rate over the term of the loan, or for a predetermined portion of the loan. In this case, the lender has paid for the cap, and will probably include its cost in the interest rate or fees associated with the loan.

In order to be protected from decreases in interest rates (for invested funds), a *floor* is structured into an option, so that the option buyer is paid if the reference rate declines below the floor strike rate.

EXAMPLE

Hammer Industries has a $25 million 3-month loan that currently carries a fixed interest rate of 7.00%. Hammer's bank refuses to grant a fixed-rate loan for a longer time period, so Hammer plans to continually roll over the loan every three months. Recently, short-term interest rates have been spiking, so the CFO decides to purchase an interest rate cap that is set at 7.50%, and which is comprised of two consecutive options, each with a three-month term.

At the expiry date of the first option, the reference rate is 7.25%, which is below the cap strike rate. The CFO lets the option expire unused and rolls over the short-term loan at the new 7.25% rate.

At the next option expiry date, the reference rate has risen to 7.75%, which is 0.25% above the cap strike rate. The CFO exercises the option, which forces the counterparty to pay Hammer for the difference between the cap strike rate and the reference rate. The calculation of the amount to be reimbursed is:

(Reference rate – Strike rate) × (Lending period/360 days) × Notional amount = Profit or loss

or

(7.75% - 7.50%) × (90/360) × $25 million = $15,625

Of course, the cost of the option reduces the benefits gained from an interest rate option, but still is useful for providing protection from outsized changes in interest rates.

Tip: From an analysis perspective, it is useful to include the premium on an option with the amount of interest paid on a loan and any proceeds or payments associated with an exercised option, in order to derive the aggregate interest rate on any associated debt being hedged.

The cylinder option described in the last chapter for foreign exchange risk can also be applied to interest rates. Under this concept, a company purchases a cap and sells a floor, with the current reference rate located between the two strike rates. The gain from exercising one option is used to partially offset the cost of the other option, which reduces the overall cost of the hedge. The three possible outcomes of this *collar* arrangement are:

1. The reference rate remains between the cap and floor, so neither option is exercised.
2. The reference rate rises above the cap, so the company is paid for the difference between the reference rate and the cap strike rate, multiplied by the notional amount of the contract.
3. The reference rate falls below the floor, so the company pays the option counterparty for the difference between the reference rate and the floor strike rate, multiplied by the notional amount of the contract.

The functioning of a collar arrangement is shown in the following exhibit, where the cap is set at 5% and the floor is set at 3%. No option is triggered until the reference rate drops to 2% in one of the later quarters, and again when it rises to 6%. In the first case, the company pays the 1% difference between the 3% floor and the 2% reference rate. In the latter case, the company is paid the 1% difference between the 5% cap and the 6% reference rate.

The Operation of an Interest Rate Collar

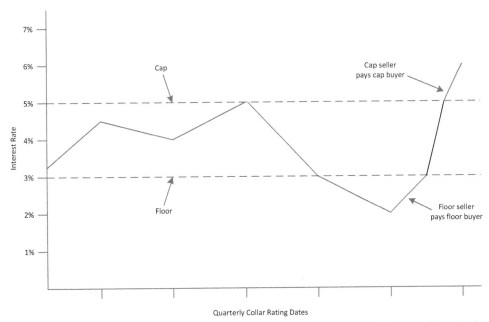

Quarterly Collar Rating Dates

From the perspective of a company using a collar arrangement, the net effect is that interest rates will fluctuate only within the bounds set by the cap and floor strike rates.

A variation on the interest rate option concept is to include a call feature in a debt issuance. A call feature allows a company to buy back its debt from debt holders. The feature is quite useful in cases where the market interest rate has fallen since debt was issued, so a company can refinance its debt at a lower interest rate. However, the presence of the call option makes investors wary about buying it, which tends to increase the effective interest rate at which they will buy the debt. Investor concerns can be mitigated to some extent by providing for a fairly long time period before the issuing company can trigger the call option, and especially if the call price is set somewhat higher than the current market price.

Interest Rate Swaptions

A swaption is an option on an interest rate swap arrangement. The buyer of a swaption has the right, but not the obligation, to enter into an interest rate swap. In essence, a swaption presents the option of being able to lock in a fixed interest rate or a variable interest rate (depending on the terms of the underlying swap arrangement). Thus, the CFO may suspect that interest rates will begin to rise in the near future, and so enters into a swaption to take over a fixed interest rate. If interest rates do indeed rise, the swaption holder can exercise the swaption. If interest rates hold steady or decline, the swaption is allowed to expire without being exercised.

The two types of swaption are the *payer swaption* and the *receiver swaption*, which are defined as follows:

- *Payer swaption.* The buyer can enter into a swap where it pays the fixed interest rate side of the transaction.
- *Receiver swaption.* The buyer can enter into a swap where it pays the floating interest rate side of the transaction.

There is no formal exchange for swaptions, so each agreement is between two counterparties. This means that each party is exposed to the potential failure of the counterparty to make scheduled payments on the underlying swap. Consequently, it is prudent to only enter into these arrangements with counterparties with high credit ratings or other evidence of financial stability.

Swaption market participants are primarily large corporations, banks, and hedge funds. The most likely counterparty for a corporation is a large bank that has a group specializing in swaption arrangements.

Summary

We have described a number of tools for dealing with interest rate risk, some of which require advanced knowledge of the underlying financial instruments. Since there is a risk of incorrectly setting up and unwinding these risk mitigation strategies, it always makes sense to give priority to the *least* complicated risk mitigation strategies. Once the organization is comfortable with these alternatives, it can move on to the various interest rate hedges that can be tailored to the specific needs of the business and provide more comprehensive risk mitigation. Also, note that many of the interest rate hedges are only available for significant cash balances, which restricts their use to organizations that maintain large debt or investment balances.

Chapter 18
Supply Chain Financing

Introduction

The suppliers that feed materials and services to a company should be well-funded. A financially healthy supplier is more capable of meeting its commitments to the company, and also has more cash to invest in facilities, as well as research and development activities. Such a business is also less likely to suddenly go bankrupt, leaving a hole in the company's supply chain. An organization can contribute to this level of funding by engaging in supply chain financing.

> **Related Podcast Episode:** Episode 143 of the Accounting Best Practices Podcast discusses supply chain financing. The episode is available at: **accounting-tools.com/podcasts** or **iTunes**

Supply Chain Financing

Supply chain financing occurs when a finance company, such as a bank, interposes itself between a company and its suppliers and commits to pay the company's invoices to the suppliers at an accelerated rate in exchange for a discount (which is essentially a factoring arrangement). The following process flow shows the relationship between the parties.

Supply Chain Finance Process Flow

This approach has the following benefits for the entity that is paying its suppliers:

- The company can foster very close links with its core group of suppliers, since this can be a major benefit to them in terms of accelerated cash flow.

Because of the ready availability of cash, this may even mean that the company becomes the preferred customer for its supplier base.

- 100% of the invoice value is available for factoring, rather than the discounted amount that is available through a normal factoring arrangement.
- The company no longer has to deal with requests from suppliers for early payment, since they are already being paid as soon as possible.

Supply chain financing has the following benefits for suppliers:

- A cash-strapped supplier can be paid much sooner than normal, in exchange for the finance company's fee.
- The interest rate charged by the finance company should be low, since it is based on the credit standing of the paying company, not the rating of the suppliers (which assumes that the payer has a good rating).

The finance company acting as the intermediary earns interest income on the factoring arrangements that it enters into with the suppliers of the target company. This can represent an excellent source of income over a long period of time, so bankers try to create sole-source supply chain financing arrangements to lock in this income. In addition, the bankers can now develop relations with the entire group of suppliers that it is paying, which may result in an entirely new group of clients for a broad range of banking services.

Supply chain financing is usually begun by large companies that want to improve the cash flow situation for their suppliers. To convince a finance company to be involved in the arrangement requires the expectation of a considerable amount of factoring, which is why this approach is not available to smaller companies.

When first developing a supply chain financing arrangement, it can be difficult to make a reasonable estimate of the amount of financing that a group of suppliers will want. There are a number of factors that could drive the supplier need for cash, including the following:

- *General business environment.* If the economy is robust, suppliers will find that their customers are more likely to pay on time, and so will have less need for accelerated payments. Conversely, if the state of the economy is declining, they may be quite eager to take advantage of supply chain financing in order to assure themselves of a ready source of cash.
- *Existing terms.* If the company has negotiated lengthy payment terms with its suppliers (such as 60 or 90 days to pay), they will be more likely to take advantage of supply chain financing, since this represents a massive acceleration of their cash flow.
- *Interest rate.* If the interest rate being charged by the bank is too high, only the most desperate suppliers will take advantage of the financing.
- *Existing factoring arrangements.* Suppliers may already have long-standing factoring arrangements in place with other lenders, and so may be reluctant to shift their business over to the company's bank. This decision will probably be driven by a comparison of the factoring deals being offered.

There are on-line systems available on which a company can post its approved invoices, and which suppliers can access to select which invoices they want to have paid to them earlier than dictated by the standard payment terms.

Summary

Supply chain financing is an easy way for a larger business to improve the cash flow of its suppliers. However, this option is only available to larger companies, so the suppliers of a smaller company will have to use their own factoring arrangements to achieve the same result. The trouble with independent factoring arrangements is that the cost to suppliers may be higher, and less than the full amount of each invoice may be made available for factoring. If a company wants to help its suppliers out of this situation, it could negotiate with them to reduce the number of days that it will wait before paying them. This does not have to be a unilateral reduction in payment terms; in exchange, the company could negotiate for preferred customer status, which would move it to the front of the queue for order placement, as well as for faster delivery times.

Chapter 19
Corporate Finance Measurements

Introduction

Corporate finance activities stand apart from the normal sales and production activities of a business, and so require a completely different set of measurements. This information can be used to gain insights into where and for how long cash is used within a company, how well cash flows can be predicted, the earnings generated on invested funds, the general level of liquidity and debt, and similar matters. This chapter includes a number of corporate finance metrics that can be of use in monitoring these issues.

Corporate Finance Metrics

At first glance, the corporate finance area might appear resistant to the use of any ongoing, standardized metrics to measure its performance. After all, we are merely finding sources of cash and then using the cash in the most profitable manner possible. In reality, there are a number of areas in which metrics can be employed. Consider the following conceptual areas for measurement:

- *Cash usage*. In what parts of the company is cash currently being used? The entire management team should be aware of which areas are using and providing cash, thereby engendering a discussion of how cash usage can be improved.
- *Cash forecasting*. It is critical to understand how well future projections of cash positions are matching actual outcomes, as well as how much lending capability the company has remaining on its borrowing base, in order to properly plan for the acquisition and deployment of cash.
- *Cash at work*. From an investment efficiency perspective, it is useful to be aware of those pockets of cash not being put to good use earning income for the business, as well as the extent of the returns on invested funds.
- *Liquidity and solvency*. When dealing with lenders and creditors, one should understand the company's ability to pay over the short term. This is essentially a comparison of obligations to projected available cash, and is described as the liquidity of a business. It is also useful to examine the same capability in relation to long-term obligations, which refers to the solvency of an entity – its ability to continue as a going concern.

In short, there are a number of areas in which metrics can provide valuable information for the corporate finance function. In the following sections, we discuss specific metrics that address all of the conceptual areas just noted.

Cash Conversion Cycle

The cash conversion cycle is the time period extending from the payment of cash for the production of goods, until cash is received from the sale of those goods to customers. The activities involved in the cash conversion cycle include the purchasing of raw materials or items to be resold, their storage, the production process, payments to employees related to the production process, and the sale of goods to customers. If a company only provides services, then the cash conversion cycle extends from the date of payments to employees to the receipt of cash from the sale of services to customers. The cash conversion cycle tends to be much shorter for the provision of services.

It is important to know the duration of the cash conversion cycle, for this is the time period over which cash is invested in a business. If the conversion cycle can be shortened, then cash can be permanently extracted from the business and made available for other purposes. The steps in the cash conversion cycle that can potentially be compressed include:

- The placement of orders for goods with suppliers
- The time required for goods to be delivered to the company
- The time required to inspect and log in received goods
- The inventory holding period
- The duration of the production process
- The time required to prepare goods for shipment
- The delay incorporated into payment terms with customers
- The time required to collect overdue accounts receivable

The cash conversion cycle can be severely compressed through the use of a just-in-time "pull" system that only produces goods just as they are needed for immediate sale to customers. Many other methods for compressing the cash conversion cycle are noted in the Working Capital Management chapter.

To calculate the amount of the cash conversion cycle, add together the days of sales in accounts receivable and the days of sales in inventory, and subtract the days of payables outstanding. For example, a company has 60 days of sales in accounts receivable, 80 days of sales in inventory, and 30 days of payables outstanding. Its cash conversion cycle is therefore:

$$60 \text{ Days receivables} + 80 \text{ Days inventory} - 30 \text{ Days payables}$$

$$= 110 \text{ Days cash conversion cycle}$$

The calculations for days of sales in accounts receivable, days of sales in inventory, and days payables outstanding are explained in the next three sub-sections.

Corporate Finance Measurements

Days Sales in Accounts Receivable

Days sales in accounts receivable is the number of days that a customer invoice is outstanding before it is collected. The measurement is usually applied to the entire set of invoices that a company has outstanding at any point in time, rather than to a single invoice. The point of the measurement is to determine the effectiveness of a company's credit and collection efforts in allowing credit to reputable customers, as well as its ability to collect from them. When measured at the individual customer level, it can indicate when a customer is having cash flow troubles, since the customer will attempt to stretch out the amount of time before it pays invoices.

There is not an absolute number of accounts receivable days that represents excellent or poor accounts receivable management, since the figure varies considerably by industry and the underlying payment terms. Generally, a figure of 25% more than the standard terms allowed may represent an opportunity for improvement. Conversely, an accounts receivable days figure that is very close to the payment terms granted to a customer probably indicates that a company's credit policy is too tight.

The formula for accounts receivable days is:

$$(\text{Accounts receivable} \div \text{Annual revenue}) \times \text{Number of days in the year}$$

For example, if a company has an average accounts receivable balance of $200,000 and annual sales of $1,200,000, then its accounts receivable days figure is:

$$(\$200,000 \text{ Accounts receivable} \div \$1,200,000 \text{ Annual revenue}) \times 365 \text{ Days}$$

$$= 60.8 \text{ Accounts receivable days}$$

The calculation indicates that the company requires 60.8 days to collect a typical invoice.

An effective way to use the accounts receivable days measurement is to track it on a trend line, month by month. Doing so shows any changes in the ability of the company to collect from its customers. If a business is highly seasonal, a variation is to compare the measurement to the same metric for the same month in the preceding year; this provides a more reasonable basis for comparison.

No matter how this measurement is used, remember that it is usually compiled from a large number of outstanding invoices, and so provides no insights into the collectability of a specific invoice. Thus, you should supplement it with an ongoing examination of the aged accounts receivable report and the notes of the collection staff.

Days Sales in Inventory

Days sales in inventory (DSI) is a way to measure the average amount of time that it takes for a company to convert its inventory into sales. A relatively small number of days sales in inventory indicates that a company is more efficient in selling off its

236

inventory, while a large number indicates that a company may have invested too much in inventory, and may even have obsolete inventory on hand.

To calculate days sales in inventory, divide the average inventory for the year by the cost of goods sold for the same period, and then multiply by 365. For example, if a company has average inventory of $1.5 million and an annual cost of goods sold of $6 million, then its days sales in inventory is calculated as:

$$(\$1.5 \text{ million inventory} \div \$6 \text{ million cost of goods sold}) \times 365 \text{ days}$$

$$= 91.3 \text{ days sales in inventory}$$

The days sales in inventory figure can be misleading, for the following reasons:

- A company could post financial results that indicate a low DSI, but only because it has sold off a large amount of inventory at a discount, or has written off some inventory as obsolete. An indicator of these actions is when profits decline at the same time that the number of days sales in inventory declines.
- A company could change its method for calculating the cost of goods sold, such as by capitalizing more or fewer expenses into overhead. If this calculation method varies significantly from the method the company used in the past, it can lead to a sudden alteration in the results of the measurement.
- The person creating the metrics might use the amount of ending inventory in the numerator, rather than the average inventory figure for the entire measurement period. If the ending inventory figure varies significantly from the average inventory figure, this can result in a sharp change in the measurement.
- A company may switch to contract manufacturing, where a supplier produces and holds goods on behalf of the company. Depending upon the arrangement, the company may have no inventory to report at all, which renders the DSI measurement useless.

Days Payables Outstanding

The accounts payable days formula measures the number of days that a company takes to pay its suppliers. If the number of days increases from one period to the next, this indicates that the company is paying its suppliers more slowly. A change in the number of payable days can also indicate altered payment terms with suppliers, though this rarely has more than a slight impact on the total number of days. If a company is paying its suppliers very quickly, it may mean that the suppliers are demanding short payment terms.

To calculate days payables outstanding, summarize all purchases from suppliers during the measurement period, and divide by the average amount of accounts payable during that period. The formula is:

<u>Total supplier purchases</u>
(Beginning accounts payable + Ending accounts payable) ÷ 2

This formula reveals the total accounts payable turnover. Then divide the resulting turnover figure into 365 days to arrive at the number of accounts payable days.

The formula can be modified to exclude cash payments to suppliers, since the numerator should include only purchases on credit from suppliers. However, the amount of up-front cash payments to suppliers is normally so small that this modification is not necessary.

As an example, a CFO wants to determine his company's accounts payable days for the past year. In the beginning of this period, the beginning accounts payable balance was $800,000, and the ending balance was $884,000. Purchases for the last 12 months were $7,500,000. Based on this information, the CFO calculates the accounts payable turnover as:

<u>$7,500,000 Purchases</u>
($800,000 Beginning payables + $884,000 Ending payables) ÷ 2

= $7,500,000 Purchases ÷ $842,000 Average accounts payable

= 8.9 Accounts payable turnover

Thus, the company's accounts payable is turning over at a rate of 8.9 times per year. To calculate the turnover in days, the CFO divides the 8.9 turns into 365 days, which yields:

365 Days ÷ 8.9 Turns = 41 Days

Companies sometimes measure accounts payable days by only using the cost of goods sold in the numerator. This is incorrect, since there may be a large amount of administrative expenses that should also be included. If a company only uses the cost of goods sold in the numerator, this creates an excessively small number of payable days.

Actual Cash Position versus Forecast

A cash forecast should be as accurate as possible. If there are any variations in actual cash flows from forecasted results, they should be investigated and the findings used to improve the forecasting model.

An excellent way to monitor cash forecast accuracy is to routinely compare the company's actual cash position, prior to financing activities, to the forecasted amount. The main point of this metric should be to note the size of the difference from the expected result. An unusually large variance, whether positive or negative, should be grounds for a review. Thus, the calculation should be on an absolute basis, rather than showing a negative or positive variance.

For example, the CFO of a company compares actual to forecasted results for the last six weeks, and obtains the following information:

Week	Actual Ending Cash	Forecasted Ending Cash	Variance	Absolute Variance	Percent Variance
1	$1,237,000	$952,000	-$285,000	$285,000	23%
2	1,080,000	1,274,000	194,000	194,000	18%
3	1,591,000	1,846,000	255,000	255,000	16%
4	826,000	727,000	-99,000	99,000	12%
5	739,000	658,000	-81,000	81,000	11%
6	2,803,000	3,083,000	280,000	280,000	10%

The actual versus forecast information in the table reveals that the staff is rapidly improving its ability to accurately forecast cash flows.

Earnings on Invested Funds

In most situations, management does not want funds to be invested in high-yield securities, since there is usually a matching level of risk. Nonetheless, there may be cases where management is willing to put some cash at risk in an equity investment, which can generate equity gains or losses. Consequently, the following formula for earnings on invested funds includes market value changes:

$$\frac{\text{Interest income} + \text{Market value changes}}{\text{Average funds invested}}$$

Note that the calculation uses average funds invested, not the amount of cash invested as of the end of a reporting period. The amount of cash invested can change substantially by day, so the average investment figure in the denominator should be based on an average of the invested balance in every business day of a reporting period.

For example, a CFO is authorized to invest in both short-term debt instruments and stocks. As a result, the business earns $45,000 in interest income and $15,000 from an increase in the market value of its equity holdings. During the measurement period, the company had average investments of $3,000,000. The company's earnings on invested funds is calculated as:

$$\frac{\$45,000 \text{ Interest income} + \$15,000 \text{ Market value changes}}{\$3,000,000 \text{ Average funds invested}}$$

$$= 2.0\% \text{ Earnings on invested funds}$$

In many organizations, a much higher premium is placed on risk avoidance than on investment earnings, so it is fairly common to downplay this metric. If it is used, the board of directors should confine the company to specific types of conservative investment choices, so there is no temptation to earn outsized returns by making risky investments.

Ability to Pay Measurements

When estimating the correct amount of debt burden to maintain, it is useful to measure the ability of a business to pay its fixed costs, which include interest expenses. The following four measurements can be employed, beginning with the narrowly-focused interest coverage ratio, and then expanding the focus of the measurement in the debt service coverage ratio to include principal, and to other fixed costs in the fixed charge coverage ratio. Also, the cash coverage ratio looks at the ability to pay from the perspective of available cash, rather than earnings as reported under the accrual basis of accounting.

Interest Coverage Ratio

The interest coverage ratio measures the ability of a company to pay the interest on its outstanding debt. A high interest coverage ratio indicates that a business can pay for its interest expense several times over, while a low ratio is a strong indicator that an organization may default on its loan payments.

It is useful to track the interest coverage ratio on a trend line, in order to spot situations where a company's results or debt burden are yielding a downward trend in the ratio. An investor would want to sell the equity holdings in a company showing such a downward trend, especially if the ratio drops below 1.5:1, since this indicates a likely problem with meeting debt obligations.

To calculate the interest coverage ratio, divide earnings before interest and taxes (EBIT) by the interest expense for the measurement period. The formula is:

$$\frac{\text{Earnings before interest and taxes}}{\text{Interest expense}}$$

EXAMPLE

Carpenter Holdings generates $5,000,000 of earnings before interest and taxes in its most recent reporting period. Its interest expense in that period is $2,500,000. Therefore, the company's interest coverage ratio is calculated as:

$$\frac{\$5,000,000 \text{ EBIT}}{\$2,500,000 \text{ Interest expense}}$$

$$= 2:1 \text{ Interest coverage ratio}$$

The ratio indicates that Carpenter's earnings should be sufficient to enable it to pay the interest expense.

A company may be accruing an interest expense that is not actually due for payment yet, so the ratio can indicate a debt default that will not really occur, or at least until such time as the interest is due for payment.

Debt Service Coverage Ratio

The debt service coverage ratio measures the ability of a revenue-producing property to generate sufficient cash to pay for the cost of all related mortgage payments. A positive debt service ratio indicates that a property's cash outflows can cover all offsetting loan payments, whereas a negative ratio indicates that the owner must contribute additional funds to pay for the annual loan payments. A very high debt service coverage ratio gives the property owner a substantial cushion to pay for unexpected or unplanned expenditures related to the property, or if market conditions result in a significant decline in future rental rates.

To calculate the ratio, divide the net annual operating income of the property by all annual loan payments for the same property, net of any tax savings generated by the interest expense. The formula is:

$$\frac{\text{Net annual operating income}}{\text{Total of annual loan payments net of tax effect}}$$

There may be no tax effect associated with debt, if a company has no taxable income. Otherwise, the tax effect is based on the income tax rate expected for the year.

EXAMPLE

A rental property generates $400,000 of cash flow per year, and the total annual loan payments of the property are $360,000. This yields a debt service ratio of 1.11, meaning that the property generates 11% more cash than the property owner needs to pay for the annual loan payments.

A negative debt service coverage ratio may result when a property is transitioning to new tenants, so that it is generating sufficient cash by the end of the measurement period, but was not doing so during the beginning or middle of the measurement period. Thus, the metric can yield inaccurate results during transition periods.

Fixed Charge Coverage Ratio

A business may incur so many fixed costs that its cash flow is mostly consumed by payments for these costs. The problem is particularly common when a company has incurred a large amount of debt, and must make ongoing interest payments. In this situation, use the fixed charge coverage ratio to determine the extent of the problem. If the resulting ratio is low, it is a strong indicator that any subsequent drop in the profits of a business may bring about its failure.

To calculate the fixed charge coverage ratio, combine earnings before interest and taxes with any lease expense, and then divide by the combined total of interest expense and lease expense. This ratio is intended to show estimated future results, so it is acceptable to drop from the calculation any expenses that are about to expire. The formula is:

$$\frac{\text{Earnings before interest and taxes} + \text{Lease expense}}{\text{Interest expense} + \text{Lease expense}}$$

EXAMPLE

Luminescence Corporation recorded earnings before interest and taxes of $800,000 in the preceding year. The company also recorded $200,000 of lease expense and $50,000 of interest expense. Based on this information, its fixed charge coverage is:

$$\frac{\$800,000 \text{ EBIT} + \$200,000 \text{ Lease expense}}{\$50,000 \text{ Interest expense} + \$200,000 \text{ Lease expense}}$$

$$= 4:1 \text{ Fixed charge coverage ratio}$$

Cash Coverage Ratio

The cash coverage ratio is useful for determining the amount of cash available to pay for interest, and is expressed as a ratio of the cash available to the amount of interest to be paid. This is a useful ratio when the entity evaluating a company is a prospective lender. The ratio should be substantially greater than 1:1. To calculate this ratio, take the earnings before interest and taxes (EBIT) from the income statement, add back to it all non-cash expenses included in EBIT (such as depreciation and amortization), and divide by the interest expense. The formula is:

$$\frac{\text{Earnings before interest and taxes} + \text{Non-cash expenses}}{\text{Interest expense}}$$

There may be a number of additional non-cash items to subtract in the numerator of the formula. For example, there may have been substantial charges in a period to increase reserves for sales allowances, product returns, bad debts, or inventory obsolescence. If these non-cash items are substantial, be sure to include them in the calculation. Also, the interest expense in the denominator should only include the actual interest expense to be paid – if there is a premium or discount to the amount being paid, it is not a cash payment, and so should not be included in the denominator.

EXAMPLE

The controller of Currency Bank is concerned that a borrower has recently taken on a great deal of debt to pay for a leveraged buyout, and wants to ensure that there is sufficient cash to pay for its new interest burden. The borrower is generating earnings before interest and taxes of $1,200,000 and it records annual depreciation of $800,000. The borrower is scheduled to pay $1,500,000 in interest expenses in the coming year. Based on this information, the borrower has the following cash coverage ratio:

$$\frac{\$1,200,000 \text{ EBIT} + \$800,000 \text{ Depreciation}}{\$1,500,000 \text{ Interest expense}}$$

$$= 1.33 \text{ Cash coverage ratio}$$

The calculation reveals that the borrower can pay for its interest expense, but has very little cash left for any other payments.

Debt to Equity Ratio

The debt to equity ratio of a business is closely monitored by the lenders and creditors of the company, since it can provide early warning that an organization is so overwhelmed by debt that it is unable to meet its payment obligations. This may also be triggered by a funding issue. For example, the owners of a business may not want to contribute any more cash to the company, so they acquire more debt to address the cash shortfall. Or, a company may use debt to buy back shares, thereby increasing the return on investment to the remaining shareholders.

Whatever the reason for debt usage, the outcome can be catastrophic, if corporate cash flows are not sufficient to make ongoing debt payments. This is a concern to lenders, whose loans may not be paid back. Suppliers are also concerned about the ratio for the same reason. A lender can protect its interests by imposing collateral requirements or restrictive covenants; suppliers usually offer credit with less restrictive terms, and so can suffer more if a company is unable to meet its payment obligations to them.

To calculate the debt to equity ratio, simply divide total debt by total equity. In this calculation, the debt figure should also include all lease obligations. The formula is:

$$\frac{\text{Long-term debt} + \text{Short-term debt} + \text{Leases}}{\text{Equity}}$$

EXAMPLE

An analyst is reviewing the credit application of New Centurion Corporation. The company reports a $500,000 line of credit, $1,700,000 in long-term debt, and a $200,000 lease. The company has $800,000 of equity. Based on this information, New Centurion's debt to equity ratio is:

$$\frac{\$500,000 \text{ Line of credit} + \$1,700,000 \text{ Debt} + \$200,000 \text{ Lease}}{\$800,000 \text{ Equity}}$$

$$= 3:1 \text{ Debt to equity ratio}$$

The debt to equity ratio exceeds the 2:1 ratio threshold above which the analyst is not allowed to grant credit. Consequently, New Centurion is kept on cash in advance payment terms.

Average Cost of Debt

A company that uses a large amount of debt financing may not be aware of the average cost of the debt load that it has incurred. If so, consider deriving the average cost of debt, which could lead to an investigation of the more expensive tranches of debt, and possibly their payoff or refinancing with less-expensive types of debt.

The calculation of the average cost of debt should encompass all types of debt, which includes the costs of bonds, bank loans, and capital leases. The calculation is:

$$\frac{\text{Annual cost of interest on loans, bonds, and capital leases}}{\text{Average amount of bonds, loans, and leases outstanding}}$$

It may be easier to calculate the average cost of debt on a monthly basis, rather than an annual basis, if the amount of debt varies considerably over the one-year measurement period.

There are several issues with the collection of information for the average cost of debt, which are:

- *Lease rate*. It can be difficult to determine the interest rate contained within a lease. If the amount of a lease is quite small, its inclusion in the average cost of debt may be immaterial, and so it can be excluded. Otherwise, contact the lessor to obtain the rate.
- *Bond rate*. The effective interest rate should be used as the interest rate for a bond, rather than the stated interest rate. When a bond is sold for an amount other than its face amount, this means the associated interest rate varies from the stated interest rate. For example, if a company sells a bond for $95,000 that has a face amount of $100,000 and which pays interest of $5,000, then the effective interest rate being paid is $5,000 ÷ $95,000, or 5.26%. Thus, if a company sells a bond at a discount from its face value, the effective interest rate is *higher* than the stated interest rate. If the company sells a bond at

a premium from its face value, the effective interest rate is *lower* than the stated interest rate.

- *Other expenses.* There may be several additional expenses associated with debt, such as an annual audit required by the lender, and an annual loan maintenance fee. If these expenses would not be incurred in the absence of the debt, include them in the interest cost of the debt.

The interest rate paid does not reveal a complete picture of the borrowing instruments employed by a business. There may be restrictive covenants or conversion clauses built into these instruments that are of more importance than the interest rates being paid. For example, a covenant not to pay dividends could be of concern to a family-held business, while a conversion clause could allow debt holders to convert their debt to equity at extremely favorable rates.

EXAMPLE

Puller Corporation, maker of plastic and wooden doorknobs, has acquired a large amount of debt while acquiring competitors that make other door fittings. The CEO is concerned about the cost of this debt, and asks for a derivation of the average cost. The resulting report contains the following information:

	Annual Interest Cost	Principal Outstanding	Interest Rate	Other Features
Factory lease	$280,000	$2,300,000	12.1%	No early payment clause
Senior bank loan	1,200,000	15,000,000	8.0%	Balloon due in 24 months
Junior bank loan	975,000	6,500,000	15.0%	Risk of acceleration
Bonds	1,680,000	24,000,000	7.0%	Convertible into common stock
	$4,135,000	$47,800,000		

Based on the table, Puller's average cost of debt is:

$$\frac{\$4,135,000 \text{ Annual interest cost}}{\$47,800,000 \text{ Principal outstanding}}$$

$$= 8.65\%$$

Overall, the interest rate being paid by Puller is acceptable. However, the interest rate on the junior bank loan is quite high, since the lender is unlikely to have access to the company's assets in the event of a default. There are also covenants associated with this loan that Puller could breach, resulting in loan acceleration. Consequently, the junior bank loan is clearly the loan to be paid off or refinanced, if the opportunity to do so is available.

Borrowing Base Usage

If a company does not have large cash reserves, it must rely upon a line of credit to provide it with sufficient cash to keep the company operational. Lenders almost always insist upon using a company's accounts receivable and inventory as the collateral basis (or *borrowing base*) for a line of credit. The amount loaned to a company under a line of credit agreement cannot exceed the borrowing base. Consequently, a critical financing metric to follow is borrowing base usage. This is the amount of debt that has been loaned against the collateral provided by a company.

EXAMPLE

A business has $1,000,000 of accounts receivable and $600,000 of inventory on hand. Its lender will allow a line of credit that is based on 75% of all accounts receivable less than 90 days old, and 50% of inventory. $20,000 of the accounts receivable are more than 90 days old. This means that the applicable borrowing base for the company is:

Applicable Assets		Discount Rate		Allowable Borrowing Base
Accounts receivable of $980,000	×	75%	=	$735,000
Inventory of $600,000	×	50%	=	300,000
		Total	=	$1,035,000

The unused amount of the borrowing base is crucial, since it must be compared to any cash shortfalls projected in the cash forecast to see if a business has sufficient available and unused debt to offset negative cash positions.

Borrowing base usage requires continual analysis, since the amount of receivables and inventory to be used as collateral is constantly changing. This is a particular concern in seasonal businesses, since they tend to build inventory levels prior to the sales season, followed by a build in accounts receivable levels during the sales season, followed by a quiet period when assets are liquidated and debts are paid off. The continual changes in debt needs and asset levels make borrowing base usage perhaps the most important metric for the CFO of a seasonal business.

Summary

Many of the metrics noted in this chapter yield information that can be difficult to act upon, or which will result in changes only over a long period of time. Of more immediate use is borrowing base usage, since management must understand exactly how much cash is still available to be borrowed under a line of credit arrangement. An entity that has substantial debt obligations should also monitor the debt service coverage ratio, to see if there will be an issue with loan repayment. If so, the borrower should pay particular attention to the maturity dates of loans and the status of projected cash flows, to see if the business can indeed repay its liabilities. If not, it will be necessary to roll over loans as far in advance as possible.

Glossary

A

Accredited investor. A high net worth entity or individual; this investor is allowed to acquire shares under a Regulation D stock offering.

Affiliate. A person who can exercise control over an issuer, such as an executive officer, a director, or a large shareholder.

Angel investor. An individual who invests small amounts in fledgling businesses.

B

Beta. A measure of the volatility of a security in comparison to the market as a whole.

Blue sky laws. Laws enacted at the state level, requiring issuers of securities to register with the applicable state regulatory commission.

Book building. The process of accumulating orders from institutional investors to buy the shares of a company.

Borrowing base. The assets used as collateral against a loan.

C

Capital lease. A leasing arrangement where the lessee is effectively taking ownership of an asset.

Capital structure. The mix of debt and equity used to fund a business.

Collar agreement. A clause in a stock-for-stock purchase transaction that adjusts the number of shares paid based on changes in the stock price of the acquirer.

Comfort letter. A letter issued by auditors concerning the validity of the financial statements and other information issued by an organization.

Common stock. An ownership share in a corporation that allows its holders voting rights at shareholder meetings and the opportunity to receive dividends.

Constraint. A bottleneck that restricts the level of output from a system.

Cost of capital. The blended cost of a firm's debt, preferred stock, and equity.

Covenant. A restriction placed on the financing or operational choices of a borrower by a lender.

Crowdfunding. The use of small individual investments from a large number of investors to fund a business.

D

Death spiral PIPE. A private investment in public equity where continuing declines in the stock price obligate the issuer to issue more shares to PIPE investors, possibly resulting in a change in control of the issuer.

Debt security. A security that involves a creditor relationship with a borrower, such as bonds, commercial paper, and Treasury securities.

Dilution. A reduction in the value of shares, caused by an increase in the number of shares outstanding.

Dividend. A payment made to shareholders that is proportional to the number of shares owned.

E

Earnings credit. Interest calculated on a bank account that is used to reduce bank account service fees.

EBITDA. An acronym for earnings before interest, taxes, depreciation, and amortization.

Effective interest rate. The actual interest rate earned on an investment, which incorporates any discount or premium paid on the investment.

Employee share purchase plan. A plan under which employees can buy shares directly from their employer, usually at a discount and without paying a brokerage fee.

Ex-dividend date. The first date following the declaration of a dividend on which the holder of stock is not entitled to receive the next dividend payment.

F

Factor. A financing entity that purchases receivables from other parties.

Financial leverage. The use of debt to increase the return on equity.

Functional currency. The local currency of the country in which a subsidiary operates.

Funding portal. Any person acting as an intermediary in a transaction involving the offer or sale of securities for the account of others, that does not offer investment advice, solicit purchases or sales to buy the securities listed on its website, or compensate its employees for soliciting the securities listed on its website, or handle investor funds or securities.

H

Hedge. An investment intended to offset adverse price movements in an asset.

I

Initial public offering. The registration of shares with the Securities and Exchange Commission by a business for the first time.

Internal rate of return. The rate of return at which the aggregate present values of a set of future cash inflows and outflows equals zero.

Issuer. An entity that registers and sells securities in order to finance its operations.

L

Lease. An arrangement where a lessor allows a lessee to use an asset for a period of time in exchange for a series of fixed payments.

Line of credit. A commitment from a lender to pay a borrower cash as needed, up to a pre-set maximum level.

Liquidation preference. When an investor has the right to be paid back his investment in a business before any proceeds from the sale of the business are distributed to its founders.

Lockup period. A time period during which current shareholders are not allowed to sell their shares.

M

Master budget. The aggregated results of the revenue and department-level budgets, which includes a budgeted income statement and balance sheet.

N

Net present value. The net difference between the present value of cash inflows and cash outflows associated with an investment.

O

Offering circular. A prospectus for a new security listing.

Operational hedge. The alignment of sales and purchases within a country to avoid foreign currency transactions.

Organic growth. Growth derived solely from increases in internal operations.

P

Preferred stock. A security that receives preferential treatment in comparison to common stock.

PIPE. A private investment in public equity, where investors purchase restricted stock that is intended to be registered with the SEC.

Primary market. The issuance of new securities on an exchange.

Public entity. A business that is required to file financial statements with the Securities and Exchange Commission.

Q

Quiet period. The time period between the delivery of a registration statement to the SEC and its declaration that the statement is effective, when information releases to the public are restricted.

R

Real option. The decision options available for a tangible asset.

Receipts and disbursements method. The use of detailed cash receipts and payments information to construct a cash forecast.

Restricted share. A share that cannot be sold for a certain period of time.

Review. A service under which an auditor obtains limited assurance that there are no material modifications that need to be made to an entity's financial statements for them to be in conformity with the applicable financial reporting framework.

S

Seasoned equity offering. An issuance of securities where the securities have been previously issued.

Secondary market. A market in which securities are bought and sold between parties that do not include the original issuing entities.

Shelf registration. The registration of securities that will be sold at a later date.

Special purpose entity. An entity designed to acquire and finance specific assets, while separating the risk associated with those assets from any risks associated with the parent entity.

Stock. Ownership shares in a business.

Stock buyback. The repurchase of a company's own shares from its shareholders.

Stock dividend. Stock issued to a company's shareholders without any consideration.

Stock option. The right to purchase a certain number of shares at a later date and at a certain price.

Stock split. An issuance of shares to existing shareholders that exceeds a 20% to 25% increase in the number of shares outstanding prior to the issuance.

Supply chain financing. Interposing a lender between a company and its suppliers, with the lender offering to pay suppliers early in exchange for a discount.

Synergy. The concept that the value derived from combining two entities is greater than their separate values.

T

Target balance. A reserve amount of cash to be kept available for unexpected cash requirements.

Tax shield. The use of interest expense to offset taxable income.

Terminal value. The aggregated cash flows for the period beyond which detailed cash flows are being predicted.

Transaction exposure. The risk of changes in foreign exchange rates between the dates when a transaction is booked and when it is settled.

V

Venture capital. Funds invested in startup firms that have strong growth potential.

W

Warrant. An option to purchase a certain number of a company's shares at a pre-determined price, within a defined time period.

Working capital. Current assets minus current liabilities.

Y

Yield curve. A plotted line showing the different interest rates of bonds having different maturity dates, but equal levels of credit quality.

Index

Accounts payable
    Budgeting.. 41
    Days 41
    Policies.. 134
Accounts receivable budgeting............. 36
Accounts receivable policies 125
Accredited investor............................. 72
Accrued liabilities budgeting............... 43
Adjacent industry strategy 179
Agency financing 95
Angel investors.................................... 50
Asset-based financing.......................... 84
Average cost of debt.......................... 244

Bad actor disqualification.................... 79
Balance sheet
    Budget... 45
    Budgeted 36
Banker's acceptance........................... 161
Banks 7
Best efforts deal................................. 59
Beta.. 106
Bill of materials 128
Billing enhancements 123
Blue sky laws..................................... 64
Bolt-on strategy 181
Bond rating, planning for 23
Bonds.. 94, 163
Borrowing base................................... 86
Borrowing base usage........................ 246
Bottleneck analysis............................ 147
Breakeven point................................. 141
Budget, financing 47
Budgeting, constraint-based 148

Capital budgeting
    Overview of 137
    Proposal analysis........................... 148
Capital markets..................................... 7
Capital structure
    Analysis... 12
    Optimal 11
Cash budgeting................................... 44
Cash conversion cycle 235
Cash coverage ratio 242

Cash flow information, reliability of.....32
Cash forecast
    Medium-term 30
    Short-term.......................................27
    Use of averages in...........................31
    Variability of....................................26
Certificate of deposit..........................161
Collar agreement 198
Collection agency................................125
Collection enhancements 124
Commercial paper 162
Common stock cost.............................104
Comparison analysis 192
Complex systems analysis 151
Control premium 193
Convertibility risk 205
Cost of capital
    Adjustments to 108
    Derivation of...................................103
    Reduction of 22
    Variations 105
Coupon bond.......................................163
Covenants..20
Credit enhancements 122
Currency option 213
Cylinder option 215, 228

Days of inventory on hand 39
Days payables outstanding..................237
Days sales in accounts receivable 236
Days sales in inventory 236
Days sales outstanding 36
Debt cost 103
Debt for equity swap...........................96
Debt maturity structure 20
Debt paydown 22
Debt service coverage ratio.................241
Debt to equity ratio 243
Dilution 82
Discount rate 138
Discounted cash flows analysis...........188
Diversification strategy 179
Dividend
    Dates...167
    Payout ratio....................................169
    Policy..169

Drop shipping 129
Dunning message 124
Dutch auction 59

Early payment discounts.................... 132
Earnings credit.................................... 157
Earnings on invested funds................. 239
EDGAR system 76
Effective interest rate.......................... 165
Enterprise value.................................. 184
Equity budgeting 44
Exchange ratio 196

Factoring... 88
FDIC insurance.................................... 154
Financial leverage
    Compensation effects...................... 18
    Concept 13
    Risks.. 16
Financial management........................... 4
Financing budget 47
Firm commitment deal 59
Fixed assets budgeting.......................... 41
Fixed charge coverage ratio................. 241
Fixed price... 198
Fixed share count.................................. 198
Fixed-exchange collar 199
Fixed-price collar 199
Foreign exchange
    Forward contract 211
    Futures contract.............................. 213
    Hedging.. 209
    Netting... 216
    Reserves 209
    Risk management............................ 206
    Swaps 216
Form 1-A 73
Form C.. 77
Forward rate agreement....................... 220
Fulfillment practices............................ 130
Full service strategy............................ 178
Future value table 114

Geographic growth strategy................. 177

Hard money loan 91

Income taxes payable 43
Incremental internal rate of return 117
Industry roll-up strategy 182

Initial public offering
    Preparation for 56
    Process flow....................................58
    Reasons for and against 54
Interest coverage ratio 240
Interest rate
    Futures contract 222
    Hedging...219
    Options..226
    Risk management 218
    Swap 224
    Swaption..229
Internal rate of return 116
Inventory
    Budgeting 39
    Disposition.....................................130
    Enhancements................................126
    Financing.......................................90
    Policies 131
    Stockpiling.....................................40
Investment
    Bankers..8
    Guidelines......................................153
    Strategy...157
Investors...7
Invoice discounting.............................87

JOBS Act 75

Laddering strategy...............................158
Lease or buy decision...........................99
Leasing
    Advantages 101
    Problems 100
Line of credit.................................18, 85
Liquidation preference 51
Liquidation value 183
Loan stock..91
Loan, long term...................................93
Lockup period 64
Low-cost strategy................................181

Managing underwriter..........................59
Margin call..223
Market
    Signals 22
    Timing 19
    Window strategy.............................180
Material requirements planning 129
Maturity matching...............................158

Mezzanine financing 92
Money market fund 162
Multiples analysis 185

Nature of finance 1
Net present value 115
Net present value analysis 138
Non-bank lenders 7
Notes payable budgeting 43

Organic growth 176
Other assets budgeting 43
Outsourcing decision 150
Overallotment 60

Payback method 143
Payment
    Processing frequency 134
    Terms, renegotiation of 132
Piggyback rights 69
Policies
    Accounts payable 134
    Accounts receivable 125
    Inventory 131
    Investment 155
Political risk 205
Preferred stock cost 104
Prepaid expenses budgeting 43
Present value table 113
Primary market 164
Private investment in public equity 74
Product
    Design 127
    Supplementation strategy 177
Profitability index 142
Purchase order financing 91

Quiet period 62

Real estate value 183
Real options 145
Receivables securitization 89
Registered bond 164
Registration rights 195
Regulation A+ 73
Regulation Crowdfunding 75
Regulation D stock sales 67
Regulatory agencies 8
Relief from royalty method 184
Replication value 190

Repurchase agreement 160
Resale restrictions 79
Ride the yield curve 160
Rights offering 81
Risk-free rate 106
Rule 144 195
Rule 506(c) 71

Safety stock 128
Sales growth strategy 176
Scenario analysis 140
Seasoned equity offering 80
Secondary market 164
Sensitivity analysis 140
Shelf registration 80
Small claims complaint 124
Stock
    Buybacks 171
    Dividend 174
    Transfer agents 8
Stock-for-stock exchange 195
Strategic purchase 193
Strategy
    Adjacent industry 179
    Bolt-on 181
    Diversification 179
    Full service 178
    Geographic growth 177
    Industry roll-up 182
    Low-cost 181
    Market window 180
    Product supplementation 177
    Sales growth 176
    Vertical integration 178
Supplier reduction 136
Supply chain financing 231
Sweep structure 154

Tax shield 18
Terminal value 118
Tiered investments 159
Time deposit 161
Time value of money 111
Transaction exposure 204
Transfer risk 205
Transitory revenue 188
Translation exposure 205
Trapped cash 157
Treasury bills 163
Treasury notes 163

Unsecured financing 84

Valuation floor and ceiling 193
Venture capital 50
Vertical integration strategy 178

Warrants 69
Weighted average cost of capital 105
Working capital 121
    Enhancements 134
    Forecasting 135
    Strategy 135

CPSIA information can be obtained
at www.ICGtesting.com
Printed in the USA
FFHW011300300919
55323926-61045FF